"If this reader were not shackled by affection to her children nor chained by financial responsibility to Mr. Visa, she would leave all behind and book the next flight to Argentina to follow in the high-heeled footsteps of Marina Palmer, author of a wicked, dangerous, and divine memoir. Beware: *Kiss & Tango* is like a siren's song. It lures you in with its frank exploration of desire, longing, romantic despair, and sexual experimentation and sublimation."

—*USA Today*

"Smoldering. . . . Palmer thoroughly explores the tango and sex connection, giving readers a brutally honest and often hilarious account of the three years she danced tango . . . and the long line of Latin Lotharios she met along the way."

—*Newsweek*

"Palmer's effervescence is so contagious that a reader feels she has actually lived the life (hangovers and all). Armchair tango. Now that's escape."

—*Los Angeles Times Book Review*

"A delicious real-life read. . . . This ballsy babe's memoir will totally inspire you."

—*Cosmopolitan*

"HBO has shelved *Sex and the City*, *Desperate Housewives* is in reruns, and the American appetite for vicarious sensuality is being only partly sated. . . . So *Kiss & Tango*, a frank, explicit diary . . . seems ideally poised to fill a gap in the zeitgeist."

—*Washington Post Book World*

"Doesn't the very word tango evoke a seductive state of mind overflowing with images? Here in specific, frank, and flowing prose, Marina Palmer takes us inside her world and the world of the tango, bringing it alive and evidencing how following your passion and not being afraid to take risks in your personal and professional lives can lead to happiness. Plus it's a sexy read."

—Mireille Guiliano, *New York Times* bestselling author
of *French Women Don't Get Fat*

Kiss & Tango

Diary of a Dancehall Seductress

Marina Palmer

HARPER

NEW YORK • LONDON • TORONTO • SYDNEY

HARPER

A hardcover edition of this book was published in 2005 by William Morrow, an imprint of HarperCollins Publishers.

FIRST HARPER PAPERBACK PUBLISHED 2006.

The Library of Congress has catalogued the hardcover edition as follows:

Palmer, Marina.
   Kiss & tango: looking for love in Buenos Aires / Marina Palmer—1st ed.
     p. cm.
   ISBN 0-06-074292-5
    1. Palmer, Marina, 1969–   2. Dancers—United States—Biography.
3. Americans—Argentina—Buenos Aires—Biography.   4. Tango
(Dance)— Argentina—Buenos Aires.   I. Title.

GV1785.P25A3 2005
792.8'092—dc22
[B]   2004043131

ISBN-10: 0-06-074297-6 (pbk.)
ISBN-13: 978-0-06-074297-3 (pbk.)

06 07 08 09 10 ❖/RRD 10 9 8 7 6 5 4 3 2 1

To my ideal tango partner:

I will yearn for you always

I should not believe in a God who does not dance.
—Friedrich Nietzsche

You sure know how to pick 'em!
—My sister, Alexandra

Acknowledgments

First of all, I thank my lucky stars for my editor, Jennifer Pooley. I have found a partner at last—when I least expected it! Also, I want to say how thrilled I am to have Sharyn Rosenblum and Samantha Hagerbaumer on board for publicity, and Rachel Bressler for marketing. I'd also like to thank Lynn Grady, Lisa Gallagher, and Michael Morrison for embracing the book. To my parents, who would say I don't need to thank them, but I will anyway. Not only have they provided me with their unwavering love and support, of both the material and the emotional kind, but they have proved to be unbelievably good sports and hardly grumbled about the way I depicted them. So many friends and relatives have cheered me along the way that I cannot name them all. But special thanks to Carina, Helen, Joyce, Leo, and my cousins Bibi and Zoe for reading the darned thing when they said they would. As for Annabel, she did a hell of a lot more than read it. I can't thank her enough for her contribution, which starts but does not end with the only flattering photograph ever taken of me. I probably wouldn't have written the book at all if it weren't for my aunts, Lisaki and Titina, who were both there at the inception and whose faith filled me with strength every time I came close to crumbling. I also want to thank my friend and lawyer, Susan Danziger, who taught me the valuable lesson of the cat on the roof. To my brother-in-law and "manager," Alex, I am most deeply indebted for the many hours he has spent advising me along the way. And finally I could not have done it without my sister, Alexandra. She may not appear in this book, but I feel her presence on every page.

Kiss & Tango

Prologue

I wanted the last tango to be perfect—even though the pop music blasting out of the Tower Records across the street was going to make that difficult. But for the eighth and last time of the day, I closed my eyes to let the tango from our own loudspeaker wash over me until it penetrated that place that only *it* can reach. Instantly, it sent me into a trance so deep that I became deaf to the sound of Ricky Martin's voice, while my body temporarily escaped the chronic aches and pains from the daily battering it receives at the hands of calle Florida. I couldn't hear Pablo's voice either, when (not for the first time) he barked in my ear: "Who's leading here—you or me?" all the while keeping his I'm-madly-in-love-with-you mask firmly in place. For the tango had kept its promise as, once again, it swept me away and flew me off to a country called Bliss. And, once again, it was perfect.

Four years and nine months earlier

Abrazo

1. Embrace.

2. Tango position assumed by the partners.
When it's good it's heaven,
and when it's bad it's hell.

January 10, 1997

Where am I going?

Luckily, I wasn't left to wonder for long, as Marty, our chief flight attendant, now welcomed us aboard American Airlines flight 845 from New York to Buenos Aires—before informing us that our flying time would be ten hours and fifty minutes. Groan. I wish he hadn't done that. That's ten hours too long, if you ask me.

I tried to dispel the unpleasant news by sitting back and relaxing in my seat as he now suggested. As I did, the following thought cheered me up, somewhat: the longer the flight, the farther away it would take me from Young & Rubicam advertising agency. Unfortunately, the thought lasted for less than a split second (along with the comfort it had provided), since my mind couldn't help wandering back to the distraught call from my client, who had screamed at me only a couple of hours ago because the cost estimate for his commercial was twice that of the agreed-upon budget. There has got to be more to life. But what?

Now we were up, up, up, and away! As I leaned over the guy sitting next to me to get a glimpse out of the window, I heaved a sigh of relief. My imagination was finally free to soar high above reality and to fantasize about what lay ahead of me over the next couple of weeks. The thing I now realized is that it's difficult to fantasize about something when you have nothing to go on. Not the slightest little clue. (I decided on Buenos Aires only because my cousin Heleni and her husband, Jacques, happened to be doing a three-year stint there for his job with Paribas bank. Otherwise it would never have occurred to me as a holiday destination, it not being at the top of my places-to-visit list, like Africa, India, or China.)

As my fingers rummaged in the bag that was placed under the seat in front of me for a piece of gum, my mind rummaged around for any association at all with Argentina, but both my fingers and my mind came up with naught. Where the fuck did I put it?! Desperate for a piece of gum, I snuck a peek at my neighbor to see whether he was chewing. That's when I noticed for the first time that he was cute. Really cute. Was he a polo player? Bingo! I had just made my first Argentina-association.

How could it have slipped my mind? Argentina is the land of the fabulously handsome Polo Player, even *I* know that! I snuck a second peek at my neighbor, who *was* chewing as it turned out. He was far too good-looking to be looked at directly, what with that arm that had swung a mallet or two—if that rippling bicep under a checkered shirt sleeve was anything to go by. As for the three-day shadow around that square jaw of his, and the raven black hair that fell to his shoulders in waves, framing the most symmetrical face you ever saw . . . Did I say he was cute? What I meant to say was that he was drop-dead gorgeous! How was I ever going to pluck up the courage to ask him for a piece of gum now? I searched for opening lines that did not involve the vulgar request of something to chew on: "Hello. Sorry to disturb you, but what is your handicap?" Nope. I simply could not bring myself to do it. Anyway, I rationalized, he appeared far too absorbed in thought—he must be one of those narcissistic types.

Okay, so apart from polo, what else is there to do in Argentina? I asked myself in an attempt to still the deafening sound of my raging hormones. And that's when I made my second Argentina-association of the day and suddenly remembered the tango. I had no idea what it actually looked like since I'd never seen anyone do it, but I do love to dance, and when in Rome, or in this case, Buenos Aires . . .

I was still lost in reverie when I was interrupted by my neighbor. But lest anyone get too excited, it wasn't to pick me up but to puke me up.

Personally, I can't say I was thrilled. He, on the other hand, did not seem to mind at all the sight of his puke floating in my lap. Indeed, after he was done erupting all over me, he spent the next ten hours treating me to his life story (which had nothing to do with polo and everything to do with boring) while I tried to avoid the domino effect of the smell of his sick.

My only hope was that this was an omen of good things to come. If it's good luck to step in dog shit and good luck to get crapped on by birds, then surely it must be good luck to get puked on by strangers in planes.

January 11, 1997

As soon as I got to my cousin's apartment, the first thing I did was put all my clothes into the incinerator. Okay: that's not true, strictly speaking, but if there had been an incinerator, I would have. The smell of puke would not go away. It followed me about everywhere, sticking to me like the unwanted affection of a horny dog. Ten showers later and I had turned into Lady Macbeth: "Out, damned spot! Out, I say!"

All I could do after that and for the rest of the day was to lie listlessly on my cousin's sofa, recovering from the eleven-hour red-eye from New York. I wish they would abolish all night flights once and for all. I barely had the energy to lie down, let alone do anything more strenuous like sit up. At which point, Heleni informed me:

"We're taking you to a *milonga* tonight to celebrate your arrival in Buenos Aires."

(Oh grrrrreat . . . just what I need. A night out. And what the hell is a *"milonga,"* anyway?)

"Lovely!" is what I said.

I looked at myself in the mirror and threatened her with staying in. She wouldn't hear of it. Extreme situations (puffy eyes) called for drastic measures (an obscene amount of makeup).

"Careful: there's a bit of skin showing under there." That was Jacques, who thinks he's funny.

Feeling like a slug whose mucus has dried up and consequently finds it difficult to get from A to B, I dragged myself out the door behind them.

"We won't be back too late, right?" was my pathetic attempt at self-assertion.

"The night is young!" trilled Heleni. I looked at my watch: it was one in the morning on a Tuesday night. How much older did Tuesday nights get down here? I wondered. In New York, which is meant to be the city that never sleeps, everyone I know is comfortably tucked in and snoring away under their eiderdowns by one A.M. on a Tuesday night.

We hopped—they hopped, I crawled—into their Renault Clio and off we went to a neighborhood called Almagro, which used to be home to Buenos Aires's meat and produce market and is now its flower district. Jacques found a parking spot a couple of poorly lit and even more poorly paved blocks away from wherever it was they were taking me.

"Watch out!" said Heleni after I had almost twisted my ankle in a pothole that I hadn't been able to make out in the dark. We seemed to be headed for a building that looked very much like a sports club or a gym.

"Here we are: Club Almagro!" my cousins exclaimed in unison, visibly excited.

I wondered what was so exciting about going to the gym at a quarter to two in the morning, but I didn't want to let the side down, so I nodded emphatically and bared as many teeth as I could at a quarter to two in the morning. As we stopped at the front to pay for our tickets, I thought I smelled a mix of sweat and chlorine and hoped it was a hallucination caused by severe sleep deprivation.

The door standing between us and whatever was on the other side was made of glass. It had been painted black on the inside and the paint was peeling off in places. I could hear the muffled sound of music I did not recognize.

"What on earth is *that*?" I asked Heleni.

"*That* is tango," she said.

Speak of the devil, I thought. I hadn't expected to get my first taste of the tango so soon. My curiosity now piqued, I forgot to yawn.

"And *this* is a *milonga*," she said as we stepped inside.

Facing us, in the center of the room, was a brightly lit dance floor filled with a swirling mass of rotating bodies that were pressed together so tightly, they looked like a can of sardines come alive. They were dancing. But instead of dancing normally, they were dancing what I could only deduce was the tango. I had not expected this at all. I had known that Buenos Aires was far away. I hadn't realized it was on another planet altogether! Those who were not dancing were either sitting down at the maroon cloth–covered tables around the floor or standing by the bar in the back. And everyone, I mean absolutely *everyone*, who was not dancing was smoking, as my itchy eyes could attest. The low lights/thick fog combo made it extremely hard to see anything beyond the dance floor, but it didn't matter since I was completely taken by the spectacle in front of me.

Before tonight I had had a vague idea that the tango was a partner dance. I hadn't really known what that meant, though, until I saw with my own eyes the magic trick that transforms two bodies into one. As I watched the couples lock themselves in an embrace so tight that they fused with one another, I was reminded of the ancient myth of the hermaphrodite. These were not men and women dancing together, these were new creatures born of the union of old men with young women, tall women with short men, skinny men with fat women, and on and on, each pairing creating a unique combination of body parts. In some couples, the main point of contact was the chest. Others were stuck together at the cheek, while still others were glued forehead to forehead, as if transmitting the dance telepathically. Some bodies seemed to fit together effortlessly, while in other cases it looked like work. Some of the hermaphrodites assumed an elegant and rather dignified posture, while others looked like they were performing a dangerous balancing act in which the female half of the creature leaned in and surrendered herself to the male half, her chest propped up against his and her bottom sticking out miles in the opposite direction. Some couples looked especially precarious—for example, those where the female half was twice the size of the male half—but there must have been magic in the air, because I did not witness a single hermaphrodite topple over all night.

My attention now shifted to the faces. I noticed that almost every woman danced with her eyes closed, while on her lips was the most beatific smile I had ever seen. The men, on the other hand, were frowning. Were they lost in deep concentration—or was it pain? On occasion, their brows relaxed and they adopted a floating-in-a-cloud look, interspersed with the odd smile and even in one case, a laugh. I wondered what was going on here. What did these mood swings mean?

"I see the others," said Jacques, interrupting my train of thought. He and Heleni had arranged to meet up with some friends, who had just come in. I followed them toward the entrance, where I was introduced to the crowd. There was Roberto, Fernando and Carolina, Alfonso and his wife, Mercedes—Mechi for short. Without so much as a how do you do, Roberto went off with Mechi to the floor. They were in a terrible hurry, it seemed. And then I saw why. It was pure, unadulterated passion. I could not keep my eyes off them. Once again, it was as if a spell had been cast on me. My eyes were as stuck to them as they were to each other. I don't know how they breathed, if they were breathing at all. Maybe you don't need to breathe when you dance the tango, I thought. I certainly forgot to breathe, and I was just watching them! It was like staring into a mirror and gradually realizing that the reflection I was staring at was *mine*. That couple over there was *me*! They were expressing *me* better than I have ever expressed myself. I couldn't get over it. I never expected to find myself here, in this dance hall, at the other end of the world. I do wonder, though, how poor old Alfonso was feeling as he watched his wife supergluing herself to another man.

By the time we got home, it was six in the morning and I was finally going to be allowed to get some sleep. But I didn't feel in the least bit tired anymore. Typical!

January 12, 1997

In spite of the worst heat wave Buenos Aires has had in decades, I decided to go for a stroll this afternoon. I felt impatient to discover the city—and the only way to discover a city is on foot. I love the challenge of figuring out the layout of a new place. What I love even more is getting lost—this is less of a challenge for me—and finding myself in the opposite direction from the one I thought I was heading in, because I have inadvertently held the map upside down and turned left instead of right so that I now find myself in a maze, which makes things even more fun and invariably leads to surprises, often pleasant, sometimes not. Accidentally spending the afternoon at an open-air jazz concert in a park you don't know the name of instead of the museum that your cousins bullied you into visiting because "it is a must" is one of the more pleasant examples.

The problem with Buenos Aires is that it's impossible to get lost, really. The people are far too friendly, so that when they see you with your head plunged in a map, they immediately stop and ask you where it is you want to go. Since you don't speak any Spanish and they don't speak any English, French, or Greek, you'd think that this would limit things, conversation wise. But surprisingly, the fact that neither party speaks the other's language is far from being a deterrent when it comes to the average inhabitant of Buenos Aires, as I discovered today. For one thing, there is always sign language. In places like London, Paris, and New York, I get told off constantly for talking with my hands. But here in Buenos Aires, I have found my peers in the gesticulating department. If in addition to all the pointing of fingers, shrugging of shoulders, waving of hands, shaking of heads, and raising of eyebrows and/or voices, you add their pidgin English to my own concoction of French with Italian-sounding endings, you end up chatting the afternoon away instead of getting to where you want to go. I don't know how many people, exactly, I told, "I'm half Greek, half American, but I grew up in London and went to a French school," when all I was trying to do was find the presidential palace on Plaza de Mayo.

A dashing older man in a white linen suit and a smart straw hat came up to me and offered me a chocolate-covered candy with a soft praline filling:

"A *bombón* for a *bomboncita!*" is what I think he said. I didn't know exactly what he meant but I could guess it was meant to be sweet. I accepted the gift with a smile and kept on walking as I unwrapped it and popped it into my mouth, where it melted lingeringly. I was starting to like these people.

Finally, I found Plaza de Mayo and the presidential palace, known as La Casa Rosada, the Pink House, with its famous balcony from which the most loved and hated of all presidential couples, Juan Domingo Perón and his wife, Evita, would wave at the crowds that rallied in the square below. Perón continues to be a controversial figure to this day, with his legacy still shaping the political scene here. Just ask Carlos Menem, leader of the Peronist party and Argentina's current president. According to whom you listen to, it was Perón who either built the country or ruined it, brought social justice to the people or was a fascist and/or populist dictator. Jacques and Heleni's friends all seem to belong to the latter group. The fact that their families lost property under his regime doesn't make them his biggest fans.

As I strolled across the square, I noticed that a large white circle had been painted on the ground, inside which was the image of a headscarf. As I stood there wondering what this meant, an old woman who was feeding the pigeons came up to me and volunteered in surprisingly un-pidginlike English to tell me about the "Mothers of the Disappeared": how they had walked around in silent circles on this spot every Thursday afternoon until recently, wearing their distinctive white headscarves to protest the "disappearance" of their thirty thousand sons and daughters under the military regime that only ended in 1983.

The pigeon lady was sending shivers down my spine. But I confess they did not stay there for long. It is difficult to experience the horror of death when the sun is out and you are being bombarded with so many signs of life; when all around you is the hustle and bustle of the city, the sounds of honking horns and the rumbling of diesel engines, and people going to and from places in fast-forward or sitting on public benches, hands chattering away merrily. Everyone here seems so cheerful. It's impossible to imagine these people oppressing anybody—and frankly, I'd rather not.

I turned my back on the ludicrously pink seat of power—*pink*, whoever thought to paint it *pink*, for heaven's sake? How is one supposed to take it seriously?—and walked down Avenida de Mayo toward Plaza Congreso, which is where I eventually found the much more serious-looking Congress building. At any rate, it isn't pink, which is a good place to start.

It was lovely strolling down the wide, tree-lined avenue, where most of the buildings date back to the turn of the twentieth century. I was reminded of Budapest, both because of the imposing dimensions of the art nouveau buildings and also because of the decay they have been allowed to fall into. There is something sad about both these cities (in contrast to the cheerfulness of the people here—not in Budapest, which is second to Sweden in the suicide rankings), which, after having reached pinnacles of wealth and glory, have now faded to shadows of their former selves. But one thing that is still alive and kicking in both places, and especially in Buenos Aires, is the café. I have never walked past so many in my life.

Finally, on the verge of sunstroke, I stopped at one of them: Café Tortoni. The clientele inside looked as if it had been sitting at the elegant marble-topped tables since circa 1900. The walls were filled with oil portraits of the city's most famous literati, artists, and musicians, along with tango memorabilia, sheet music, and black-and-white photos. At the back were pool tables and even two mini-theaters where they hold tango concerts, the waiter told me. I felt much better after I had gulped down my *licuado de ananá*—basically, a pineapple smoothie—and was now ready to resume my stroll down the avenue. I was not expecting my stroll to be rudely interrupted by a great, big, bloody highway.

Technically, the 9 de Julio is not a highway. It is an avenue—in fact, as I read in my guidebook when I got home later, it is supposedly the "widest avenue in the world." But in *my* book, fourteen lanes of cars that whiz past one at 100 miles an hour qualifies as a highway. I've never been so terrified of crossing a road in my life. I felt especially sorry for poor old Avenida de Mayo, which had been cut in two and left with this big gash right down its middle. What a shame, I thought, as I imagined what it must have been like, once upon a time, to stroll happily from Plaza de Mayo to Plaza Congreso without the risk of getting run over by a truck.

I finally made it across without injury and walked north along 9 de Julio toward what can only be described as a giant prick soaring into the sky. An extremely pointy one, at that. It didn't take a degree in psychology to understand the symbolism here. I had already noticed all the postcards of the Obelisco at the kiosks everywhere. But still, I blushed to see it in the flesh. I couldn't help wondering, though, about the implications of this "big is better" mentality. Argentines do have a reputation for being insufferably arrogant (another Argentina association) and I suppose this vulgar display of power proves this point. The real question is, what was the guy who built the thing compensating for? Because, let's face it, beneath every arrogant prick lies a teeny-tiny one. It goes without saying that one would prefer to think that the size of the obelisk is a reflection of the dimensions of the average Argentine member rather than of his overinflated ego—which, as I just pointed out, is usually inversely proportional to the dimensions of said member. Which was it? I wondered.

"Get your mind out of the gutter, girl!" I chastised myself.

I kept on walking along 9 de Julio and passed the Teatro Colón opera house. I am starting to see why they call Buenos Aires the "Paris of South America." They certainly did a good job of ripping off European architecture. I hate to admit it, but the highway was growing on me. In spite of the racket and the fumes, there is something to be said for the luxurious amount of space created by fourteen lanes in the heart of a city. I noted the eclectic mix of the tasteful with the not so tasteful: the coquettishly elaborate palaces, the terrifying fascist buildings, the new glass-and-steel structures that had already started to age, the stone facades of their hundred-year-old neighbors that hadn't aged a day. And everywhere, flashing lights and giant billboards that lent unity to this landscape of order and chaos, recklessness and restraint, tackiness and splendor.

Before they finally caved on me, my legs took me down Avenida Corrientes, which reminded me of Broadway: people everywhere, pouring out onto the street from the bookstores, theaters, movie houses, or happily sitting inside the cafés and restaurants, of which there were at least two on every block. All full to bursting on a Wednesday at four o'clock in the afternoon. And we are not talking little cafés or restaurants. Each one looks as if it seats hundreds. My cousins told me that Argentina was once the fourth-richest country in the world until it went to pot under Perón. Apparently, there even used to be a French saying, to be "rich as an Argentine." But people must still be stinking rich. How else does one explain that nobody is doing any work and that they are all idling away at a café at four P.M. in the middle of the week? Or is there something in this picture I don't get?

January 13, 1997

Today I went for my first tango lesson at the Academia de Tango, housed in a charming (in a shabby kind of way) turn-of-the-century building on avenida Callao, next door to the Congress building.

I have to admit, I was a bit nervous at first. Or maybe the butterflies in my tummy and my shaky limbs were a sign of excitement. Mixed with impatience. I wanted to learn to tango ASAP so I too could not breathe in the way I had watched Roberto and Mechi not breathe at Club Almagro.

I hadn't taken a step yet and already I had finished my one-and-a-half-liter bottle of Evian. It continues to be scorching hot, and as a result it was a sauna in there, the concept of air-conditioning not yet having made it into the building. I don't mind being hot; in fact, I love the sultry touch of my sundress clinging to my skin—especially when I think that if I were in New York right now, I would be buried alive under three layers of wool. I was rather enjoying the tingly sensation of the sweat that trickled from the nape of my neck, via my armpits, down the inside seams of my dress, taking a detour toward my bottom, continuing its journey down my thighs, then along my calves, from whence it splashed imperceptibly onto the floor. It was a pleasant sensation. The only thing that made me a bit uncomfortable was the thought of imposing my sticky, salty self on some poor stranger. But I needn't have worried.

Forty-five minutes after the official starting time, the class had not yet started. This seemed to go down perfectly well with the couple of other students in the room, who didn't lift an eyebrow. I don't think they even noticed that we were off to a late start. I found this both frustrating and refreshing at the same time. Frustrating because I am a victim of my upbringing in London, where Time and the Imperative of Being On It is the national obsession. Refreshing because I'd love to be liberated from the aforementioned obsession and the constant worry of being late. The thing is, it takes Time (and Work) to adopt this nonchalant indifference to Time. Which is why I decided to go cold turkey—I don't believe in half measures—and took my watch off then and there. And I haven't put it back on again. In fact, I am seriously considering throwing it away.

When our teacher, Flavio, finally appeared, the first thing he did was close all the windows, thereby cutting off our oxygen supply. Maybe my wish about not breathing was being taken too literally. He did this to silence the racket from the street below and to keep out the car fumes that were asphyxiating us. That's what I call being caught between a rock and a hard place.

There was not a single man in the class apart from the teacher. Great. How am I going to dance the tango without a man? I wondered.

I wasn't.

Flavio explained that before you can dance the tango, you need to learn how to walk.

"There is a famous saying: 'It takes only twenty minutes to learn a figure. But it takes twenty years to learn to walk.' "

(In Argentina, maybe. But where I come from, honey, it takes about a year, I wisecracked in silence, before giving in to an internal temper tantrum. I didn't come here to learn to walk, for heaven's sake! I've been managing on my own quite well for almost thirty years now.)

I was on the verge of asking for my ten pesos back, when he put the music on. He told us that we were listening to Carlos Di Sarli, who directed one of the most popular tango orchestras in the forties and fifties, at the height of the golden age of tango. The tempo was that of a slow and deliberate heartbeat and the melody was exquisitely melancholic, oozing with nostalgia.

And so we walked. One step per beat. Right foot, then left foot, then right, then left. One foot in front of the other in a straight line. When we had reached the wall, we started again, but backward this time. It's not easy to walk backward in a straight line, by the way. And again. I don't know how many miles I walked, but gradually, the nostalgia of the tango became my own. With each step, my heart filled with the sublime sadness that had traveled through time to find me here in this high-ceilinged room with the dusty parquet floor. Something was happening to me. Something I can't really explain. I felt myself lifted up into a cloud. I was at one with myself and everything around me. It was a moment of pure happiness. Happiness as I've never felt before.

January 14, 1997

When people say that looks aren't everything, they are lying. And men who think they are exempt from the beauty contest are fooling themselves because it's a myth that women don't care about the way men look. They care a lot. And here in B.A., I've died and gone to heaven. I can't get over how beautiful the average *porteño* is—that is what I've been told the inhabitants of Buenos Aires are called, since technically this is a port town, though I have yet to see anything resembling a port according to my definition of one.

Being fully aware that beauty is in the eye of the beholder and that not everybody has the same eye, I cannot expect other beholders to take my word for it when I say that this city contains the most beautiful men per capita (we're talking both quantity and quality). To that end, I have devised an index that will hopefully enable others to draw their own conclusions:

BEAUTIFUL MEN INDEX (PER SQUARE MILE):
Athens: 0 *
Rio: 4 **
New York: 8***
Paris: 15

London: 17 ****
Venice: 79 *****
Buenos Aires: 86

* You might find one or two in Greece, but you'd have to go to Mykonos for that—and chances are that he's foreign and/or gay.

** However, it must be said that *cariocas* do wear the best (i.e., white and therefore see-through when wet) bikinis. I wish men all over the world would follow their example. It really does save everybody a lot of time and disappointment.

*** When it comes to the male aesthetic, I'm afraid to say that New York is pretty average. But what do you expect in a species whose sole preoccupation is work? I blame it on all that artificial office light—it's absolutely ghastly for the complexion.

**** One cannot deny that England, being an island, is subject to the vagaries of inbreeding, nor that in the vast majority of cases, the sad result is atrocious ugliness. But when they get it right, boy do they get it right. In fact, it is most surprising the consistency with which they do breed beautiful thoroughbreds, otherwise known as English roses. Of course, the index is not weighted to include factors such as sex appeal, skills in bed, and the ability to talk while dangling a cigarette from the lips. If it were, Paris would instantly jump three notches in the ranking.

***** Note the close competition Venetians give *porteños*, confirming my theory that Argentines are really just Italians on a beef diet.

January 15, 1997

Yesterday, I discovered the hell that is partner dancing when neither of you knows what you are doing—and when one of you doesn't smell too good. My back is in agony after lesson number two. I spent an hour and a half in the most inconvenient position. If the brute has a name, I would prefer to forget it. Unfortunately, I will not forget so soon how his left forearm kept my waist locked in a death grip, forcing me to thrust my pelvis forward, where it really did not want to go, while his right hand—the clammiest I have ever had the misfortune to hold—levered my own left one toward the sky, literally yanking it out of its socket.

Adding insult to injury, he kept barking orders at me:

"Cross now! Cross now!" he said, thereby exposing me to the perils of his putrid breath.

I showed amazing grace throughout my trial, if I say so myself. I was still intoxicated from my first lesson. Nothing, not even this dragon, could erase the memory of that. And sure enough, following this test by the Cruel Gods of Partner Dancing, came my reward. Flavio finally took pity on me and tore me out of the arms of Herr Two Left Feet (he was German). My gratitude for having been rescued from a plight worse than death knew no bounds.

I didn't need to fight to stay upright anymore. I could relax into the arms of my knight in shining armor. He did all the work, while I did nothing at all. Instead, I lay back and closed my eyes like a cat that is being stroked. Any minute now I would start to purr. I surrendered myself to this stranger as I have never surrendered myself to any man before. I was more fused with him than I had been with my mother in her womb: we were One. He could read my mind, knowing better than I what I wanted and when, anticipating what would give me pleasure by instinctively taking me to where my feet wanted to go. He heard the music with my ears, interpreting it exactly as I would have, stepping on the beat that I would have stepped on had I been dancing alone. It was impossible to say who was leading and who was following. We wanted the same thing at the same time with all our body and soul. Time and space vanished. There was no past, no future: we were in the present and I was free.

Until the track ended, whereby Flavio dropped me like a sack of potatoes. The lesson was over, he announced. I was still in a daze, the sack of potatoes not having landed back on earth, so I wasn't able to say if what I had just experienced was real or if it had been a dream. Whether it was true love or a beautiful mirage, which, by definition, evaporates into thin air as soon as you try to touch it. But what I did know was that I intended to go back for more—because, real or not, it felt bloody fantastic.

January 16, 1997

"Let's go to San Telmo," said Heleni. "You'll love it; it has this great flea market on Sundays."

If there is one thing I can't stand, it's flea markets. I've never been much of a shopper, and especially not when it comes to things liable to contain fleas. On the contrary, my shopping philosophy has always been: if it glitters, it's gold. If it doesn't, don't buy it.

It was elevenish by the time we arrived in San Telmo. As we walked through the cobblestone streets along the main drag, calle Defensa, Heleni told me that this used to be where the rich lived before the yellow plague hit at the end of the nineteenth century, forcing them to beat a retreat to Barrio Norte, the North District, which is where *"gente como uno,"* "our crowd," still lives today.

We walked past one antiques store after another, countless art galleries, and what were once the mansions of the city's patrician families. In spite of all the antiques stores and the hordes of camera-toting tourists they inevitably attract—it's funny how even though I am a tourist myself, I find Tourists Who Are Not Me offensive and feel strongly that they should be deported, whereas I . . . well, it's different, isn't it?—the neighborhood, as I was saying, does manage to retain its authentic flavor. Perhaps that's because most of it is in an advanced state of dilapidation and for some reason dilapidation = charm.

As we walked and talked, I admired the many dilapidated = charming buildings that had once been red, pink, blue, yellow, and green and that were now various shades of ocher thanks to the double effect of time + grime. Funnily enough, this only served to enhance rather than diminish the playful grace of the exteriors, the stucco ornamentation around the windows, the intricate floral designs of the wrought-iron railings on the balconies that jutted forth from the facades. Stopping in front of one particularly delightful example, the elegant stonework of which was in the poetic process of crumbling apart, we were able to sneak a peek through the French doors and see a bookcase full of dusty, leather-bound books, a massive mantelpiece made out of carved mahogany, and a crystal chandelier that hung heavily from the ceiling above. The only sign of life was the Siamese cat lazing inside the alcove of a bay window.

At last, we came upon Plaza Dorrego, the main square. It was noon by now and the sun was at its peak. Making matters hotter still were the throngs of people shoving and squeezing, pushing and squishing past each other in the narrowest aisles you ever had to shove, squeeze, push, and squish through. The stalls had turned into literal heat traps thanks to the overhead blinds that kept any air at all from circulating. But if you think this was enough to put off the flea-market aficionados from their treasure hunt, think again. Personally, I doubted very much that they would find anything remotely treasurelike among what to my admittedly untrained eye looked like mountains of garbage. I didn't doubt, however, that they would find lots of fleas.

"Taxi! Take me to Chanel!" was the cry I was repressing as best I could.

As I followed Heleni, wondering when it would be okay to say: "You were right: I love it. Can we go home now?," while saying sorry every two seconds to the people who were stepping on my feet and elbowing me in the ribs, I noticed that many of the stands were displaying the picture of somebody I didn't recognize.

"Carlos who?" I asked.

"Gardel," repeated Heleni.

"Who's he? A saint?" It wasn't a bad guess, given all the plastic flowers and votive candles placed in front of what to me looked like icons. He really could have been: I've never seen such a charismatic display of dimples in my life.

"Not quite. He is—was—a tango singer," said Heleni. That's all the information she was able to provide me with, since as she herself admits, she is not a leading expert in matters pertaining to the tango.

We stopped at the stand of a particularly devout follower of the singer-saint, judging by the size of the shrine erected to him. The owner of the stand looked to be in his late seventies and, in spite of the impossible heat, he was wearing a black, long-sleeved shiny polyester shirt that showed off nicely the dandruff that was falling from his greasy salt-and-pepper hair onto his shoulders. He was smoking an unfiltered cigarette, and when he opened his mouth, I was able to take note of the effects of the habit on his teeth, which were the same color as some of the houses we had passed on the way.

With Heleni acting as interpreter, I asked him to tell me about Carlos Gardel. I wanted to know what was so special about him. The man at the stand literally rubbed his hands with joy at the prospect of converting the two infidels standing before him.

"Have you never heard of el Zorzal Criollo?" he asked in disbelief.

"*El zorzal* is a kind of bird. A thrush, I think. And *criollo* refers to the first Spanish settlers of Argentina, so that when you say of something that it is *criollo*, it's a way of saying that it is authentic Argentine," Heleni filled in.

"And thrushes have nice voices?" I asked Heleni, since, frankly, I have no idea.

"Yes, I think we can safely assume that," she said.

"No, I'm ashamed to say that I haven't," I said to the guy at the stand. "But it's never too late to learn."

And with that, the floodgates opened and Walter, for that was his name, gave us the unabridged version of the singer-saint's life. Mercifully, his life was short; otherwise we would have been there all afternoon.

"They say that Gardel sings better every day," he said.

"Hang on a minute. Do you mean to say that he is alive?" I asked, confused all of a sudden.

Walter, taking immense delight in my innocence, let out a chuckle that made his midriff shake like Jell-O.

"No, no, no . . ." His mood swung suddenly to profound sadness as he shook his head despondently. I felt I should condole with him. Perhaps the singer had died recently—maybe this was another Princess Diana scenario—and Walter was still in mourning. But when he told us that Gardel had died in a plane crash in Colombia in 1935, I was impressed. This was definitely no ordinary tango singer we were talking about. More than sixty years had passed and he was still being mourned.

I often wonder how long it will take for people to stop mourning me after my death. On a good day, I give them a month to forget that I was ever born.

I noticed that Walter spoke about "Carlitos" almost exclusively in the present tense, the ultimate proof that the man is a legend. Although they often end up prematurely mangled—in fact, it seems to be a condition sine qua non if you want to become one—legends never die.

"Without Gardel, the tango would have stayed in the slums for good," he pronounced. Since this comment drew a blank from the ignorami before him, Walter was forced to elaborate that before Gardel, no respectable Argentine could be seen doing it, unless safely hidden away in a brothel in one or another of the slums. It was considered far too naughty to be practiced in public, and frankly, I can see why. Heleni whispered to me that to some extent this is true today. None of her friends from the so-called good families would dream of being seen at a *milonga*.

But when French high society fell in love with Gardel and everything to do with the tango, including the dance, the Argentine snobs, who had pooh-poohed it until then, changed their tune, Walter was saying in a "Tango History for Dummies" voice.

Now Walter took out a black-and-white postcard and waved it under our noses:

"See this picture? Carlitos is shooting the movie *El Dia Que Me Quieras*—"

"Who is the little boy beside him?" I interrupted.

"*That* is Astor Piazzolla," said Walter. Suddenly, he cleared his throat and launched a huge glob that narrowly missed Heleni and landed a couple of inches away from my open-sandaled foot.

"Ah, yes! Piazzolla! Of course! I've heard of *him*!" I said, relieved to know something for once. "He's famous," I said, not realizing I was digging myself in deeper.

Here Heleni had a tough time keeping up with the expletives that my innocent remark had precipitated. One thing was clear, and that was that Walter did not approve of Piazzolla.

"I was in the front row when Amelita sang that . . . piece of garbage, *'Balada para un loco'* [Ballad for a Lunatic]. I will never forget it. It was in November of 1969. But there are times in life when you must defend what you believe in."

"How?" I asked.

"With tomatoes," he said. "The ripest ones I could lay my hands on. Of course, you had to feel sorry for Amelita." Now his voice turned nostalgic, like that of a soldier deep in his war memories. "What a night, though!" he sighed, his voice fading into the past.

Heleni and I were winking at each other frantically. It had been educational, but it was time to go. As I was paying for the postcard, which I wanted as a souvenir, I couldn't refrain from asking one last question: "Is Carlitos married?"

I had developed a crush on him—there is nothing sexier than a dead legend in a black-and-white photo—and this naturally made me curious about his marital status.

"No, he is faithful to his mother," said Walter, as if this were the most normal thing in the world. "Of course, he has many girlfriends, but he has never married, out of respect for her. She is the great love of his life."

"Hmmm . . ." was all I said. I didn't think that Walter needed to know how I feel about mama's boys, even if they are of legendary proportions. But looking on the bright side, at least I achieved instant closure. . . .

January 17, 1997

They say the hole in the ozone layer is right above Argentina. The sun is so intense down here. You'd think that people would wear sunglasses to protect their eyes. But they don't. This was a mystery to me at first. Especially when I compare it to New York, where people wear sunglasses all the time, even at ten o'clock at night. But I have solved the mystery. If people wore sunglasses, they wouldn't be able to play the staring game. There isn't a street in Buenos Aires where it is not practiced. I would even go so far as to say that it is more popular here than soccer. And that's saying a lot.

I think it's got something to do with the Italian blood flowing through almost everyone's veins. They play the game, however, with a lot more panache than their Italian cousins, whose idea of seduction is to pinch your bottom as you are trying to get across the street. The Argentine player is in a class of his own. It's all about the eyes, and the men here are supremely talented in this department. They are able to undress you and caress you and say a thousand words with just one look. And unlike their counterparts anywhere else in the world, they are often quite nice to look at themselves, as I think I have made abundantly clear, so that you are quite happy to return the compliment. Which is why I've thrown away my sunglasses: it would be such a waste to wear them, ozone layer or no ozone layer. And if this leads to premature crow's-feet due to constant squinting . . . so be it!

January 19, 1997

Why the fancy neighborhood is built around a cemetery is anybody's guess. At first, I found the idea morbid and wondered how my cousins could stand living in such close proximity to the dead. But now I have gotten used to the idea. In fact, I rather like it. What better—i.e., quieter—neighbors could one have? Since it's usually good to be on friendly terms with the neighbors, I decided that the time had come to pay them a visit. There was one in particular I wanted to meet: Eva Duarte de Perón.

As I walked the couple of blocks over to the Recoleta cemetery, I drank in the atmospheric cocktail of the streets. The Paraguayan/Bolivian/Peruvian maids, in uniforms, were pushing strollers containing blond, blue-eyed cherubs, their faces standing out in an uninterrupted sea of white. This is disconcerting for someone who is used to the multicultural patchworks of New York, London, and Paris. I couldn't help drawing uncomfortable parallels with the Aryan utopia. And yet, if I am honest, I have to admit that I also find comfort in a world where time has gotten stuck in the 1950s. Where things don't change—or if they do, not fast. It's almost as comforting as eating rice pudding with a tablespoon. I let out a wistful exhalation, otherwise known as a sigh—rice pudding tends to have that effect on me—when a bus rumbled past and let out a black fart of diesel so stinky that it made inhaling again physically impossible for what felt like too long.

I held my nose for another thirty seconds just to be on the safe side, hoping that the noxious fumes would soon be absorbed by the luscious green leaves of the trees that lined the sidewalks. Sitting underneath them at the cafés were the manicured and/or pedicured and/or face-lifted and/or Botoxed and/or tummy-tucked and/or breast-enhanced ladies who, by the look of their moon-shaped faces and ridiculously sharp cheekbones, had all been to the same plastic surgeon. They were drinking *cortados*—espresso coffees "cut" with milk—while exchanging the day's gossip. Strolling past them, the old men showed off their not-so-bygone elegance, with their three-piece suits, panama hats, and soft leather shoes. They did not appear in the least bit affected by the heat wave.

I admired the adolescent girls, Lolitas each and every one of them, their hair loose and faces shiny. They walked confidently from the hip as they talked on cell phones, apparently unaware of their breathtaking beauty. And everywhere you looked, skirts and high heels. Women here are so feminine that even when they are wearing pants, they look as if they are wearing skirts. I think the optical illusion is due to the way they move. They don't walk, they dance in the street or as they wait at the traffic lights to cross the road.

Take this one, for example. She was waiting at the curb, feet turned out like a ballerina, heels rolling inward at a slight incline and just grazing each other. When the light changed, her knees brushed together softly as they extended and contracted like an elastic band, giving each step a delightful springy quality. Watching her in motion, I understood why the tango is Argentine.

I had arrived at the gates of the cemetery and went inside. When I was finally able to locate Evita's tomb in the labyrinth of mausoleums and marble statues, I found it covered with flowers that were wilting in the heat of the sun. As I stood reading the inscriptions on the plaques donated by the numerous associations of ardent admirers, I noticed a woman weeping as she offered up her bunch of flowers. I couldn't help but be impressed by the fervor Evita still inspires today. Love her or hate her, it's impossible to ignore her. And once again, the magic formula for being remembered decades after your death seems to be: unbelievable amounts of charisma + untimely death (due to cancer in this particular case). I felt like asking the weeping woman how she felt about her idol's fondness for Christian Dior dresses, but then I thought better of it. Anyway, I already knew the answer: love is blind. It's as simple as that.

On my way home, I stopped off for my daily ice cream at Freddo's. It's become a ritual. I don't know how all the girls manage to keep their size-two waists here. It's a real mystery. Making matters even more fattening, they insist on piling the huge scoops so high that (a) it's impossible to keep them from toppling off the top of the cone, and (b) there is no way you can finish your ice cream before it drips all over your clothes. So you gobble your two giant banana-split/chocolate-chip scoops in order to beat the rate at which they are melting, but that still isn't fast enough so you briefly contemplate putting the whole thing in your mouth, but even *your* mouth is not big enough for that. And in the end, having lost the daily struggle, you get home in a yellow-and-brown-stained T-shirt wishing somebody would tell them that bigger is not always better.

January 21, 1997

It depresses me to think that I will be leaving in a couple of days, so I try not to think about it. But I do need to take gifts back to everyone in New York, no matter how little I want to think about it. Heleni told me that the best place for gift shopping is calle Florida, the main pedestrian street in downtown Buenos Aires. You'll find everything you need there, she said. I wanted to make this shopping expedition as quick as possible since I hate the antiseptic quality of pedestrian streets, to the point where I would almost prefer to go to a flea market. But try as one might to avoid them, it's not always possible to bypass these commercial booby traps. Sometimes you have to shop with the flow.

I went by Galerías Pacífico, a department store-cum-mall. Out in front of it, a huge crowd was congregated around something I couldn't see. Everybody seemed absorbed by whatever it was. I could hear the sound of tango music and a woman's voice amplified by a microphone. I am not usually interested in street performances—they normally fill me with pity—but my curiosity had been awakened and so I pushed through the crowd to the front—when you are only five feet two, you learn to do that.

Two men, one old and one middle-aged, were dancing together. They were wearing gray pants with white stripes, embroidered black waistcoats over shiny black shirts, white neck scarves, and black fedora hats, and the crowd was loving them. They were dancing a *milonga*, a faster-paced and happier version of the tango. Don't ask me why everything is called *milonga* in this country. It just is.

When the dance ended and the applause had subsided, a woman wearing a dangerously short skirt went up and grabbed the middle-aged man—boy, were we in for an explosive treat! Their dancing had a confrontational, angry quality to it as their legs cut in and out of each other like blades in slick, incisive movements, reminding me of the fight scene in *West Side Story*. Timing was of the essence here: one second too early or too late and those kicks could do some serious damage to an unsuspecting shin, or worse. I flinched a couple of times as one or two of the less precisely timed kicks came too close for my/his comfort. For example, after he put his hand on her bum as he nodded at the audience, she responded in kind by sending a back kick between his thighs that, frankly, looked completely off the mark—unless, of course, her heel was meant to land where it landed. But amazingly, he didn't flinch. Either his balls are made of steel or they have become numb from years of getting the shit kicked out of them.

Afterward they posed for photos as the old man passed a hat around, waving it under people's noses until they got the message. I fished around for whatever coins I had in my wallet and placed them in the hat. The old man wrinkled his nose and gave me an unmistakable "Is that *all?*" look. He pulled out a bill of five pesos (five dollars!) to suggest what he thought would be a more appropriate contribution.

What cheek! I thought as I took his suggestion and placed five pesos (five dollars!) into the hat.

I pushed my way back out of the audience and walked past the tacky tourist shops, the low-end jewelry stores, the high-end fur boutiques, the hungry men handing out flyers for discounted hamburgers or cut-rate cell phones until I found the store I was looking for: Havanna.

It's hard to describe *alfajores*. They are too big to be cookies and too compact to be pastries. They come covered in chocolate icing or powdered sugar and their insides are filled with *dulce de leche*, which is basically caramelized milk, though that is not doing justice to it, and to make a long story short, you die and go to heaven with every bite. I bought ten boxes (each one containing a dozen). Not for me, off course. They are *gifts*, remember?

By the time I was done with my shopping and passed back in front of the Galerías Pacífico on the way home, the *Pacífico Tango Show* had packed up and the crowd had dispersed. In its place, a living Statue of Liberty was getting ready for his shift and was spray-painting his face green. And as I watched him, I wished I didn't have to go home soon, or ever, for that matter.

January 23, 1997

Last night, I danced with a stranger. Jacques had to act as a go-between because I was too shy to close the deal myself. Normally the woman is supposed to look at the guy she wants to dance with. If the feeling is mutual, he nods at her. It's called the *"cabeceo."* It's a safe way for a guy to ask a woman to dance without anyone else seeing him. This way, if he is turned down, he doesn't lose face. The system is designed to spare the fragile male ego. But what about *my* poor ego? The idea of debasing myself by staring at a guy is too horrible to contemplate. I've never done it, and I'll be damned if I start now. I don't want to go fishing, thank you very much! I want to be swept off my feet by surprise.

It was my last night in Buenos Aires. We were back on Plaza Dorrego in San Telmo, where they hold an open-air *milonga* on Sunday evenings after they've cleared the square of the flea market. I couldn't believe that it had been a week already since our encounter with Walter and my short-lived love affair with Carlos Gardel. I felt a sudden pang at the thought that tomorrow I would wake up from this dream and find myself back in my nightmarish existence as an account executive at a large New York agency. I put this miserable thought to sleep again as quickly as possible. I did not want to let it or anything else ruin the magic of this balmy evening.

We sat down at a candlelit table under a tree on the edge of the square and ordered *choripanes*. These are hot dogs, basically, though thicker and shorter than the U.S. version—and once again I found myself daydreaming about the implications. You can't walk a block in Buenos Aires without the ubiquitous smell of grilling fat wafting up your nostrils—and I have to admit that it is enticing, even though it does make you want to go home and wash your hair.

The dancers were already circulating in the middle of the square in an anticlockwise circle—Jacques told me that it's called the "line of dance." Beneath the surface of the music, I was sure I could hear the sawing song of the crickets, adding their own rhythm to the tangos that spilled out of the amplifiers. Couples, like reproducing cells, formed and split, to form again with others in a permanent cycle. Although I was anxious to put into practice what I had learned in my first few lessons, I was too nervous, as I have already mentioned, to do anything about it. I was resigning myself to being a wallflower when Jacques said:

"See that guy over there?" He was pointing to a huge fellow. Actually, huge is an understatement: the guy was clinically obese.

"It's difficult not to see him," I said.

"Oscar is his name. He's a great dancer and a really nice guy. How about if I ask him to dance with you?"

Beggars can't be choosers. And at least this way, I was avoiding the calamity of all calamities: being picked by someone and then dropped after that someone realized his mistake—i.e., that I couldn't dance. Tango dancers, you see, are *really* fussy about who they dance with. There is an obvious pecking order: at the top of the pyramid are the gorgeous, skinny girls who look as if they were born in the even skinnier heels they are wearing. At the bottom are the old, the ugly, and the tango infirm, and no matter how unpleasant the truth, I belonged in the third category. So by asking Oscar if he would dance with me, Jacques was asking him for a HUGE favor.

Oscar, bless his soul, bore the imposition with infinite grace and immediately took me in his hefty arms. He was so massive that all I needed to do was relax and let the weight of his body take me wherever it wanted to go. In spite of the great difference in our volumes, dancing with this gentle giant felt completely natural. I hoped I was not alone in enjoying the experience. I will never know, since it is impossible to get inside somebody else's head. But I try anyway. Part of me thinks that if I enjoyed dancing with him so much, then he must have enjoyed it too. But another part of me—the part that is depressingly aware that each and every one of us is an island unto himself—knows that rarely do two people experience the same feelings at the same time, no matter how much they like to project their feelings on to each other. So as part of me fantasized that Oscar and I were in the moment together, the other part of me worried that it wasn't much fun for him to be dancing with a complete beginner. But I will say this for him: he did his utmost to disguise his boredom by giving me constant encouragement as he stroked my back before placing his left palm in the hollow between my neck and shoulders. I closed my eyes and elected to suspend disbelief, opting to believe in the lie instead.

"*Que divina!*" he sighed. I didn't say anything, but he was starting to look divine to me too—of course, it helped that I had my eyes closed. In spite of these harmless attempts at seduction, I felt safe with him. In fact,

I have never felt safer than in the arms of this mountain of a man. It was quite a revelation, since never before had I associated safety with the opposite sex. This was a milestone for me—a huge one, in every sense of the word.

Before we had set off for the *milonga*, Jacques had given me a briefing on tango protocol, on the dos and don'ts. A set is comprised of three to four tangos, he had said, and etiquette requires you to complete a set with a partner before switching to another. Do not under any circumstance thank him before the end of the set or he will be deeply insulted, he had warned me. Four tangos had seemed like a lot in theory. But in Oscar's arms, it was nothing at all. In fact, they went by far too quickly for my taste. I had to force my eyes open and pry myself apart from him, even though I had not the faintest desire to do so, even though what I really wanted to do was to go on and on all night. I put a brave face on it, though, and even managed a smile.

"Thank you, Oscar. That was really lovely," I said in my pseudo Italian, hoping that he would understand. He did, apparently, because he replied that the pleasure had been all his. And the strange thing is, I believed him—he said it with such sincerity—while knowing at the same time that it couldn't possibly have been true.

Escorting me back to the table—that too is etiquette—he "handed" me over to Jacques before disappearing again in search of another partner. The man is a dancing machine!

"I see you've worked up quite a sweat there!" said Jacques.

I had not noticed because I was still on cloud nine. I looked down at my dress, noticing just then that I was drenched. I couldn't have been any wetter had I just taken a bath with all my clothes on.

"I'll have you know, it's not *my* sweat," I said under my breath. "If this was *my* sweat, you'd be rushing me to the hospital."

Poor Oscar. It wasn't his fault it was boiling hot and that he had turned into a massive lump of perspiring flesh. But I will say this for him and Argentines in general: no matter how much they sweat, they don't smell bad. I was amazed when I took the subway here for the first time: not a single foul whiff anywhere. They must wash twenty times a day.

All pleasures come with a price tag, I said to myself. And those ten minutes of pure, humid love had been worth every penny.

I couldn't have wished for a lovelier end to my trip. Speaking of which, I have to pack since my flight leaves in a couple of hours. It saddens me to think that since Heleni and Jacques are going back to Paris in a couple of months, I may never come back here again. For one thing, Argentina is so out of the way. And for another, there are so many other places I still want to go: Africa, China, India . . . But I will never forget my time here. Buenos Aires has given me a gift that will always remind me of it, a gift that I am taking back with me in my suitcase, along with the eight remaining boxes of *alfajores:*

The tango.

Gancho

1. Hook

2. Tango figure whereby one partner inserts his or her leg between the other's, hooks it around an inner thigh, and squeezes. This feels rather pleasant if well executed.

Enganchado/a

To be "hooked," as in to be crazy about someone or addicted to something—the tango, for instance.

January 25, 1997

On my way back to work this morning, I thrashed though the crowds on the sidewalk for the twenty blocks that constitute my morning commute to Fortieth and Madison. I knew exactly when the traffic lights would turn red for me and I crossed anyway. I feigned oblivion of the couriers on their bikes, who swerved at the last minute to avoid hitting me, and I played deaf to the horns of the drivers, who had all woken up on the wrong side of the bed. Since it was hailing, I wielded my umbrella, which served as both shield and weapon, sending pedestrians, terrified of having their eyes poked out, flying out of my way.

I had some notion of the discomfort I was causing in my wake, but it was vague. I was listening to *"Bahía Blanca"* by Carlos Di Sarli on my portable CD player. And the sound of the tango was beaming me back to the hot and dusty studio in Buenos Aires and making me unconscious of everything outside myself, including the bitter cold that threatened to bite off my fingers. Without realizing it, I must have been practicing my tango walk, crossing here and executing a *boleo* (kick) there, because I sensed that people were giving me that sideways glance they give to the schizos. But I didn't care. I was happy!

I floated back into the Y&R building, and it seemed as if nothing could affect this newfound serenity, not even the muted lighting, the dark blue wall-to-wall carpeting, or even the mahogany paneling, all of which normally have an immediate impact on my mood, as if someone were turning my inner dimmer switch to low. Today, nothing and nobody could switch me off. I felt alive!

Before taking the elevator up to my floor, I went to the cafeteria to grab a styrofoam cup of what passes for coffee. I noticed how glum everybody else looked, but today I wasn't going to let their mood get me down. I was going to remain elated in the face of the muted smiles and muted tones of these people who had once been but were no longer my fellow convicts. Like Clint Eastwood, I had broken out of Alcatraz. The tango had set me free!

When my colleagues asked me how my vacation was, I answered: "Great!" without going into further detail. I wanted to keep my secret, feeling it was too precious to share with any-old-body. By talking about it, I would dilute the intensity of my happiness. Yet I could not keep the twinkle out of my eye or stop the sides of my mouth from touching my earlobes when I said, "Great!" No matter how hard I tried, I could not help looking as happy as I felt.

I took the elevator, carefully avoiding eye contact with all the vacant gazes that reminded me of how I used to feel in 1996 B.T. (before tango) and got out on the twenty-third floor. My secretary was already sitting at her desk in the area outside my office. I had forgotten what a depressing sight that was: she already looked bored and the day hadn't even begun. As she looked for my mail and messages, I told her she really needed to get herself to Buenos Aires ASAP. That was cruel of me, I realize. But I didn't mean it to be.

The first thing I saw as I stepped into my office—it's more of a cave than an office, really, since it doesn't have a window (which is handy for afternoon naps)—as I was saying, no sooner had I stepped into my cave than I saw the red, flashing light on my phone that screamed at me like a police siren: "Voice mail! Voice mail! Voice mail!" This is only to be expected when you come back from a two-week vacation. What is not to be expected, however, is the violence of the bombardment via loudspeaker once you push Play. Think Pearl Harbor.

8:50 A.M.: "Hey! Hope you had a good one. Okay, so the deal is, we need to go over the budget again. And we need to talk pre-production. Welcome back!"

My client. Shit. I'd forgotten about the shoot. In fact, I'd forgotten all about my client, not to mention his stupid canned pasta.

February 8, 1997

I have just gotten home from work and Jacques has called to tell me that Oscar is dead.

Luckily he broke the news more gently than that. It happened in the middle of a *milonga*, apparently. He was eating a pizza when he had a heart attack. I'm the one who is heartbroken, though. My first tango partner, gone, just like that. To think that only a couple of weeks ago I was in those big, warm arms and that they have gone cold forever. For once, I am not exaggerating when I say that he danced himself to death. It reminds me of the girl in the fairy tale with the red slippers. Or those poor bears in Bulgaria that they beat with a stick and that dance and dance and dance till they drop dead from exhaustion . . . What an exit! Speaking of exits, how *were* the ambulance men able to carry his corpse out of there? Another mystery to be solved along with how they built the pyramids . . . If I weren't feeling so sad, I'd be happy for him. In fact, I'd be jealous. What better way to die? The lucky thing gets to spend the rest of eternity in the arms of one partner after another at a never-ending *milonga* in the sky.

March 10, 1997

I've signed up for tango lessons at three different studios. I go to the first because that's where Al Pacino went to learn to tango for *Scent of a Woman*. To the second because they taught Madonna for *Evita*. And to the third for luck. I am running around the city like a headless chicken to make all my classes and I have never been happier or more confused in my life. Each teacher tells me to do things differently and swears that he or she is the only one who knows the right way to tango.

One says: "Stick out your chest!" and "Lean into your partner!" He explains that this is the way that the *compadritos* used to dance. They were the *gauchos*-turned-gangsters who, when they left the pampas for a life in the city, traded in their baggy *bombacha* pants and cowboy hats for pin-striped suits, white scarves, and fedoras. They may have been dressed like dandies now, but they had kept their knives and their fierce attitude. These guys liked to show off, and instead of walking like everyone else, they went around with a swagger, their bowlegs bent at the knees, bringing them closer to the ground, their weight thrust forward like raging bulls and their chests pumped out like cocks ready to battle. According to this teacher (Teacher A), *el pechito Argentino*, as it is known, is the basic posture in tango.

Translation: if the guy sticks his chest out, I've got to stick mine out too. It's for the sake of balance, so that he doesn't fall on top of me. As a result, our bodies form a triangle, chests together and hips apart, creating a certain tension, quite a pleasant sort of tension, I might add . . .

This all sounds convincing. So I do as I am told: I stick out my boobs and I lean like the Tower of Pisa.

"No, no, no, it's all wrong," says Teacher B, reprimanding me severely. She insists that follower and leader each maintain his and her own axis. There is to be no leaning at all. "That's all nonsense. People used to dance like that. But things have changed. The tango has evolved—just like everything else," she says. I was glad that my friend Walter from San Telmo wasn't in the room because he would have attacked Teacher B with a ripe tomato on the spot. AHHH! I'm going mad!

The only cure for insanity is to shop, so I went to Capezio and bought myself a pair of "tango" shoes. They are a far cry from the sexy stilettos I saw on the women's feet in Buenos Aires. But I don't think I could stand, let alone walk, in those. My new ones will have to do the trick for now. A little heel goes a long way, I am discovering. It really helps, despite what one might think. It's not just about looking sexy. It suddenly becomes possible to walk backward without bobbing up and down. And since you spend most of your time walking backward, while the man walks forward as he pushes you out of his way, you want to avoid bobbing as much as possible because it's a complete no-no to bob. Teachers A, B, and even C agree that you must always keep your head level. You simply can't do that in flats, unless you are on the balls of your feet all the time, which is extremely painful after five hours of dancing. Trust me.

More exciting, though, than my new shoes are my new fishnets. I cannot claim any practical reason for that purchase. They just make you feel terrific. Like you're making love to yourself every time you dance.

"Tango is a sensual dance. Let your thighs brush against one another with each step," says Teacher C. That is a lesson I shall retain forever and practice *always*, no matter who says it's wrong . . .

April 26, 1997

Last night, I did something really scary: I went to a *milonga*. *Alone*. Yes, I often go to the movies alone. It doesn't bother me because, apart from the few embarrassing minutes in the beginning before the lights go out, it's dark and everyone is concentrating on the film, so they soon forget about the loser in the fifth row with no date and no friends. Yes, I often walk into a restaurant or a bar alone. But it's always to meet someone there. The fact that someone is invariably late and I am always punctual, meaning that I spend, on average, fifteen minutes having full-scale panic attacks, certain that I am about to be stood up, is neither here nor there. Last night was a whole new ball game. There was no someone to look forward to. And we're talking about a well-lit kind of place. But I had no choice. If I wanted to dance the tango, I would have to go to the dark side (which, I reiterate, was not dark enough for my taste).

Il Campanello was one of those seedy-trying-terribly-hard-to-be-glitzy Italian joints in the West Forties. A cheap version of the Rainbow Room. The tables were covered with elegant white tablecloths, while the chairs were made of white plastic—to go with the tablecloths, I presumed.

This interesting combination skirted a dance floor, at one edge of which a three-piece band was playing. The trio consisted of a *bandoneón*, which is *the* tango instrument par excellence and which used to be made in Germany but is no longer made anywhere. It's a kind of high-pitched accordion that produces the lament so characteristic of the tango. Nowadays, you can only find decrepit ones in antiques stores. I remember seeing a couple at the flea market in San Telmo. The other instruments in last night's trio were a guitar and a key board.

I had changed into my heels and was sitting at the bar, sipping a drink that I didn't really want. But I needed something to look busy. I felt self-conscious, and if I didn't give my arms something to do, they would have dangled at my sides awkwardly. I was sure that everybody was looking at me and feeling sorry for this poor girl who was all alone. I sat with my back to the dance floor. I didn't want to look at anybody, lest they think I wanted to dance (which I did), since I didn't feel entitled to lure them under false pretenses. After all, I don't even know if I'm supposed to stick my chest out or keep it in. I was stirring my martini, thinking it best to just keep stirring because alcohol is terrible for my balance and the last thing I needed was to be drinking and dancing, when I was approached by a man with an outrageous tan, in his mid-sixties, wearing a three-piece suit (he must be Argentine) and spats (I wasn't sure anymore), and a diamond stud in his ear (I was even less sure).

"*Hola, rrrrrubia!* I am Arrrrmando. What's your name, my darrrrr-ling?" (Argentine.)

Was he talking to me? I turned around to see if there were any blondes in the vicinity (*rubia* means blonde—it's one of the first things you learn). And then I remembered that I am a blonde. I have been a blonde for six months now. I still can't get used to it. I love the results, though. I've never gotten so much attention in my life! It's true: Blondes *do* have more fun.

I'm so out of practice when it comes to flirting, though. Nobody flirts in New York City. I imagine the guys are worried about getting sued. So I found it refreshing to flirt with Armando, regardless of the fact that he was thirty-five years older than my target group. I had to hand it to him: this old dog certainly knew how to turn on the charm. I wouldn't be at all surprised if I were told that all Argentinos attend compulsory charm school. Either that or they are naturally gifted!

We sat chatting at the bar for a while. He was telling me how he had come to the States twenty years ago for work and had ended up staying. You'd never guess from his accent that he has been here that long. He is a psychologist—like half the population of Argentina, according to what I've heard. When I asked Armando if it was true that there are more shrinks per capita in Buenos Aires than anywhere else in the world—even more than in New York City!—he confirmed it. I was surprised. The Argentines I met while I was down there didn't strike me as being neurotic at all. In fact, I thought they seemed extremely well-adjusted. Too happy, if anything!

Out of the blue, Armando volunteered that he was recently divorced. I nodded sympathetically and changed the subject, in case he got the idea that I was at all interested in his marital status. I asked him instead how he had gotten started dancing the tango. He leaned forward and, invading the space that my face had been occupying so that my face was now forced to seek a more remote location, he confided to me that when he was a student in Buenos Aires, and was *still* handsome—he was fishing, but I didn't take the bait—he had worked in a tearoom where single ladies (old hags?) whiled away the afternoons in the arms of young men who charged by the dance. In other words, he had been (still was?) a gigolo and the tan made complete sense. As he spoke, his hand had crawled along the side of the bar and was now firmly placed on top of mine.

"*Mi amorrrrrr*, dance with meeee," he said. The way he said it, it sounded like I'd be a fool to refuse him. I wondered whether I would be presented with a check at the end of the set. Nonetheless, I accepted.

We found a tiny space on the crammed floor and waited for the trio to start playing again. When it did, he grabbed me by the waist and . . . it was love at first dance. Again?! I couldn't believe it. So soon after dear old Oscar, may he rest in peace. To think that out there in the real world, one can wait in vain one's whole life for love at first sight, while in here, it happens all the time. Also, I'm starting to notice a trend: The freakier the partner, the more likely you are to love dancing with him. Here I was once again connecting perfectly with someone who was a far, FAR cry from my physical ideal. How was I supposed to explain that I was currently swooning in the arms of someone I wouldn't normally have touched with a ten-foot pole? Someone old enough to be my father? Surely it was a bit late in life to be developing an Electra complex?

What is happening to me? I asked myself. This didn't stop me, though, from asking myself what Armando's rate was for a full night of tango versus one set. And whether he might give me a discount.

When the set ended, he led me back to the bar. I was relieved because it didn't look as if he was going to charge me anything at all. But I should have known better.

"Que barbara!" he cried—I must remember to look that word up. "You're going to be a grrrreat, grrrreat dancer!" he said.

"Do you think so?" I said ecstatically.

"You arrre light as a featherrr! And you surrrender yourrrrself with such abandon! A rrrreal pleasurrre to dance with!" he said.

It's true: I have taken to the business of surrendering to strange men like a fish to water. Armando is not the first partner to have commented on it, so it *must* be true. I'm starting to think that it's because I'm so afraid of being vulnerable in "real life" that I compensate for it with such gusto on the dance floor. Tango is a great substitute for love. I don't need my therapist to tell me that. Or Armando, for that matter.

The band started up again and he was gone in a flash. He needn't have disappeared so quickly! But I didn't have time to stay miffed for long. Now that Armando had broken the ice, the other men, who had been watching to see if I was at all decent, came flocking and, to make a long story short, I didn't stop dancing until two in the morning. By the time I called it a day, I had forgotten all about being afraid of remaining a wallflower. I had also forgotten all about Armando.

May 19, 1997

But Armando had not forgotten about me, as I discovered a couple of days ago at Dance Manhattan, where he flew me to heaven once more, so that once more I found myself thinking:

What is happening to me? I was more perplexed than ever. Which did not keep me from dancing five, yes *five*, sets with him. I know you're not supposed to dance that many with the same guy, because it gives him the wrong impression. But it felt too good to refuse. Why not have my cake and eat it too? I thought.

Surely, if I squeezed ten other partners between the five sets I danced with him, it would telegraph a lack of romantic interest. My thinking went that this would be the elegant way of communicating that while I enjoyed dancing with him *an awful lot*, it would not stop me from enjoying other men too. I thought I was being smart. Unfortunately, that is usually what one thinks when one is being a total idiot.

There is no getting away from it: tango thrives on ambiguity. That's what makes it so addictive. It's the *not* knowing if it is real or make-believe that keeps you going back for more. Try as one might to penetrate the mystery of it—and boy do the guys try—all one can do is skim the surface. Desire is awakened but not quenched in an endless foreplay—a foreplay that is never consummated by sex. Well, not then and there. I'm convinced that when people talk about safe sex, they are referring to the tango. Imagine having your fire lit 24/24 and never being able to extinguish it. "Frustrating" is an understatement.

As I swooned in Armando's arms, still feeling safe in the ambiguity of our embrace, I hoped things might stay that way. I hoped he understood that although the surrendering-to-him bit was real—while being make-believe at the same time—it was made possible only because it was safely confined to the limits of the dance floor. I hoped he realized that I could give myself entirely to him only when I was dancing because *and only because* the tango gave me permission to do so.

"Let's have dinnerrr, my darrrrling," he whispered in my ear, his lips brushing against the right side of my neck, just beneath the earlobe.

(Oh dear. He's taking the surrendering thing literally.)

I would have screamed "Help!" had my cheek not been glued to his. I needed to find a diplomatic way out of dinner as quickly as possible. Unfortunately, trying to come up with excuses not to have dinner with people is terrible for one's concentration. The net result was that I kicked him in the shin when he tried to lead me into a *gancho*.

"Oops! I'm soooo sorry, Armando!" I cried, horrified by my blunder.

"Neverrr mind, my darrrling! You can make it up to me by having dinnerrr with me this week," he said. He's the type who would say such a thing.

"Thank you soooo much, Armando. That would have been lovely! But I'm afraid I'm booked solid this week," I said as warmly as I could to make up for the fact that I was rejecting him. That was clear enough, wasn't it? No ambiguity there, right? Armando begged to differ.

"*Rrrrubia!* Arrrre you leaving already? Let me take you home!" he said, intercepting me on my way out. Shit. I had tried to leave without saying good-bye, to hammer in the point. But my plan had been thwarted.

"Thank you soooo much, Armando! But you needn't trouble yourself. Really. I'll take a cab," I said, feeling uneasy and sensing danger. Apparently, what is clear for some is murkier than a swamp for others.

"No, no, no! I insist!" he said.

What was a girl to do? My last remaining hope was that I had misinterpreted his honorable proposal. Argentine men are incredibly gallant toward women, as I noticed when I was down there. They take pride in being *caballeros*, i.e., knights in shining armor, and continue to open doors, pour the wine, let you go first in any line-type situation, and generally shower you with the little attentions that make a big difference. I wish men everywhere would take their lead: Why should feminism be an excuse for bad manners? But I digress.

Maybe he's being a gentleman, went the wishful thinking as I got into his car.

It was a miracle we made it home without an accident. His hands didn't touch the steering wheel once the entire time, since they were too busy wandering up and down my legs. Finally we were outside my building—praise ye the Lord! I tried to make my getaway as quickly as possible, frantically extricating myself from the seat belt that had become tangled up while yanking the car door open at the same time. But he was quicker than me—his lips were making a beeline for mine— which left me with no choice but to get physical too.

"Please, Armando. Don't," I said as sweetly as I could as I placed both arms on his chest and pushed, hard. I could have used less force, it's true.

"You don't know what you arrrre missing," he said curtly, sitting back upright in his seat and staring ahead at the street. The good news was that my body language had worked. The bad news was that he was sulking. He didn't get out of the car to escort me to my door, as any Argentine man would have done, a sign that he was deeply offended.

If only you hadn't surrendered so convincingly, I told myself. But then, you wouldn't have been dancing the tango. Since by definition, tango = surrender = catch-22.

After the guilt came the anger: How could he have thought he stood a chance? Hadn't he looked at himself in the mirror recently? Couldn't he see that he was forty years older than me (thirty-five: same difference)? What was the (old) man thinking? other than *Viagra*!

And then the blame. It was all the fault of those young girls who *do* go out with them. By giving lecherous geriatrics the wrong idea about their attractiveness, they are making life unpleasant, not to say unbearable, for the rest of us. I, for one, am sick and tired of shooing away salivating old dogs. *Basta!*

July 27, 1997

I used to be a popular guest at dinner parties. You could always count on me to regale my neighbors at the table with stimulating conversation on any topic, ranging from film and art, to politics and social issues, to religion and philosophy. But those days are long gone. Because, much to the distress of my friends, the only thing on my mind these days is the tango, which I'm afraid has had a serious—read: negative—impact on what was once my riveting conversation. Just as it's taboo to tell a girl you're bored of listening to her incessant meanderings regarding her ex, my friends don't dare interrupt the flow when I've started obsessing out loud about my favorite topic. I have noticed, however, that they do get that crossed-eyed "I'm-bored-to-distraction" look on their faces after what feels to me like two seconds but to them two hours, no doubt. What do they expect? I'm a *milonguera*! That's what they call addicts like me who go out dancing every night of the week. And as with any addiction, there is a price to pay.

First of all, my feet. They are killing me. Actually, it is I who am killing them. The poor things are the victims of the worst kind of domestic abuse, and if they had fingers, they'd be on the phone to the hot line for the prevention of cruelty to feet, so it's a good thing they don't (have fingers, I mean).

On the bright side of being a junkie: I have lost my appetite. I can't eat a thing. I force a few morsels down my throat every now and then to provide my poor body with enough calories so that it doesn't let me down in the middle of a tango. But I have completely lost interest in what used to be my sole reason for living: a good meal. I have never, ever, not even when I thought I was experiencing the worst love pangs, lost my appetite. If this is what it feels like to be in love, then I've never been in love before. It is a great diet. Nutritionists ought to be recommending it.

The effects of love on my sleeping patterns, however, I find less happy. I can't sleep a wink. (Except in the office, where I have no trouble at all.) I am turning into a ghost. Or rather, it is the tango that is the ghost haunting me and making it impossible for me to rest. After four or five hours of nonstop dancing, I lie awake in bed unable to get the music out of my head. Sometimes, I don't even make it into bed. I become Audrey Hepburn in *My Fair Lady*, when she sings, "I could have danced all night." I twirl around my bedroom, hopping onto the bed and pirouetting in and out of the curtains. Unfortunately for the neighbors, my voice isn't dubbed like hers.

September 3, 1997

Help! I'm turning into Dracula: I come out only at night and the sight of garlic fills me with horror. Long gone are the days when I could give in to the mouthwatering pleasure of a nice, thick, crusty piece of garlic bread. Spaghetti *al pesto* is out. You can forget about any of the Italian sauces, for that matter. Along with all French dishes—and most Greek ones too. In fact, there are few cuisines in the world that don't rely heavily on garlic. And those that don't, use onions. Even the English have learned to cook, and now put garlic in everything. What does that leave me with? Dry crackers.

Nowadays, it is painful to go to a restaurant because I can't order most of the things on the menu—and I'm the type of person who likes most of the things on the menu. But I'm off to a *milonga* afterward and it would be unacceptable to show up with garlic breath.

Bad breath is a tango dancer's obsession. It is a foe that must be wiped out at all costs. I thought I was the only one to fret about it. But I'm not. I think that Wrigley's and Orbit must make their healthy profit margins thanks in very large part to the tango community. I forgot to mention Halls. Few tango dancers would be caught dead without gum or mints in their pockets. And if they run out, they become more frantic than a smoker out of cigarettes.

"You don't have any gum, do you?" implores a forgetful soul.

When you hand it to her, her relief and gratitude are comparable to that of a baby whose mother has finally bothered to change it out of its soiled diapers.

Finally, knowing that the guy I am dancing with, who chews as he dances, is as afraid of offending me as I am of offending him has helped me overcome my own bad-breath anxiety. It is comforting that I am in the company of a fellow vampire.

October 6, 1997

Last night at Sandra Cameron's, I had a ball. I erased a guy from my "to-do" list! I will not rest until I have "done" every guy who has yet to dance with me because he is more advanced—or thinks he is.

Alas! There is no escaping the pecking order, and a follower, no matter how impatient she might be, must bide her time and pay her dues before a leader will do her the honor of asking her for a dance. Given that there are far more women than men on the scene—those who thought the ratio was bad in the rest of the city haven't been to a *milonga*—it's the guys who have the power to pick and choose. Last night must have been my lucky night because I got picked and chosen by one of the best dancers. Ecstatic doesn't even begin to describe how I felt!

I had been pining for John, a staff reporter for the *New York Times*, for weeks. I was starting to lose hope that he would ever ask me, when bingo!, he nodded in my direction from across the room and I went running to him like a Labrador puppy. And when he took me in his arms and we embarked on a *salida*, I said, Thank you, Lord, for making me a girl! In spite of all the frustrations that come with being a follower—i.e., not being able to invite a guy to dance with you, not being in control on the dance floor, and generally having to assume the passive role—when it's good, it's so delicious that it is worth every humiliation and frustration in the world. You would *pay* to come back as a follower if you had had the misfortune of being born the wrong gender. I'm not exaggerating. Following is far better than leading. How do I know? Because I've taken classes as a leader to see what it feels like on the other side of the fence. You never know: it might come in handy one day. If I were to decide to turn pro, for example. Something I have been daydreaming about lately . . .

To make a long story short, John was as divine as he looked from afar—which is not always the case. And to top it all, he was extremely generous with the compliments:

"How come we haven't danced before? What took me so long to ask you? Wow! You are wonderful, amazing, fabulous, blah blah blah . . ."

If I sound blasé, I don't mean to. On the contrary, my ego soared so high that I was afraid it would float off into outer space. I have never been so thrilled to tick anyone off my list in my life.

October 7, 1997

Last night when I went to Belle Epoque, I was expecting to experience the same high as the night before at Sandra Cameron's. Stupid of me, I know.

John was there. John, who only the night before had raved about my dancing and made me feel like a million bucks. You would think that somebody who had been so effusive would want to repeat the experience at the first possible opportunity, wouldn't you?

Not so.

In fact, I am starting to detect a pattern. When somebody spends all night telling you how marvelous you are, you can be 100 percent sure he won't look in your direction the next night. Or if he does happen to turn his head toward you by mistake, you can raise all the eyebrows you like, smile to high heaven, and nod your head as if you have a bad case of Parkinson's, he will pretend he has no idea what you want. Which is exactly what John was doing to me right now. As a result, my ego, which only the night before had been launched like a satellite to the moon, came crashing back down to the ground.

Anyway, he had terrible BO, was all I could come up with to console myself.

To make matters more depressing, I tried to "do" a couple of other dancers on my list, who were there to tantalize me like candy in a candy store. But I could not get my hand on a single M&M. Not even a brown one. It was as if they had held a meeting beforehand and agreed to boycott me in order to make sure I didn't get too big for my boots. Even Armando was in on the conspiracy. I suppose it's only to be expected. I did briefly consider going up to him and saying hi, but I couldn't find an opportunity since he spent all night in the arms of a girl who was even younger than me.

December 1, 1997

I'm finding it more and more difficult to juggle work and tango. Everybody keeps asking me if I'm okay because I look so pale and I keep yawning every two seconds. Also, I feel bad because I have been cranky with my assistant, no matter how hard I try not to be. But boy, does she get on my nerves!

For starters, she is unbearably chirpy in the mornings, and this morning was no exception when she gave me a ten-minute rundown on last night's rerun of a rerun of *Friends*. I looked as interested as possible and then, when she'd finished relating her vicarious life experience, I asked her to edit a reel of all the advertising of canned pasta that has ever aired on the seven continents, including the South Pole, figuring that this would keep her busy for a while and keep me from having to hear about last night's episode of *Seinfeld* (because I saw it).

Actually, I have been taking tips from George in how to sneak naps at the office. Every afternoon, I lock my door, stretch out on the thick carpet, and take five minutes. Not having a window in my office has turned out to be my job's biggest perk. Unfortunately, five minutes is all I can squeeze in, what with my client's incessant calls and my assistant's constant rapping to ask if there is anything she can do for me. See what I mean about her being annoying? I really need to put a "Do Not Disturb" sign on the door.

January 27, 1998

When Armando ignored me (along with everyone else) that night not so long ago at Belle Epoque, I assumed that that was the end of that. This was because I had not taken his Latin breeding into account, whereby the more one resists them the better they like it. I bet that if a poll were conducted among Latin lovers, nine out of ten would say they prefer the chase to the conquest. Meaning that just as I thought I was off the hook, the fun was about to begin.

Since the embarrassing events that took place in his car outside my home, he has been showering me with attention and flowers, phone calls and chocolates, and I have to admit, not being at all used to this kind of behavior—I usually go for the ones who treat me like shit—it does make a pleasant change. So much so that every time we dance, I, myself, find it harder and harder to distinguish love *on* and *off* the dance floor.

"What is happening to me?" has become my mantra.

In all probability, his ignoring me at Belle Epoque has something to do with it, there being no bigger turn-on than being ignored. But the real turning point came when we danced again a few weeks later at Dance Manhattan: the relief that he still wanted to dance with me was like an aphrodisiac. Suddenly, the age gap, which before had seemed completely insurmountable, looked perfectly surmountable. Hello, Electra complex!

"*Que piel!*" Armando said between two tangos.

"What does that mean?" I asked.

"It means you and me, *amor mio*, we 'have skin'—Spanish for chemistrrrry," he purred.

The thing about chemistry is that you don't choose whom you have it with. Often it's with the people you'd least like to have it or anything else with, for that matter. If the connection I had felt dancing with Armando the first time at Il Campanello had been intense, the electricity in the air now threatened to short-circuit the building. I'm discovering that there's nothing like thinking you're never going to dance with somebody again for the sparks to fly. The long and the short of it is that this time around, when he insisted on taking me home, I was *this* close (my thumb and forefinger are almost touching) to hopping into the sack with him. There is only so much skin a girl can resist. But I was saved by the smell.

You know how old people go stale? No matter how much cologne Armando doused himself with—I think he bathes in it—it couldn't cover up that sickly sweet smell of putrefying flesh. In spite of my fear that he would not forgive me a second time, I followed my nose instead of my heart and sent the poor man packing once more. When it came to the crunch, I couldn't bring myself to do it.

But the good news is that there was no need to worry. Far from spelling the end of our tango affair, my sexual rejection of him has only enhanced his desire to dance with me. Making it that much better when we do. And since he doesn't expect me to behave any differently—deep down, he actually *wants* me to reject him!—it's the perfect arrangement. What more could a girl ask for?

Having said that, I do worry about how close I came to falling into bed with somebody I wouldn't normally want to touch with a ten-foot pole. I was saved from making a terrible mistake in this case, but what if it happens again? What if I "have skin" one day with a partner who isn't completely repulsive? It is only natural to fantasize that if a guy makes you feel great on the dance floor, he might be able to do so under/on top of the bedcovers as well. I suppose all I can do is hope that I am this lucid the day a moderately attractive man flies me to tango heaven. Or that his skin smells like Armando's.

March 17, 1998

I don't know when it started. But it has hit me hard. This craving for a tango partner. One my own age. One I might conceivably fall in love with.

"Why do you need a partner?" is the first thing people ask me when I tell them that I'm looking for one. It's not really a surprising question if you consider that these are the same people who say "flamenco" when they mean "tango"—or "flamingo" as somebody wrote to me the other day. You really do have to wonder about somebody who writes "flamingo" for "flamenco" for "tango." To be fair, I was once just as naive. I shudder to think that I could have remained stuck in a state of tango ignorance forever. I can't imagine my life without the tango and yet, I might never have gotten onto that plane to visit my cousins in Buenos Aires. Was it chance or destiny? I don't know. But whatever it was, it points in one direction. It's true what they say: You do not choose the tango. It chooses you. And I thank it from the bottom of my heart for admitting me to its ranks!

March 19, 1998

It has occurred to me that I am not 100 percent clear as to what exactly I am looking for in my hypothetical partner. I think it might help to find the needle in the haystack, if I had an inkling of what the needle looked like. It would make sense therefore, in order to make the search as efficient as possible, to lay out the specifications one by one. So, here goes:

1. Height: Candidate must be between a half to a whole head taller than me (in heels)—but no taller, because otherwise I won't be dancing with him but with his belly button. It goes without saying that candidate should under no circumstances be shorter than me.
2. Build: Candidate must be neither too fat—because that would make the couple look awful—nor too skinny—because that would make me look awful (i.e., fat).
3. Face: This is not as crucial a factor, thanks to (1) the distance between stage and audience, and (2) the magic of lights and make up. Having said that, for own viewing pleasure, it would help if candidate were gorgeous. Also, it does make it substantially easier for one to fall in love with candidate if he has a nice one, thus ensuring the proper cement for the foundation of long and happy partnership.
4. Personality: Candidate mustn't have one.

Oh, this is silly. I realize, as I write, what a futile exercise it is. I can't possibly define my ideal partner. Because the magic of tango has nothing whatsoever to do with the outer package and everything to do with chemistry, or "*piel*," in Armando's words. Look at Gloria and Pablo, who are absolutely marvelous together: she's fat and he's skinny. Or Carlos and Vanina: she's tall and he's short. When these couples dance together . . . deep sigh . . . you don't see any of that. Only at first glance is tango a physical manifestation. When you look deeper, the couple transcends the physical plane altogether to become disembodied. So much for the "outer" specs.

As for the other stuff: heart, personality, intellect, drive, values, and all the other things that make up a human being, it doesn't make the slightest bit of difference what one is looking for since, let's face it, one always ends up with the total opposite anyway. Or is it me?

April 3, 1998

I think Armando has finally gotten the message. Better late than never . . . Some time has passed since I last had to foil one of his attempts at seduction. I am happy to report that we are now a platonic item. He continues to adore and spoil me—which I wouldn't have expected, frankly—and in exchange I have to listen to him vent about Vilma, his psychotic girlfriend, a forty-something mother-of-two accountant who conveniently lives in Long Island. And who appeared from out of the woodwork no sooner than it had become clear that he and I would be "just friends."

Anyway, we were at a practice session on Wednesday. I was wearing my favorite pink-and-white-flowered seventies-style nylon pants. My wardrobe is starting to feel the effects of tango, what can I say? And then on Thursday, I saw him again at another lesson.

"You'll never guess!" hissed Armando between two attempts at the figure the teacher was showing us. "Vilma phoned this morning. She was hysterical. She called me a lying son of a bitch. And some less nice things as well. I told her to calm down. 'What have I done, *mi vida?*' I asked her. She was yelling so much, I couldn't understand a word she was saying. And then she said: 'If you don't know what I'm talking about, think pink pants.'"

He paused. I realized I was supposed to see. But I didn't see at all—it was foggy. He repeated the part about the pink pants a dozen times or so. I suspected that they were somehow relevant, but I could not put two and two together. Finally, he reminded me of my attire the previous night, which you could loosely have described as "pink pants."

"But how did she know?" I gasped.

"She's having me followed by a prrrivate detective, *querida*!" cried Armando.

"She doesn't trust you?!" I said. He didn't think it was funny.

"Whose side arrre you on?" he barked defensively.

"Yours, *querido*! Why, yours, of course!" I said.

I do hope the pictures turned out well—i.e., that my bottom doesn't look too fat in the so-called pink pants. To think that had I never stumbled on the tango, I would have been wearing my regular black jeans, which are so much more flattering.

April 19, 1998

Going to the *milonga* is no longer as much fun as it used to be. The stakes have gotten far too high. Now, in addition to wounded egos, when the dancers who were flocking to you last night are flocking elsewhere, you must contend with the dreadful thought that you may never find anybody with whom to spend the rest of your dancing life and will thus be left to rot on the proverbial tango shelf. As if you didn't have enough reasons to feel like shit. Now you have double the reason to feel like double the shit.

Take last night for instance. I was at Dance Manhattan. I scanned the place (which wasn't easy, given how dark it was) and quickly concluded that there was nobody of any short-term (tonight) or long-term (the rest of my dancing life) interest. Except for Frank. The new assistant tango instructor at the studio and the only person in the joint I hadn't ticked off my list yet. I knew his name, but he didn't know mine. Actually, I don't think he was even aware of my existence.

Okay, so I had found my reason for being at Dance Manhattan. Now I had to make him aware of it. But either because it was dark in there, or because he simply pretended not to notice that I was looking at him, Frank refused to cooperate. Which made me all the more adamant that I should get him. Frank is not one of those guys who will dance with a

girl just because she is pretty. Because if we are honest, that is what it
boils down to. A guy will dance with you either because you are a good
dancer or because you are pretty, but preferably because you are both.

Call me arrogant, but I have gotten to the point where I am able to
look in the mirror and not want to throw up. I am what most people
would call attractive. And I know it, though I do sometimes forget. But
even the newly self-confident me is not immune to tango's vicious attacks on her self-esteem. I know that I am not the only woman—in fact,
I'm sure that this is true for *all* women who dance tango—who is convinced, on a regular basis, that she must be the ugliest cow on earth and
that that is why so-and-so will not dance with her. To bolster your mood
when so-and-so is being an uncooperative bastard, you find all sorts of
excuses for why he's left you to rot on the bench:

"He must be tired after having danced nonstop with all those women
(none of whom was me.)"

"He's playing games in order to pique my interest."

"He's got performance anxiety and is afraid to dance with a goddess
(me)."

"That bitch he's dancing with has cast an evil spell on him, blinding
him to the frantic signals I am sending in his direction."

"He can't see me because it's dark/crowded/I'm wearing black and
have disappeared into the background; I'll never wear black again."

As you sit on the bench, you turn into the prosecuted waiting for the
verdict of the jury (Frank and his kin). Will you get a reprieve or will it
be death row?

And last night, it was death row.

April 22, 1998

I spotted him the second I walked into the *practica*. It was impossible not
to see the tall, lithe figure gliding gracefully across the floor. Frank's
technique was as flawless as his looks. There was something ethereal
about both of them. As I leaned down to tie the straps around my

ankles, I kept one eye glued on him at all times and in the process almost twisted my neck.

I had finished tying up my shoes, but not with obsessing about how I would get him to ask me to dance. So what did I do? What I always do when I find a guy attractive: I ignored him. I didn't look in his direction once. Now, if he had looked like either Oscar or Armando, I would have had no problem whatsoever in staring at him until he gave me the *cabeçeo*. But luckily for him, he did not look anything like Oscar or Armando.

I had resigned myself to spending the rest of the evening wishing he would ask me to dance, while feeling wretched because he didn't, while kicking myself for being so incredibly stupid, when I looked up and there was his hand, reaching out to me. If this wasn't divine intervention on a grand scale—absolute, irrefutable proof of His existence and much more convincing than any of Descartes's theological proofs—I didn't know what was.

I followed Frank onto the floor like an automaton. I was terrified that I would let the side down. In fact, I was sure that I had forgotten how to dance. As we waited for the music to start, I settled into his embrace. It smelled delicious—of musky cinnamon that made you want to gobble him up on the spot. I looked up into his almond-shaped eyes and noticed their soft hazel coloring. They were kind eyes. The fullness of his lips and the evenness of his white teeth only confirmed the gentle impression. His straight-to-the-point nose, on the other hand, projected strength and confidence, while his high forehead lent a wide-open quality to his whole face. It was a face that was extremely easy to look at, framed as it was with the most gorgeous light brown locks complete with just the right amount and length of sideburn. And was that a pierced ear? I hadn't noticed it before. Was it his right or his left ear? I ought to ask someone once and for all which is the gay ear and which the straight because I can never remember.

The music started, and without further ado, he proceeded to put me through a complex series of figures that I had never encountered before. To my huge relief, I realized that (a) I *hadn't* forgotten how to dance, and (b) I *was* able to follow him—rather well, if I say so myself. To be perfectly honest, I enjoyed dancing with him in the way one enjoys a challenge. I can't say that it was the most intense connection I have ever felt. Each smooth step was perfectly executed, but he wasn't dancing from the heart or the gut or wherever the passion they call *"el sentimiento,"* that special feeling that finds its expression in the tango, resides. But who cared? I was in the yummy-smelling arms of the most handsome and highly accomplished dancer in the room—My Future Partner?

We had barely exchanged a single word, apart from the cursory "hi" in the beginning and "thank you" at the end of the set, when Frank asked me: "Do you want to go out for dinner sometime this week?" Was this a double theological whammy or what?! And to make matters more surprising still, he actually sounded shy and/or nervous. Surely, *I* was the one who was supposed to feel shy and/or nervous. This role reversal was so unexpected that it threw me for a loop. Until only moments ago, *he* had been the object of desire and *I* the pursuer of the object. Now, here was the object in the palm of my hand and I wasn't quite sure what to do with it. I was about to do a U-turn and start running in the opposite direction when I caught another glimpse of his pierced ear, so I said yes.

May 2, 1998

Frank called me on Tuesday for a Saturday-night date. Has he read *The Rules*, or what? He suggested Barolo on West Broadway and I said, "Perfect." When I arrived, he was there waiting for me. I didn't have to wait for him to show up late, as is usually the case. For some reason, instead of pleasing me, this was a source of intense irritation (I didn't let on—he didn't need to bear the brunt of my neurosis). How was he to know that it wasn't meant to be this easy?

But he was really cute . . .

Anyway, after we'd had a drink at the bar, we were shown to our table in the garden. I soon realized that Frank's shyness when he'd asked me out was not circumstantial but a permanent state of affairs. He is very quiet. So quiet that our date was in danger of turning into a trip to the dentist's. It was like pulling teeth. As always happens in these situations, I developed a bad case of verbal diarrhea to compensate. I spent all evening staving off the threat of an uncomfortable silence around the corner of each sentence.

But he was really cute . . .

It must be said that he is a very thoughtful fellow. Whenever I dropped my napkin, which was often, he would stoop to pick it up. He always made sure my glass was full, and asked me numerous times whether I liked my food. How was the poor thing to know that I don't like to discuss the food on my plate, preferring instead to eat it?

But he was really cute . . .

Finally I found a topic that brought out the chatterbox in him: cars. As I spent half my time listening to him talk about things that were of absolutely no interest to me (it's not at all easy to stifle a yawn when the person you're trying to stifle it from is looking straight at you) and the other half desperately looking for ways to cover the silence, I mourned the evening not so long ago when I had pined for the elegant figure in the distance who did not know I existed.

But he was really cute . . .

Finally, dinner and our first/last date came to an end and I did a splendid job of disguising my relief. He asked me if I was in the mood to go to a *milonga*. I apologized profusely for being too tired, at the same time as I waved down my runaway cab and threw myself into it, thereby preempting any idea he may or may not have had of giving me an end-of-first-date kiss.

But he was really cute . . .

May 10, 1998

Frank was at Dance Manhattan last night. The bastard hadn't called me after our date, which, I must admit, surprised me since I had gone to such great lengths to look fascinated by the Formula One. But apparently I was not the only one to be doing a fantastic job of covering up boredom. That, at any rate, was the only explanation I could think of for his not calling me. So imagine my astonishment when at the end of the set that we danced in silence he asked me out *again*! Is he a sucker for punishment, or what?

But more astonishing still was my reaction. At the exact same time I was thinking, Over my dead body, my lips uttered the words, "Yes, that would be lovely."

One might be tempted to interpret my acceptance of the invitation as a bout of temporary insanity with suicidal leanings. But actually, it makes perfect sense if you take into account the following five motives:

I had no decent excuse prepared since I hadn't thought I would need one.

I simply didn't have the heart to say no after he had picked up my napkin off the floor so many times.

I was afraid that if I said no, he would never dance with me again.

He didn't call and thus immediately regained all the attractiveness points he had lost during the date itself.

He smelled of Vetiver.

None of the above answers the more critical question of what on earth we are going to find to *talk* about on date number two. I don't think I can sit through another lecture on the superiority of Michelin over Dunlop tires.

May 15, 1998

The verdict is in: Frank is straight as an arrow, and I say this with the utmost confidence. How refreshing it is to come across one of the last of the dying breed of the Male Who Is Most Definitely Heterosexual Beyond a Shadow of a Doubt. It doesn't happen every day, that's for sure.

I know, I know, I know: I *shouldn't* have. Call me a slut-who-doesn't-wait-till-the-fourth-date, but I have a perfectly valid excuse: I needed to find a way out of the conversational dead end—and fast. It was all I could come up with, so sue me. Worse still—I know this is very wrong of me—I can't help patting myself on the back for what turned out to be perhaps the most inspired decision of my life so far.

Frank more than compensated for my guilt feelings about breaking *The Rules*. He may not be the most skilled conversationalist in the world, but last night I discovered that when it comes to body language, he is more than fluent. As soon as he put his warm, tingly hands against the hollow of my back, I realized that I had been wrong about him. When he proceeded to gently glide his fingers up the inside of my thigh and down again, up and down, never quite reaching their destination, I realized just how very, very clever he was. And when he pinned my arms up above my head against the headboard, so that no matter how much I wriggled and writhed, I could not escape his powerful grip, nor his tongue, which was giving me goose bumps all over, I thought, Mensa!

As for his body, it was to die for. Beginning with its aroma of freshly ground coffee beans. The guy smelled of sex. My nose could not get enough of his armpits, nor of the other places where it went to seek its olfactory treasure. And while we're on the subject of these other places, they were as smooth as his dancing. That's because he shaves down there. Talk about being a pro! It made such a nice change not ending up with pubic hair between one's teeth or stuck in one's throat. In fact, he asked me to return the favor.

"I'd be delighted," I responded with a twinkle in my eye.

Oh, and another thing: His ear isn't the only thing that is pierced. I couldn't believe my luck.

"Are you ready to be enlightened?" he asked me.

"I was born ready!" is what I would have answered had I been able to answer anything at the time. But my mother told me never to talk with my mouth full.

Needless to say, I'm in love.

Who needs to talk? Talking is so overrated.

July 11, 1998

Frank brought me breakfast in bed this morning. Along with the waffles dripping in maple syrup and accompanied by a fruit salad, the freshly squeezed orange juice, and a perfectly executed cappuccino, he had placed a single, long-stemmed red rose on the tray. Is this guy for real? I suspect he must be a figment of my imagination, which until today was the only place where men brought girls breakfast in bed.

Of course, bed is the only logical place for him to bring me my breakfast. Since we haven't managed to make it out of there since our second date.

"So there!" I say to *Rules* girls everywhere.

It's not that we haven't tried. Once, we even made it as far as the bedroom door. But we said "Fuck that" and hopped right back into bed again. The path to enlightenment is a long one. And I'm not complaining.

There is something fishy going on, though, I can smell it. No doubt, the gods are preparing a nasty surprise, which they are planning to spring on me any day now. I can't believe this stroke of luck. It's bound to run out soon. The question is, when? But I mustn't give in to these negative thoughts. Luckily, having sex all the time helps in that department. I've become rather good at not thinking anything at all, negative or positive.

There is only one drawback to having one's libido satisfied on a, shall we say, regular basis, and it is that my need to dance the tango has diminished proportionately. Confirming my no longer sneaking suspicion that tango and sex are mutually exclusive. How *can* they coexist? Tango thrives on desire—not on its satisfaction—and once desire is quenched, there goes the tango. It's a shame, really. But I've made my bed, so I might as well do everything but sleep in it.

Seriously, though, we are going to have to get out of bed at some stage. For one thing, it's impossible to practice back *sacadas* (displacements) between the sheets. I simply cannot believe that I've found My Partner already! It didn't take long at all, when you think about it. In the meantime, I might as well enjoy the honeymoon while it lasts, right?

September 2, 1998

When I mentioned to Frank the other day that we should start practicing and that I had an idea for a choreography to *"Libertango"* by Piazzolla, he looked at me as if I were speaking Greek. All he could do was repeat what I was saying with a blank expression on his face, which did not make him look very intelligent:

"Practice? Choreography? *'Libertango'*?" he echoed. I could have strangled him.

When I asked him point blank whether he wanted us to practice together, whether it had occurred to him that we might make a tango couple, whether he liked the idea of us being partners, his countenance continued in the same expressionless vein:

"I hadn't really thought about it, to be honest," he said. Now I wanted to rip him to shreds, after strangling him.

"Well . . . would you think about it?" I asked as casually as if I were asking to know the time—while wanting to smash his fucking watch with a hammer into a million little pieces.

"Yeah, sure. I'll think about it," he said without looking at me.

"Oh good," I said. (You do that, you prick.)

Why couldn't I just leave it at that? Why did I have to go and dig myself into a deeper hole? Why did I have to go and ask him THE QUESTION? Why?

"I love you, you know," I blurted out, my cheeks burning. Somebody had to take the plunge, after all.

No response. Apparently, I wasn't speaking Greek anymore but Chinese.

"Do you love me . . . at all?" I asked, trying hard not to whine and not succeeding.

"Hmmm . . . maybe . . . ," he responded at last. The sensation in my cheek now spread like wildfire to the rest of my face, while I concentrated on not throwing up.

I can't believe it has taken me this long to see that Frank's face is a big fat liar. His kind eyes and open brow weren't telling the truth. They were conniving to hide his stone-cold heart from me—a heart he holds clenched tight as a fist. He looked so sweet and innocent, but he is far, far from either sweet or innocent. Now I know: he is the devil. Will somebody please explain, then, why this makes me want him more, instead of less?

October 3, 1998

Last night, Frank got out of bed, put his clothes back on, and in the blink of an eye was out the door. I was furious. Not because we had had the best sex or anything. To be honest, I think we have reached the end of the path. And it doesn't seem any lighter at this end than it did at the beginning. It's amazing how even with what starts off as the most stimulating sex, you end up thinking, Been there, done that! while he is doing whatever it is he is doing to you.

But that wasn't the point. The point was that the bastard was going to a *milonga* while I had to stay at home to be fresh in the morning for a job I hate. I waved him off cheerfully, a smile on my face and murder in my heart. He wasn't supposed to want to dance tango after sex. Even so-so sex. I didn't, so how could he?

The thought of him dancing with other women is bad enough. But going out with him on those rare nights I make a brief foray into what used to be my playground is worse. Going to a *milonga* has become unbearable. What was once my springboard for flights into a world of fantasy has become the diving board into a toxic pool of pent-up rage and poisonous hatred.

The last couple of times have gone something like this: Frank and I arrive at the salon together. We dance the first set. And it's okay. Not terrible, not great, just okay. We know each other too well. Tango is a dance to be danced between a man who has not seen her wax her bikini line and a woman who has not listened to him snore all night. Tango is that place where he is strong and she is beautiful 24/7. It is not that place where he is too shy to assert himself, for example, in a movie theater when the people in the row behind you won't stop talking, or where she looks and smells like garbage in the mornings.

We invariably end the set with a bitter taste in our mouths. We try to hide it from each other, but we know that together we do not possess the magic to take off in flight. We are chained to the ground by a big, fat rock. And so we go our separate ways and spend the rest of the evening in the arms of other partners. I make sure to dance with a dozen, at the least. I put on a show of looking ecstatic, but it's a farce. I can no longer dance with my eyes closed. They have become paranoid. They dart around the room, searching him out to supervise every move of his hand on a partner's back or waist. They calculate the millimeters (if any) separating him from her. They analyze the degree of pleasure written on both their faces. Going to a *milonga* used to be an escape from pain. Now it has become the mine from which the salt is extracted before it is poured directly into my gaping wound. The sight of Frank giving and receiving pleasure in the arms of another woman is more than I can bear. And yet not only do I bear it, I can't take my eyes off it.

October 15, 1998

It was mortifying: My boss caught me red-handed, sleeping during a focus group. Actually, I'm surprised I managed to stay awake for as long as I did. No matter how many pages and pages of notes I took afterward, it was impossible to convince him that I was fascinated by the discussion going on on the other side of the two-way mirror between a dozen housewives aged twenty-five to forty regarding the nutritional habits of their ketchup-smeared brats. Nor does it do anything to help my relationship with him. He has long suspected me of being the fifth column. Now he has all the ammunition he needs to bring me down. What he doesn't realize is that I would love for him to fire me. I don't think he will, though. I can't help doing a good job, even if I do take the odd nap here and there. It's the overachiever in me.

The real tragedy is that I did not fall asleep because I had been dancing the night away. Then I wouldn't have minded so much getting caught: it would have been worth the humiliation. No, I fell asleep because I didn't sleep a wink last night. Or the night before. Or the night before that . . .

While I toss and turn without respite, Frank lies there peacefully beside me, enjoying the deep sleep of the innocent. He doesn't even suspect the torment that is keeping me awake: Why doesn't he want to be my partner? Why? Why? Why? What's wrong with me? Why doesn't he love me? Me? Me? Me?

These are the questions that spin around in my head all night long and that do not rest until the alarm goes off at eight A.M. I get up, bleary-eyed, as he continues to snore away under the covers because he doesn't need to get up *like I do* because he doesn't have to sell his soul *like I do* because he gets to dance the tango *like I don't*, while I have to sit through endless focus groups and meetings followed by more focus groups and more meetings. The bastard. I hate him.

Which is why the only moment of rest I got today was when I fell asleep during the focus group. I was dreaming I was back on Plaza Dorrego, dancing with Oscar, when I was rudely awakened by my boss with a sharp nudge to my ribs. My dream of dancing was quickly replaced by the *danse macabre* of questions that had started up again where they had left off: Why doesn't he want to be my partner? Why? Why? Why? What's wrong with me? Why doesn't he love me? Me? Me? Me?

November 2, 1998

Frank asked me to watch him practice a choreography he and his tango partner are preparing for a gig next week. When I was forced to watch him dancing with other women at the *milonga*, I thought I had already reached Dante's twelfth circle of the Inferno. I thought it was impossible to sink any deeper into the bowels of jealousy and torment. How naive, how carefree I was back then.

When he announced to me that he wanted to start practicing, I almost bumped my head on the ceiling with joy.

At last! I exclaimed, relieved that my suffering was finally about to come to an end. Patience *is* a virtue. It was only a matter of time before he came around. All that worrying for nothing, I said to myself.

However, my joy was dashed in the very next sentence. His new partner's name is Isabel and she is my nightmare come true. She is a giant stick insect. I mean this in the beautiful sense of the word: she is tall and skinny. In other words, she is everything that I am not and hence the ideal me if I were allowed to come back again and start all over. Making matters worse, this dark beauty is an excellent dancer.

So how do I show him that this does not sit well with me? I smile. It's the English way of dealing with adversity: "Stiff upper lip, old chap." I think I've been overdoing it, though, because I can't wipe the grin off my face. It's gotten stuck. Somebody call the paramedics!

I sat on the sidelines, watching Frank and Isabel do *their* choreography.

How euphonic: Frank and Isabel. Frank and Isabel. Frank and Isabel, I said to myself, twisting the knife deeper and deeper into my stomach.

They had chosen what is perhaps the most shattering piece of all: "*La Yumba*," by Osvaldo Pugliese. I get the shudders every time I listen to it, which is a lot. As I sat there watching them do their thing, I had the fascinating experience of being simultaneously transported to heaven by the music while being nailed firmly in my coffin by the spectacle in front of me. Before finally being confined to hell. Talk about being pulled in different directions. Once "Frank and Isabel" had finished tormenting me, they asked me in unison:

"So? What do you think?" They were unable to contain *their* excitement. I awoke from the daydream that featured eyes being gouged out and hair torn from scalps.

"It's wonderful!" I enthused.

The effort has drained me of any last remaining drop of blood. In fact, I think I'll go and lie down now. When the paramedics get here, somebody ought to tell them I also need a blood transfusion.

November 20, 1998

I was afraid of the truth, but the truth was not afraid of me. And the truth, no matter how hard I have tried to sweep it under the carpet, is that I wanted Frank to want to dance with me, not with her. Not with Giant Stick Insect. After I don't know how many nights of insomnia, I finally gave in and did what every woman does at least once in her life and regrets immediately afterward: I gave him an ultimatum: "Dance with me or else." I didn't put it quite like that, but that was the gist of it, and well . . . the answer was "or else"—i.e., I have shot myself in the foot.

Our ways parted by the Bethesda Fountain in Central Park. It was a scene worthy of a Hollywood movie, featuring enough tears to fill the fountain. There really is no more romantic place for a breakup. A shame it isn't deeper, though. I was about to throw myself in it when I realized that the water would barely have reached my ankles, making it rather hard for me to drown myself.

The highlight of the scene has to be when he said: "I love you. Always have and always will." A real tearjerker. Fat lot of good that does me now.

In retrospect, it was a pity he didn't dump me on a Saturday afternoon in the summer. Then I wouldn't have had far to run to seek solace, the *milonga* at the Bethesda Fountain being one of my favorites. As bad luck would have it, though, he dumped me on a cold and gray wintry Monday afternoon, so I was going to have to wait five long hours before going to Dance Manhattan in order to throw myself into the merciful embrace of the tango.

In fact, the last thing we did before prying ourselves apart was to divvy up the *milongas*. I got Dance Manhattan, Sandra Cameron's, and Belle Epoque. He got Triangulo, DanceSport, and Danel y Maria's. It was my idea. I simply can't bear the thought that I might bump into him at one of them. He wasn't happy and tried to talk me out of it, but when he saw that I wasn't going to budge, he didn't insist. He felt guilty. Good.

I haven't danced with as much intensity as I did that night in a long, long time. Being emotionally devastated did wonders for my tango. Also, it helped that I hadn't danced in weeks, which is years in tango parlance. And since the last time I had gone out, I had spent all my energy checking up on who Frank was dancing with, it hadn't counted.

So for the first time in ages, I was able to give myself up to the comforting arms of a dozen or so strangers, each one of whom performed his unique alchemy on my soul, thereby transforming my sorrow into sweetness.

And as I passed from one healing embrace to another, I made a couple of mental notes:

1. Stick to dancing.
2. Forget about sex (it's even more overrated than talking, anyway).

December 8, 1998

My boss always likes to start the day with a game of telephone. This morning's request was a list of the top-twenty cartoon shows on the kids' networks. As soon as he hung up, I picked up the phone again and called my assistant, who in turn called the media department, who called me back an hour later so that I could call my boss, who relayed the information to my client's boss (with God knows how many distortions), who passed it down to my client, who then asked me for another useless piece of the useless puzzle, and so forth and so on. It made the time go by, I guess.

Then, at eleven o'clock we switched to musical chairs, the rules of which are as follows: you go around and around from one conference room to another until the music stops—except the music never does stop, being on continuous play, as it were. And so you keep going from meeting to meeting to meeting to meeting. For instance, today we spent three hours discussing the relative merits of Spider-Man versus Ninja Turtles since my client is launching cartoon-shaped pasta in a Machiavellian ploy to lure unsuspecting mothers and their innocent offspring into eating their vile product. I swear we spent a good forty-five minutes in heated debate on what was cooler: spiderwebs or multicolored space suits. The decibel level soared as the room became divided between the camp that (strongly) felt that the popularity of the Ninjas, who currently hold the number one spot in the rankings, would rub off on the brand, and the camp that felt (equally strongly) that Spider-Man is the ideal spokes-character for the brand since "he is a classic and won't go out of style." When forced to give my two cents' worth, I did a quick "eenie meenie minie mo" and landed on Spider-Man. When I pronounced the character's name, it was with such conviction and compelling reasons that even my boss, who no longer bothers to disguise the fact that he hates me, looked pleased. But the debate raged on and was still raging by the time we were scheduled to go into the next meeting, so it was agreed that another meeting would be held tomorrow to discuss the issue further.

Why can't they leave me out of their stupid meetings? I can't stand these constant interruptions to my favorite game of all—the one I play all day long on the computer: solitaire.

December 31, 1998

I was lying down on my therapist's couch, moaning as usual. About not having a boyfriend because he dumped me (okay, if you look at it objectively, I'm the one who dumped him—but I was not in the mood to look at it objectively). And about having a job that I hate. And yet, in spite of all the effort I was putting into my moaning, the session was turning into a disappointment.

Given the symbolism of the day—it being New Year's Eve and all—I had been hoping for spectacular fireworks on the analytical front. But none appeared to be forthcoming. Beth, my therapist, was not up to par. I could tell that she wasn't inspired. She seemed elsewhere. I don't know if it was because she was bored by my mental meanderings or distracted by the festivities that lay ahead. Perhaps she was wondering if the champagne she had purchased with my monthly fees had been delivered yet. And whether it was chilled or whether she'd put it in the freezer for ten minutes before uncorking it for her guests.

I interrupted her inner monologue with a longer than usual pause. It took her a few seconds to notice, but finally she snapped to attention. I could feel that she was looking desperately for something to say. Anything at all.

"What would you do if money *weren't* a concern?" was what she came up with. (My moaning had shifted to the crap-job-dimension of my existence for the final five minutes, after having focused entirely on the crap-love-dimension of my existence for the first forty-five minutes of the session.)

Give me a break! Is this the best she can do? I really think she could make somewhat of an effort, for Pete's sake! Needless to say, I was not happy with my therapist at that moment.

But that's precisely when *it* happened: the epiphany. It was as if a ton of bricks of sadness had come crashing down from the ceiling I was staring at, to bury me alive on the couch. It knocked me out. But before I entered into a coma, a word popped out of my mouth.

"Tango." *I* didn't say it. *It* said me.

And that's when the crane elevated me out of the rubble of sadness. It lifted me up into the light. I was no longer buried alive. Oh joy!

It was all so clear, so simple: I was going to quit my job, move to Buenos Aires, and find myself a partner. One who wanted to dance with me instead of giant stick insects. I don't know why I hadn't thought of it before. What was the big deal?

I was so elated by my breakthrough that I told Beth she deserved to drink every last drop of champagne in the world. She didn't know what I was talking about. Never mind.

January 24, 1999

I'm free from the shackles of advertising at last! I can't believe I finally plucked up the courage to do it. What took me so long? I ask myself. In retrospect, I was crazy not to do it sooner. I feel exhilarated!

I called my parents, in London, to share the wonderful news with them. My mother first. When I told her that I had quit, she didn't sound very exhilarated. In fact, it would be more accurate to say that she freaked out, especially when I told her *why*.

"Tango?! You're not serious, darling."

"Yes I am, Mummy. Perfectly serious."

"But you can't be. *Nobody* dances tango. Not professionally. I've never heard of anything so silly. Keep it as a hobby, if you like. But you don't want to become one of those people who live at night and sleep during the day—you can't possibly; it's a *ghastly* way to spend one's life. Not to say what it does for the complexion."

"Yeah. I know. But—

"Darling, it's the *wrong* sort of environment. With the *wrong* sort of people. And you know it. You even said so yourself."

"I know I did. But now I've decided that tango is far too important to worry about how people hold their knives and forks."

"Don't be ridiculous. Of course, it's important how people hold their knives and forks [big sigh of frustration]. If only I had sent you to an

English school. I should have taken you out of the French *lycée* before it was too late. You would have grown up normal. Why can't you be more like my friends' children? And what are they going to think when I tell them that my daughter has gone off to become a tango dancer?"

"It doesn't really matter to me what they think."

"How could you say such a thing? That's selfish! Don't do this to me!"

I tried to explain to her that I wasn't doing this to *her*. Yes, I admitted I was being selfish. Finally, I have awakened from my long sleep. I am no longer doing an imitation of the living dead. I have come alive! Wasn't that fantastic news? I asked her.

Apparently not. The time had come for her to pull out her trump card:

"How do you expect to meet anybody if you're dancing tango all the time? Look what happened to me and your father." I didn't know how that was relevant unless she was telling me that they got divorced when I was two because she had been dancing tango behind his back? I didn't think now was the time to ask.

After having paused for dramatic effect, she continued her scathing attack: "How are you *ever* going to have babies? You're no spring chicken anymore. You've got to think about these things."

(Thank you, Mummy. There isn't a day I don't, I didn't say.)

Of course she *would* bring babies into it. She's Greek, after all. The thing is, being my mother's daughter, I'm Greek too and I can't help thinking about the baby aspect of things. No one is more aware than I that tango is not exactly conducive to making them. And no one is more terrified than I by the prospect of remaining barren for life.

After we had slammed down our phones on each other, it was time to call my father. I'd gotten to the bit about becoming a professional tango dancer when the line went dead.

"Are you still there, Daddy?"

"Yup, I'm still here," responded a ghost from the other side of the grave.

"Well? . . . What do you think?"

"What I think is: how are you going to pay your rent in New York? Dancing *tango*?" I didn't particularly like the deprecating tone he used when he pronounced the word "tango."

"You've got to start thinking about your future, young lady."

(I think about my future plenty, believe me, I could have said, but what was the point?)

Of course, he'd bring up the practical side of things. He is American, after all. Money, money, money. But, being my father's daughter, I'm American too. Why does he think it has taken me so long to pluck up the courage to take this step? Of course, I'm scared. I'm scared shitless! Does he think I relish the idea of not having enough money to live on? Does he not realize how nervous it makes me that what used to be my trust fund would now fit into the piggy bank he gave me for my seventh birthday? True, I haven't told him about the nights I sleep on the floor in preparation for the days ahead when I will be a homeless bum living in the gutter. It's probably best for him to think of me as irresponsible and carefree.

"Well, actually, there's something else I want to tell you . . ."

"Yes?"

"I'm moving to Buenos Aires."

The line went even deader than before. "Look on the bright side, Daddy: the rent is much cheaper there . . ."

For some reason, this did not cheer him up.

"You're picking up and moving to the other side of the world on a whim?"

"It's not a whim."

"And what about your education?"

"What about it?"

"I didn't put you through Cambridge for you to throw it all away like this."

I didn't think now was a good time to remind him that he hadn't paid a penny for my education since tuition at English universities is free.

"Cambridge graduates become tango dancers all the time," I quipped.

I didn't hear any laughter at the other end of the line. But I thought it was funny . . .

February 9, 1999

Last night I watched *Manhattan* for the millionth time. You know how Woody Allen decides to quit his job in TV to write a novel? He moves out of his apartment because he can't afford the rent anymore. And into a dump, where the water comes out of the tap brown and he can't sleep because it's so noisy. I watched him quit his job in dismay:

"No! No! Don't do that! Big mistake!" I yelled at the TV.

But he didn't listen to me. Then, when he couldn't sleep because "it's quieter out in the street" than it is in his apartment, I got an attack of the I-told-you-sos.

You should have kept your job. What were you thinking? and more along those lines.

Now why is it, do you suppose, that I am more protective of Woody than I am of myself? I've made the same "sacrifice" he has. Except that I'm moving from my comfy one-bedroom in a doorman building on the Upper East Side to God only knows what kind of accommodation a continent away. I'm guessing rathole.

I'm fully aware that my life is going down the tubes, according to other people's perception of things. Let's face it: I am a dropout. I bet they are all shaking their heads behind my back in dismay:

"It's *such* a shame. She was *such* a clever girl. And now look at her. How did it all go so wrong?" they say.

What they don't know is that I've never been happier. I am not a slave to material possessions the way they are, nor does my sofa own me as it does Annette Bening in *American Beauty*. But I still can't help being upset about poor old Woody. Really, it's *such* a shame. He was *such* a clever man. And now look at him. How did it all go so wrong?

February 21, 1999

This morning, I almost died of a heart attack. I received my bank state-
ment in the mail. What's the point of a trust fund if it runs out on you
just when you need it most? Just when you have finally understood how
to put the money to good use? Where did it all go—the money that
didn't go straight into my therapist's pocket? This is most inconvenient.
By my estimate, I might be able to survive on what's left for a year—or
eighteen months if I skip meals. And then what?

I'll be poor is what.

And with that not very comforting thought in mind, I decided to go
for a walk. I went up Madison Avenue, past Calvin Klein, Valentino, Ar-
mani, Ralph Lauren, Gucci, Christian Dior, etc., and for the first time it
dawned on me that I would be walking past them for the rest of my life
since I would never be able to afford to go inside. The realization came
like a punch to the stomach. It made me reassess the whole entire
dropping-out business. Not that I live to wear designer labels. Far from it.
But one thing my father has taught me is to keep all doors open—Chanel
included. Especially since half the women in my family have their permanent address there. While the other half live at Yves Saint Laurent.

Now it hit me: there were consequences to my decision. And they
were nerve-wracking. By quitting my job and aspiring to dance the
tango professionally, I was, in effect, waving good-bye to the privileged
life I had expected to enjoy until death did me part from Versace. I was,
in effect, condemning myself to being persona non grata in all of the
above establishments. And if ever I had the audacity to step inside one
of them, the sales assistants would no doubt treat me the same way they
had treated poor Julia Roberts in *Pretty Woman*. I knew this was pathetic
of me, but I couldn't help it.

Living without fancy clothes is one thing—as I said, I don't care
about the clothes. If I'm whining, it's more about the principal of the
thing than the thing itself. But living without traveling—say good-bye
to India, China, and Africa!—without four-star restaurants and expensive wines, without going to the theater, to the opera, to concerts, and

especially to the movies three times a week; living without going to my shrink (also three times a week); without going to the pool or to yoga or to tai chi (by taxi); without skiing or winter holidays in the sun; living without the future penthouse on Fifth Avenue and without a nanny for my children—in summary, living without these things is quite another. Of course, I was only joking about the penthouse, but not about the nanny. I am deadly serious about that. Not that I'm ever going to need one the way things are going, but that is beside the point. Once again, it's a matter of principal.

It's true: I don't need to live in a luxury apartment. Really, I don't. Neither is it essential to own country houses and/or ski chalets and/or beach houses, the way my sisters do. But I wouldn't say no to a roof over my head. It doesn't even need to be a very big one. I'll be lucky, though, if I have a cart to call my own when I'm seeking shelter from the rain under somebody else's doorway. In a nutshell, I wasn't looking forward to my life as a *nouveau pauvre*. In fact, my exhilaration level had dropped considerably since the phone calls I'd made only a month ago to my parents.

I found the whole idea even less appealing when I compared what was soon to be my life in the gutter with the glamorous life of my forbears, who, when they weren't too busy gallivanting around casinos, swinging off chandeliers, drinking each other under the table, and sleeping with each other's mistresses, had a marked tendency to marry royalty, free the oppressed, and die gloriously flying missions over enemy borders. I had always felt that I had a lot to live up to, growing up around these ghosts. Now my plan to become a tango dancer put a serious dent in my dreams of grandeur. It was going to be difficult to be grand with mud all over my face.

The final straw came when I pictured myself pushing a pram containing two dirty-faced and underfed babies into a crowded subway car before walking up six flights of stairs at the age of eighty and not making it to the top due to a coughing fit (I had emphysema).

"It isn't too late!" I cried. If I wanted to backtrack, there was still time. I had not yet done The Irrevocable. I had only *thought* about it. Big difference! I could still change my mind. Phew! What a relief!

No sooner had I heaved the sigh of relief than I realized that I wasn't going to change my mind. In the words of I don't know which self-help guru, I was going to feel the fear (absolute terror) and do it anyway.

"At least you got *that* out of your system," I thought before adding a "Fuck Yves Saint-Laurent!" out loud, for good measure. I had not intended the lady-who-lunches, who happened to be exiting the store with more shopping bags than arms at that moment to take it personally. I felt bad as I watched her teeter away as fast as she could up Madison Avenue in her Manolos, while clutching tightly onto her Hermès bag. Oh well . . .

February 24, 1999

On second thought . . . I don't much fancy the prospect of lying in a puddle of my own blood in the middle of a street in Argentina and being left there to die because I don't have any health insurance because my trust fund has dried up and I've been disinherited to boot.

It was time to storm the arsenal. I wasn't going to go down to the gutter without putting up some sort of fight. One of the only good things about being broke is that you can go for broke, having absolutely nothing to lose. So in I went and out I took the only weapon that hasn't gotten rusty in all these years since leaving university: persuasion.

"Daddy, it's me again," I said.

"Yes?" he said. That's all: just "yes." Not a good start.

"I know you don't think it's a good idea for me to go off to Argentina to study the tango," I started. Note use of the verb "study."

"Damn right, I don't think it's a good idea. I think it's a bad idea. In fact, I've never heard a worse one," he said. Shit. He *is* going to disinherit me.

"I hear you," I said, because it is key in any negotiation to let the opponent feel he is being "heard," no matter what bollocks comes out of his mouth. "I do see how from your point of view my choice must seem a little . . . eccentric. Not to say outright crazy!" I paused to gain momentum. After all, the tough part still lay ahead.

"I'm glad to hear that you are still in possession of part of your mental faculties," he said. Good: we were making progress.

"In spite of appearances, I want you to know that I *have* been thinking about my future. A lot. Believe it or not, I *do* want to be successful." Another pause. It never hurts to pause. ". . . but on my own terms." Pause. He wasn't saying anything. Difficult to read. Better go back to talking. "I truly believe that one can only be successful by doing what one loves." No need to quote actual passages of *Do What You Love and the Money Will Follow.* "By the same token, it is impossible to be successful doing something that makes one miserable. The long and the short of it is that I will never shine in advertising. I simply don't love it enough." Understatement of the century. Pause. "Whereas tango—"

"Yes, *tango?*" There he was again, using that tone I didn't particularly care for. But we were all about advancing the argument at this stage of the game. Not about creating one. (Overlook the tone and move on, I said to myself.)

"As I was saying, I know that I have it in me to be good. Very good."

"I don't doubt that. What I want to know is how the hell are you going to live off it?" Oh dear. Had I sown the soil prematurely? Were the crops going to fail me?

"Good question. Granted, I will never become a multimillionaire dancing the tango. But it's certainly possible to make decent money."

"What do you call decent?" Now we were talking!

"A hundred dollars an hour for private lessons, at least five hundred per workshop, and when performing, a salary of two thousand a month—that's *net*, i.e., after taxes with all expenses, travel, lodging and food included, so it's basically pocket money." A golden rule in any negotiation: do your homework. He didn't say anything. But underneath the silence I detected pleasant surprise. "Of course, it's not like banking, but we're not talking peanuts, either." Hammer it in while it's hot.

"That's not bad," he conceded.

"No, it's not. The thing is . . ."

"What?"

"You know how everybody does their MBA?" (First mention.)

"Yes?"

"Well, the way I see it, the next couple of years are an MBA equivalent . . ." (Second mention.)

"An MBA equivalent, hey?" I wish he wouldn't do that. It puts me off my concentration when he repeats everything I say.

"Yes, an MBA equivalent." (That makes three and whatever you do, don't stop now.) "It's *exactly the same* as going back to school. Think about it: (a) I will be taking the theory that I learn in the classroom and applying it directly in a practical setting; (b) I will have put myself in the ideal networking environment—as you yourself have said time and time again, getting a job is about who you know—"

"What are you saying?" he said in his cut-the-crap voice. So I did.

"Daddy, what I'm saying is that I need you to *subsidize* me while I *study* the tango—you know you would if I were going to do an MBA [four]. Look at it as an investment, same as you would an MBA [five]. But a teeny-tiny one compared to the average cost of an MBA [six]. It's a win-win situation! Seriously, you should thank me for going to live in Buenos Aires, where the cost of living is substantially lower than it is at Harvard. Not to mention the forty grand a year you're *saving* on the MBA itself!" And that made seven! The magic number of times I stuffed the letters "MBA" down his throat and the only thing of value I ever learned in all my years in advertising.

As we shook hands over the phone, I knew that he had only pretended to buy my crap. Because he's not stupid. He knows that I know that he is supporting me because he can't bear to think of me in the gutter any more than I can. But this way, he has saved face. And I get to be a spoiled brat for a couple more years. Hooray!

Now that my father was so much happier about my decision, I didn't think it was fair to leave my mother feeling down in the dumps. So I called her too. The name of this persuasion game was to convince her that by pursuing something that makes me happy, I'm far more likely to find a poor sod to marry me. To that effect I shared the findings I had just come across in a *Vogue* article I had read over somebody's shoulder about how being happy causes your hormones to secrete an enzyme that keeps your skin looking young and smooth.

"You see, Mummy, I'm not over the hill *yet*," I said. That cheered her up. "You wait and see: I am going to make you the most beautiful grandchildren, and that's a promise." And this did the trick.

If only I could persuade myself. But I had said the magic word, meaning that between the two of them, I now have a monthly "stipend" of $2,000 to "study" the tango. This should be enough to keep my head dry and my stomach filled with crackers in Buenos Aires. I wonder if it's enough for health insurance if I stretch it?

March 1, 1999

Fuck. I can't sleep. Whose stupid idea was it to move to Buenos Aires, anyway? What if I never find a partner? Who in their right mind is going to dance with a foreigner who doesn't have it in her blood? I don't stand a chance. They are never going to take me seriously. I'll be the laughingstock of the *milonga*. They'll send me packing. I know it. "*Gringa*, go home," they will say. Without a job. Without an MBA. Without a penny to my name. Just older. More wrinkled. Unmarriageable. A spinster. My parents were right. Better to stay here and forget about the whole thing. I'm canceling my ticket first thing in the morning. Now go to sleep.

Sacada

1. A motion in tango in which one partner invades the other's space and "displaces" him or her from it. It looks better than it sounds—trust me.

2. A woman who is not in her normal emotional or mental state—i.e., who is "out of her mind," having been driven there, more often than not, by a tango partner.

March 3, 1999

Hooray! I'm here! (The ticket was nonrefundable.)

I can't complain about the flight this time around since nobody puked on me. And now, here I am already sunbathing on Oliver's terrace while taking in the stunning view of the Plaza Congreso. He's lent me his place while I look for something permanent. I'm so glad I went up to him that day in New York and asked him whether he was related to the president on the $20 bill. He is the SPITTING image of Franklin. It *is* Franklin, isn't it? Talk about corny pickup lines. That was my lame but oh-so-effective attempt to get him to ask me to dance in the days when he was still on my "to-do" list. He raised an eyebrow at my cheek, but it worked and we danced and it was great and we have become fast friends. And now, here I am in his place and I feel like the luckiest girl alive!

When he told me that he had bought a "pied-à-terre" down here, I never imagined this! It isn't a pied-à-terre, at all! It is a *"pied-au-ciel,"* a foot-in-the-sky. Actually, it feels more like a boat floating in the sky. And we haven't gotten to the part that makes it so special. Its biggest claim to fame is that it is attached to one of Buenos Aires's landmark cupolas on the Avenida de Mayo. I can't wait to go to bed tonight. Not only because I'm my usual zombie self after the red-eye, but because my bedroom is *inside* the cupola. What a dream!

I decided to go for a stroll as soon as I had lugged my two unliftable suitcases up the six flights (the elevator wasn't working and
the stairs reminded me of my premonition the other day). I needed to
make sure that my being in Buenos Aires wasn't a dream. So I turned
right out of the building and walked down the avenue toward the 9 de
Julio. I couldn't get over the fact that I had done it! And to celebrate,
I squinted through the glaring rays at every man who passed by me
on the street. I'm glad to report that the staring game is as popular as
ever!

I still haven't drunk it in yet that I am really here. It feels unreal. Actually, it's almost as if I have never been here before. Not because the
city has changed. But because I have. It's as if the person who came here
on holiday two years ago was not me, but somebody else. And I can
scarcely remember who she was, nor put myself in her shoes—the ones
she wore before she traded them in for high heels.

On my way back to Oliver's place, I bumped into my cousin's friend
Roberto, by accident, who happened to be walking back to his office
downtown from a business lunch. He couldn't believe it when he saw
me. "What are *you* doing here?!" he exclaimed. I told him that I had
come back to devote myself full-time to the tango and that he was partly
responsible, since it was my original vision of him superglued to Mechi
that had sparked this passion of mine. He was delighted. Anyway, he
says he happens to know someone who owns an apartment in the building opposite and that it is about to be vacated. I've only been back ten
minutes and already I may have found somewhere to live! It's all being
made so easy. A sign that it was meant to be. And I thought I might
never come back.

March 4, 1999

I was nervous about going back to Club Almagro alone. For one thing,
I barely know this city and I don't speak the language (that's two
things), and this makes it nerve-racking getting into a cab and asking the
cabbie to take you somewhere. I've noticed that hardly anyone speaks

English. Which is good because I'll be forced to practice my Spanish—the day I have some to practice.

I made sure to prep beforehand and bought a map of the city from a *Kiosko*. I wanted to see where it was exactly my cousins had taken me that night that changed my life—has it been two years, already? I had no idea since I never pay attention when I'm sitting in the back of other people's cars. While I was at it, I decided to map out all the tango places to which I have been told to go. There are about twenty of them, so it took me an hour or so to pinpoint them all. They are spread out all around the city, which is intimidating even for me, who has lived in my fair share of sprawling cities.

Of course, even after an hour spent with my nose plunged in the map, I had no idea where I was going. But wherever it was, it looked far-awayish. As I rolled on my fishnets, my heart began to thump uncontrollably. It had been a long time since I'd had an attack of wallflower phobia. I thought I'd overcome my fear for good. But I wasn't in New York anymore. I was playing in the big leagues now. What if nobody asked me to dance? What if I sat there all evening and nobody came to save me from my disgrace? It's been known to happen. I've heard many a gruesome tale of women sitting on their bottoms all night long. *Porteños* are ruthless, or so I've been told. Armando told me that being a wallflower is *planchar* in Spanish, which means "to do the ironing," and there is nothing I hate more.

Speaking of which, I needed to iron the wrinkled dress that I had only just unpacked and that I planned to wear. Once I had done my chore—there really *is* nothing I hate more—I got dressed in front of the mirror. "That'll have to do, I suppose." I did hope the little black wrap-around dress with a low-plunging V neck wasn't too short by local standards. I didn't want to cause offense by revealing either too much cleavage—not that there's much to reveal—or too much leg, of which there is a bit more.

"The bait mustn't be too obvious to be effective," I said to myself.

Then I got a bad case of the heebie-jeebies. What's the point of wearing a dress that flatters your legs? Nobody is going to see them be-

cause they are going to be stuck under the table all night. I didn't even
know enough to know if I was being paranoid or realistic.

I hailed a cab, and the rudiments of Spanish that I have managed to
teach myself were wiped clean from my mind. I switched to my tried-
and-true mix of Italian and French. The cabbie either feigned to be or
truly was unaware of the fact that I do not speak his language and proceeded to talk my ear off for the entire journey. And the club was far-
awayish indeed. One might even omit the ish. I didn't understand a
word of what he was saying, but nodded, oohed and aahed, and said *si*
whenever he paused for breath, which was not often. After about twenty
minutes, he decided that my time had come to shine linguistically, so he
asked me something. I assumed it was the usual question: "Where are
you from?"

So in a Spanish that was fractured in at least ten places, I gave him
my spiel. He was fascinated.

"A *gringa* who has come to Buenos Aires to dance tango! Well, well,
well . . . Fancy that!" he chuckled. Now I could do no wrong.

We finally got to our destination, having taken God knows how many
detours (I was at his mercy—he could have taken me to Timbuktu).

"Your Spanish is so good, dear!" he exclaimed as I gave him his tip.

Suddenly, it had been worth every detour. His words—whether true
or bullshit—had given me the confidence to enter Club Almagro, head
held high. Though what my language skills had to do with my tango
skills was not clear, even to me.

I was relieved to see that nothing had changed. Everything was exactly as I had left it. The glass door through which I gained admittance to
mecca once more had not been repainted, so the black paint was still peeling off in large flakes. This reassured me. I don't know why, but it did.

Once I was inside, it all came flooding back. The shock to the system it had been when I had first laid eyes on the tango. I had forgotten
just how gorgeous the local talent is. It is not a good idea to compare
oneself with a *porteña* because one cannot emerge favorably from the
exercise. It is a sure recipe for inadequacy of the incurable kind. But
one does, regardless. You can spot these knockouts from a mile away.

They are the beautiful, small-framed, and skinny ones with the long, glistening black manes, who wake up looking beautiful. They are not overdressed like the foreign pilgrims, who have all gone to the same store and bought the same shimmering dress with tassels and the same two-toned shoes. In fact, *porteñas* tend to underdress—i.e., they wear as few clothes as possible. Crop tops are in, and I see why. They show off these nymphs' annoyingly flat bellies and perfectly tiny waists. The titillating tops that look as if they are about to fall off any minute hang precariously onto their wearers by a thread. More precisely, by thin straps that zigzag across the most feminine backs you ever saw. Also the fashion, I noticed, are low-sitting, hip-hugging pants or skirts, which barely make it over the pubic line. And as for the hips they hug, they are as perfectly petite as the rest of these girls. In hindsight, it was silly of me to have worried about causing offense. I was dressed for church by comparison. In fact, I felt completely inappropriate in my outfit that did far too conscientious a job of covering up tits, ass, knees, and belly button.

"There is not much I can do about my hips—short of surgery." I sighed. My wardrobe, however, is an easier fix, I said to myself.

My attention turned to the guys now. They were less demoralizing. *Porteños* are all so beautiful that one wants to fall in love with each and every one of them and doesn't know where to start. The symmetry of their features reminds me of classical Greek statues. In fact, they look a lot more like classical Greeks than any modern Greek I have beheld. And when their bodies are in motion, they become even more beautiful, if that is humanly possible. Which it is not. From whence I deduce that they are not mortal, but gods or heroes.

Everyone on the floor (I mean the Argentines—the foreigners had ceased to exist) looked professional. It was like trying to look into the sun. I couldn't for fear of being blinded. No, that's not right. They were more like stars in a distant galaxy, a million light years away. As I stared at them, I wondered if my partner was up there among them. And if so, how I would get him to notice me down here. It was absolutely imperative that I get myself properly outfitted at once. After all, like an astronaut, I was preparing for a journey into outer space, requiring me to pay close attention to my suit.

By the way, my worst fears did not come true. Which is why I have them. If I think of all the bad stuff that might happen, then it won't. The bottom line is that I barely sat down all evening. My first dancer was a ninety-year-old—I'm not exaggerating—called Adolfo (I swear), whose claim to fame was that he was one of the first performers ever to bring tango to the stage. It was actually rather scary dancing with him. I kept worrying that I might break him, he was so fragile. Or that he might croak on me the way Oscar had. Except that Oscar had had the decency to wait for me to leave the country first. It was unpleasant, but at least it served the purpose: to show off my calf muscles, which are my best feature (after my eyes). Then, I got invited by lots of men. But they didn't count since they were all from this galaxy . . .

March 7, 1999

Before going to the *matinée*, which is a *milonga* that takes place in the afternoon, at Confitería Ideal, I had urgent business to attend to. In addition to my new sexy red zigzaggy top, I needed to buy a pair of tango shoes. I had been lucky at Almagro but I did not want to push my luck. The guys had been forgiving once, but they might not be as forgiving a second time. By this I mean that tango dancers are shoe fetishists. The men even more than the women. It's the first clue they look for in order to answer the million-dollar question: can she dance (meaning, is she a *good* dancer)? He will judge her according to her shoes. I hate to think of the number of good candidates I have lost simply because I was not wearing the right ones. There are no two ways about it: good shoes = good partners = speedy improvement.

So off I ran to Flabella, the most famous tango shoe shop in B.A. I spent an hour agonizing over which ones to choose since I liked every pair on display—apart, perhaps, from the gold-and-silver lamé ones with the ten-centimeter heel (I don't know how many inches that is, but it's too many)—much to the distress of the shop assistant, who quickly tired of assisting me. Finally, though, my nature prevailed and I went for simplicity in the form of a classic pair of shiny, black-patent ones with the traditional T-strap in front. Most important, I am able to walk in them without wobbling (too much). They are sexy in the sophisticated sense rather than in the slutty sense. I left the store feeling thrilled with myself and my good taste.

My feet properly armed, I crossed the road and went over to Confitería Ideal. It is a wonderful place: a tearoom, built at the turn of the century. It's falling to pieces, which only adds to its charm. The floors are made of marble, the ceiling is (barely) held up by baroque pillars that look as if they are made of candy floss, while retro globe lights hang like bunches of grapes from the ceiling, except they are not retro because they have not been replaced since 1966. Neither have the dancers, by the looks of them. White-haired men in three-piece suits dance with their blue-rinse-haired wives. Glitter is passed from middle-aged cheek to middle-aged cheek. Foreign ladies, come from afar in search of love, dance with *porteño* playboys ready to sell it to them for as much as it's worth to each lady. Armando would do well here. Time has stopped in this enchanted palace and the music confirms it.

I had just danced with a man they call Chiche, who spent the entire set grinding his false teeth in my ears—not the most pleasant of sounds—when I noticed a short, chubby man, somewhere in his seventies, who looked like someone trying to look smart. He wore a jacket and tie, but his shirt was frayed at the collar and his trousers were made of polyester. His dyed black hair needed retouching at the roots and the teeth that hadn't fallen out yet were yellow from chain-smoking. But to me, he looked like Apollo. It was his dancing, you see: his style was so elegant, contained and sober. It was pure 1940s.

My set with Chiche was over and I absolutely had to dance the next set with Apollo. Since he was sitting at one end of the overcrowded salon and I at the other, I stared at him fixedly until his eyes found mine. Then I raised my right eyebrow (for some reason, my left doesn't work as well) and sent him the following telegraph: "You're next." He got the message and nodded back at me, which prompted me to look at him with a mix of surprise and flattery, as if it had been his idea all along.

The stranger came over to collect me at my table at the start of the next *tanda*. I noticed he was limping. I was worried that this might affect his dancing. I needn't have been. It was spectacular, and once again, my instinct had not failed me. In fact, I am starting to notice a trend: the chubbier the partner, the more comfy he is to dance with. But I am getting ahead of myself, not for the first time and probably not for the last.

I got up and coolly walked to the floor with him, feeling like a queen in my brand-new shoes. He took me in his arms and we got cozy as we waited for the music to start. It did, and we set forth on our journey together, lifting anchor and setting sail with a beautifully executed *salida*.

And then I fell down.

Luckily, he was there to catch me before I hit the marble. It was my new shoes: they had gotten stuck.

"You must put Ba-se-leena," he said.

"I beg your pardon?" I didn't understand what he was saying. Was this meant to be English?

"Ba-se-leena is good. You try. You see," he persisted. I think it *was* meant to be English. What on earth was "baseleena"? I repeated the word a number of times in my head. And then I got it.

"Oh! Vaseline!" I exclaimed, my face going beet red. That was rather forward of him, I thought. Weren't Catholics squeamish about things like that? "What do you want me to do with Vaseline?" I asked him, just to double-check.

"On your shoes. Mine too. They got . . . how do you say? . . . sticky. I almost fall. And then I put Ba-se-leena. It work!"

"Oh. On my shoes. Of course," I said, feeling embarrassed. Dirty mind!

We stumbled to the end of the set, and as soon as it was over, I ran out to find the nearest pharmacy. And he was right: Ba-se-leena was exactly what I needed. When I came back, Hector, for that was his name, very sweetly gave me and my new patent-leather shoes (now smeared in

Vaseline) a second chance. And this time it was smooth sailing all the way . . .

March 13, 1999

I went back to Ideal, hoping to find Hector there, and to my immense delight, he was. He spotted me as soon as I entered the salon and immediately gave me the nod. I was thrilled. I was less thrilled, however, when I realized quite *how* happy he was to see me again. As I pressed up against him, waiting for the music to start, I marveled at the vigor of the erection in one so old, while praying this would not turn into another Armando scenario.

Ignore it, I said to myself, it might go away.

The set ended and Hector led me back to his table. Once again, I noticed his limp, which disappeared only when he danced. I asked him in my pidgin Spanish what was wrong with his leg. I think (but cannot be 100 percent sure) he said something about having had a double hip operation, which goes to show that nothing will stop a tango addict!

Etiquette would normally have required him to escort me back to my table, but I was still dizzy and had no idea where my table was, so I followed him over to his, like a lost sheep. He said he wanted to give me something. We sat down and he took out what looked like an enormous ledger from a satchel and opened it. It was bound in soft leather and it contained women: women collected over forty years and fifty-six cities, he said. Women from Buenos Aires to Boston, Los Angeles to Lausanne, Tirana to Tiananmen Square. I was surprised by all the places one can find women to dance with. And apparently, today was my lucky day: I was being inducted into the ledger. Hector, who is as picky as any collector, explained to me that not everyone he dances with is ledger worthy. I think this was his way of telling me what an honor it was that he was bestowing number 3,997 on me. Truth be told, I've never been so honored to come 3,997th in my life!

But that is not all. Each member of this exclusive (though steadily growing) club receives an official wallet-size card with her ID number. On the back there is Hector's picture and a poem: "To me, you are not just a number. I will treasure the unique moment that you and I shared on this day forevermore. You will always have a special place in my heart."

"You too, Hector!" I said after I had read the poem.

Afterward, it occurred to me that Hector must be a very happy man indeed. When you think about it, 3,997 are a lot of special moments.

It also occurred to me that the *matinées* at Ideal are not where I am going to find my partner, where the average age is eighty-seven. If I'm going to find my needle, I need to roll around on the right haystack. Time to stop wasting time, already!

April 10, 1999

I rolled out of bed two weeks ago and into the apartment in the modern doorman building across from Oliver's place that I now call home. It's a lot more luxurious than anything I could afford for $500 a month in New York, that's for sure. So the parents ought to be grateful. I'm really quite low maintenance, if they think about it.

Also, I'm glad I haven't moved far, since I've become friends with the waiters at the café on the square and with the guy who works at the *locutorio* (a telephone and Internet center). He has a crush on me, I think. He is reading *À la Recherche du Temps Perdu*—in Spanish, obviously—because I told him that Proust is my favorite author—if that's not devotion, I don't know what is. Then there's the old man who runs the kiosk on the corner, who hands me a candy every time I walk by, and the two brothers at the laundromat who wash my dirty underwear and who gave me a cassette the other day of Charlie Garcia, the father of what they call *Rock Nacional*. And then there are all the other shopkeepers and familiar faces to whom I blow kisses on my way to and from tango. Actually, I have become a kind of neighborhood mascot. People are not used to foreigners here, so I stand out. I hope not like a sore thumb, though. Having so many new friends who don't speak a word of English is doing wonders for my Spanish. I bet it sounds like chalk screeching against a blackboard to their ears. They are all incredibly supportive, though, and don't hesitate to lie through their teeth about how well I speak.

There are six doormen in my building and they are all adorable. Even if they do wonder what my job is. The night porter in particular gives me funny looks. He sees me coming back at six or seven every morning, sometimes accompanied by a guy—a different one each time. Usually, the guy doesn't come farther than the gate. If he does, it's just for a coffee, but the night porter doesn't know that. And my new clothes don't help matters, I'm sure. Salvatore (that's the night porter) smiles at me in the most conniving way. I really ought to set him straight. But what do I tell him? "I'm not a hooker, the way you think I am"? I need to ask somebody how you say "hooker" in Spanish.

I love my new apartment because it has a balcony. I spend every "morning" (I get up at two P.M.) sunbathing on it as I absorb my three cups of coffee before going to dance at La Pavadita at around four o'clock. I apply myself hard to this task since it is of utmost importance that I be crispy brown all year around to bring out the sparkle in the sequins I plan to wear.

April 14, 1999

I met Valeria the other night at Gricel, when we were asked if we minded sharing a table and we said we didn't. She is a twenty-five year-old art school graduate who has been an aspiring professional tango dancer for a couple of years now. She has also studied ballet since before she could walk, and it shows. She is as graceful as a swan: tall, blond, and simply ravishing, with a strikingly long neck. If she weren't so sweet, I'd want to wring it.

I've noticed that my Spanish is improving rapidly. Partly because it is so similar to French. And partly because I have no choice. I was impressed that I understood at least 50 percent of what she said, which is remarkable, if I say so myself. In fact, I've noticed that you

don't even need to understand that much to get the gist of what somebody is saying. Which proves that most of the words we use are su-
perfluous. After marveling at the fact that I could understand so much
of what she was saying, I marveled even more when I caught myself
in the act of using some very sophisticated words and complex gram-
matical constructions that I didn't know I knew. I couldn't believe
some of the words that were popping out of my mouth. Where had I
picked them up? I wondered. In other cases, I made a conscious effort
to use words or expressions I had heard others use or that others had
explained to me when I had asked them what they meant. Here is a
case in point.

"So how do you spend your days?" she asked me.

"Me rasgo el higo," I replied. I didn't expect the following reaction at
all: her eyes widened, her jaw dropped, while her hand reached up to
cover her mouth. She held the pose for a few seconds before finally
bursting into hysterical laughter.

"Where did you learn to say *that*?" she asked while gripping her
sides.

"Somebody I was dancing with yesterday," I said. I wondered what
was so funny.

"Do you know what it means?" she asked, finally pulling herself
together.

"He told me it means 'I scratch my belly button' and he said it is like
saying 'I laze around doing nothing all day.' Why? Did I say it wrong?"
I asked her innocently.

"Not at all. But did he mention that it also means 'I masturbate'?" she
inquired.

"No, actually. He didn't!" I said before we both cracked up laughing.
I'm going to kill Pablo the next time I dance with him!

Yesterday, Valeria invited me to her place for *mate* with *alfajores*—
I hadn't had any since I'd ODed on the eight boxes of Havannas I'd
taken back to New York as "presents." I had forgotten how delicious
they were. My hips are going to have to stay well clear of them.

Having said that, it's rude to refuse when they are being offered to you, which is why I made sure to be polite—all three times they were offered.

Valeria lives in a charming but rundown studio that an artist friend of hers is letting her stay in. It's a glorified squat. But she doesn't seem to care at all about the lack of basic amenities. Who needs central heating or hot water when you have *mate* and tango? *Mate* was the bitter pill that I had to swallow, with the sugar-coated *alfajor*. It is a kind of tea, but it's not just tea. It's much, much more than that. It is part of the traditional Argentine lifestyle. The ritual consists of putting bitter-tasting leaves, called *yerba*, into a gourd—this is what they call the *mate*—pouring hot water on it, adding sugar according to taste—or not in this case—sipping it out of a metallic straw, and then passing it along to the others, in a circle, like one would with pot. But the rules of conduct are stricter than they are for the passing around of a joint. The thing to remember is that when people offer it to you (which they will), say "Yes, please" and then try not to make a face when the bitter liquid burns a hole in your stomach. And when you've had far more sips of the foul drink than you wanted in the first place, indicate to the host that you have had your fill by saying *gracias* (before you escape to the bathroom to wash your mouth out).

After we had drunk our *mate*, we rolled up the carpet and put on our heels, and Valeria took me through the two-hour exercise routine for walking, with embellishments, that she does every day. Also, she says it's really important that I take up ballet if I want to dance professionally. The men won't take me seriously otherwise, she says. And I drink it all in. But unlike the *mate*, I don't spit it out when she's not looking.

April 20, 1999

Last night at Niño Bien, I met a fellow by the name of Marcelo. He had light brown whiskers and the same color shoulder-length hair, which he played with constantly. He flicked it back with his head, twirled it with his fingers, put it up in a ponytail, brought it back down again, shook it out, put it up again, only to let it loose once more before running his fingers through it suggestively. He did this all night long. It was hypnotizing.

As for his height and build, they were perfect.

He came up to me at the table I was sharing with a stranger and spouted something to me in Spanish:

"I'm sorry, could you speak more slowly please? My Spanish is not very good," is the only thing I can say with a flawless accent.

He looked surprised. It must have been my sexy new shimmering pink crop top that fooled him. I'd be happier, of course, if it flaunted less belly and more button, but that's another story.

"You no *porteña?*" he said in Spanish. Did he think that if he butchered his language, I would understand him better?

"No, me no *porteña.*" At least I had permission to butcher it back.

"You on holiday?" he continued, mouthing each word carefully, after he had introduced himself.

"No, me no on holiday. Me live here now," I said, abandoning any attempt at grammar.

Marcelo looked pleasantly surprised. I have to say, I was starting to like him.

"How old *you* are?" he asked me. All of a sudden, I liked him less.

"How old *you* are?" I echoed back. I was trying to buy some time while I thought of how to answer.

"Twenty-one," he said. Damn, my time was already up. "So, how old you are?" he repeated.

"Twenty-one?" I said tentatively, which is why it came out sounding like a question. My brain freezes when I panic. I expected him to call me a liar to my face. But to my amazement, he believed me. I had gotten away with it. I must be in better shape than I think. The one problem is that I am now stuck with being twenty-one. It is going to be tricky to keep up the pretense. I need to erase the last ten years from my memory as well as the last five countries I have lived in. I hope he doesn't catch on.

He really is a beautiful dancer. I wonder if he's up for grabs . . .

April 23, 1999

I went to Almagro last night, and there he was: Marcelo! And he apparently was as pleased to see me as I was to see him. He took possession of me immediately. I love it when men do that. It's so sexy. I wish all men knew how I long to be treated like an object.

We were dancing now, and Marcelo was whispering sweet nothings in my ear. It tickled—it was his whiskers. The sweet nothings were a translation of the lyrics of the tangos to which we were dancing. Even if I did speak Spanish, I wouldn't have understood them because they are mostly in Lumfardo, the argot of Buenos Aires. It was originally developed as a code by criminals who did not want the police to understand what they were saying.

We were dancing to the sad tale of Yvonne, a French ingenue who is brought over to Argentina by a scoundrel who seduces her and then duly dumps her, so that she is forced into prostitution to survive.

> *Ten years they passed since you . . .* como se dice? *. . . sail*
>   *from Francia,*
> *Mademoiselle Yvonne, now they call you "Madame."*
> *You are sad when you drink your champagne . . .*
> *Your suffering is pure like snow . . .*
> *And the Argentino who bring you from Paris . . .*
> Se borro *. . . he left without saying good-bye . . .*

The translation may have been somewhat lacking from a purely linguistic perspective, but this was amply made up for by its rendering. Marcelo's delivery was heartfelt as he squeezed here to emphasize a particularly sad bit and caressed there to highlight a particularly touching bit.

When I first heard the tango in this very place two years and three months ago, it had been the music that had wrenched my soul from its socket. I had not needed to understand the lyrics to experience the loss, longing, and nostalgia it conveyed. In fact, I did not believe that understanding the words could add in any way to the sublime sadness I already felt. But I had been wrong. As Marcelo translated the lyrics—no matter how inadequately—the pathos of the music was enhanced, so that dancing to it became even more exquisitely painful than it had been before. With the added support of the lyrics, the music provided an even greater dimension to the sadness, while the embrace of a stranger provided even greater comfort. As a result, the perfect circle of pain and relief was made even more perfect, and catharsis more cathartic.

I don't know whether or not to ask Marta, my Spanish teacher, to teach me Lumfardo. On the one hand, I want to be able to understand the lyrics of the tangos I dance to. On the other, if I understand them, Marcelo won't have any excuse to tickle me with his whispers anymore. And that would be a shame.

May 4, 1999

I've started taking ballet lessons. Valeria was right: it's the only way to be taken seriously as a tango dancer. The guys won't even consider you as a partner unless you say yes without blushing when they ask, "Do you take ballet?"

Everyone agrees that Miguel Angel Bravo is the maestro to go to.

"He's the best. You'll love him," Valeria promised me over *mate*. (It's amazing how quickly one acquires the taste. I'm becoming addicted to the smoky bitterness of the leaves. My only complaint is that it stains the teeth. Mine are already starting to look like Hector's.)

I entered the dance studio already feeling self-conscious in my tights and leotard. Ballet reminds me of what a clumsy, stocky sherpa girl I am, not the graceful swan I want to be. The wide back and broad shoulders that others think are sexy are a source of constant shame. Not to mention the stumpy little legs and muscular thighs. Okay, I admit, I have divine calf muscles, which give the optical illusion of nice legs, but it's an illusion. Why oh why couldn't I have been born tall and lean, like my sister? Why am I saddled with this muscular body that makes me feel like a man in drag, especially when I am forced to stuff it into a leo-tard?

Memories come flooding back to me. I am five years old again. That's when I experienced the trauma of failing my first ballet exam. I can trace most of my neuroses back to that day. Indeed, ballet has been a veritable fountain of humiliation. I remember how I felt every time I looked in the mirror as I struggled to perform my *pliés*:

"Why do the other little girls look so much more graceful than me?" I didn't express my inadequacy in these words—I was only five at the time—but that's basically how I felt.

My teacher agreed with me.

"Look at her posture! It must be corrected before it is too late," she warned my mother. "Suck in your tummy, dear! And stick your bottom in!" She was addressing herself to me now as she poked me in the stom-ach with her cane before using it to pat my bottom. It felt like a spank.

My mother agreed with me too. I was nine now.

"I don't want my daughter to dance on point [like every other girl in the class]. Her thigh muscles are huge as it is, and I don't want them to develop even more," she whispered to the teacher.

I am an elephant, was the thought that went through the head of the nine-year-old.

So here I am, back to face the enemy, over twenty years later. I have built up some sort of defense system in the meantime. But although my self-esteem has improved somewhat, I'd prefer not to test it more than is absolutely necessary.

So here I am, back in leotard and tights, facing the mirror and wish-ing I was dead. I don't know which is worse: the psychological pain caused by my reflection or the physical pain I am about to endure (I don't know it yet). It's a good thing I was born a masochist.

First it is time for the "warm-up" exercises.

I sit with my legs spread while the teacher pushes my nose into the ground, so that I am licking the dirt off the floor:

"Do you feel the stretch?" he asks me.

I don't respond because of the pain that is ripping me apart at the seams.

"Good girl!" he says.

Later, he grabs my head when I least expect it and yanks it to the left with both his hands.

Crack! goes my head.

"Ahhhhhh!" go I.

"Did they tell you that I'm also a chiropractor?" he asks me.

I don't respond. I am in a state of shock.

"Good girl!" he says.

Now it is time to get serious.

"I want you to lift your right leg and stretch your arms back behind your head, grabbing hold of your foot with both your hands, like so, and lifting your leg gently behind your arched back, like so," he says as he uses me to demonstrate to the rest of the class. He is forcing my leg to go in a direction it was specifically designed not to go in.

"I'll let go now, okay?" he asks me.

"Yeeeessssss!" I scream. My spine is on the verge of snapping in two.

"Good girl," he says.

The contortionist has finished her act. Now it's time for her to go to the bar. Send in the clowns! The sight of me doing *pliés, relevés, tendus,* and *rond de jambes* is so grotesque it makes me want Miguel Angel to lift my leg up behind my back again. Things continue to get steadily worse. He orders us to come to the middle, where we must execute arabesques and *souplesses, pas de bourrée,* and *ciseaux, échappés* (jumps), and *fermés.*

Finally, the class ends with seventy-two *échappés* in the fifth position: I am a *jumping* elephant, I correct myself, twenty years later.

The class is over and I clap along hypocritically with the rest of them. Never again, I swear to myself.

"Good work," says Miguel Angel. I have gone up to him to say my adieux.

"Do you really think so?" I say in disbelief.

"Absolutely! You show great promise," he says.

"I do?" I drink in his praise like a very thirsty five-year-old.

"So what did you think of the class?" Valeria asked me the next day.

"Miguel-Angel is *great;* you were right. In fact, I've signed up to go to him three times a week."

May 10, 1999

La Glorieta is an open-air *milonga* that takes place every Sunday evening in a turn-of-the-century bandstand. It sits on a hill in the middle of a park that is filled with jacarandas, the native tree of Argentina. And on a day like yesterday, the leaves and the grass were made more fragrant still by the light autumn rain that was falling pitter-patter above our heads onto the glass-and-metal roof as we danced.

I was taking a break and went to stand by the railings, where a young crowd had congregated. They all wore jeans and looked a bit the worse for wear after a heavy-duty Saturday night out. It seemed to be one big clique. Every time a new person showed up, or left, he or she kissed all the others hello or good-bye. Even the guys gave each other a big smack on the cheek along with a warm hug—it's not considered gay, apparently. You kiss on only one cheek down here, but that's still a lot of kissing. I tried to listen in on their chatter, but I still find it really hard to understand when lots of people talk at the same time. Or when they are not talking slowly for my benefit.

And then I saw him: Marcelo, fiddling with his hair as usual. The surge of lust, which traveled from my belly to my knees and back again, was impossible to ignore.

"*Che, flaca!* Dance with me!" he said. Flattering as it was to my ego to believe that he thought I was thin, he didn't necessarily. *"Flaca"* (which does indeed mean thin) is a common term of endearment and may or may not be an apposite description of one's physique. It's better, though, than being called one of the variants: *"gorda," "loca,"* or *"negra"* (fat girl, crazy girl, or black girl respectively), all three of which I have been treated to on more than one occasion. Frankly, I would much rather they didn't call me anything at all. I was not going to refuse him, though, no matter what he called me.

We danced the most divine set, during which all I could do was hope that he might ask me to practice at the end of it (the first step toward being his partner) and pray that he was not already shacked up with the girl who was eyeing us from the railings as we danced. I can't say they were the friendliest pair of eyes I have ever seen. I swear they reminded me of the shower scene in *Psycho*.

Afterward, we went back to join the group, which was hanging out at the railings. The girl immediately came up to him, looking visibly annoyed. She said something to him in Spanish, which I didn't catch. He said something back, looking deeply irritated with her. Then she went off in a huff, while he stayed behind, acting as if nothing had happened. He proceeded to introduce me to everyone: all aspiring professional dancers, and all between the ages of sixteen and twenty-two. (I don't plan on turning twenty-two for a very long time.)

Five minutes after Miss Psycho had left, Marcelo went back to tickling me with the translation of more tangos, accompanied by the sound of the raindrops. Sadly, he didn't ask me to be his partner. But I can wait . . .

May 19, 1999

La Viruta was packed like a tin of sardines and so dark that it was impossible to spot anyone unless you had brought your night-vision binoculars, which, stupidly, I had left at home. I was dancing with partner number twelve—that's the minimum quota per night: fewer than twelve partners and I get cranky—when who should I bump into but Marcelo, who was dancing with one of the "Glorieta girls"—but not Miss Psycho.

He came to get me at the beginning of the next set. He didn't ask me if I wanted to dance. Neither did he ask for my permission when in the middle of the second tango, he locked my right hand behind my back, thus narrowing the already nonexistent gap between us. Nor did he say please before he started to explore my bottom with his free hand. Any moment now and he was going to take all my clothes off without even a thank-you. And I don't think I would have done anything to stop him. I was putty in his arms. I had goose bumps all over and it wasn't just the whiskers.

But I was saved by the "*Cumparsita*." That's the national anthem of tango, which they play at the end of all the *milongas*. It was six-thirty in the morning and the halogen lights went on, signifying that it was all over.

"Want to go for coffee and *medialunas*?" he asked. That he bothered to ask was confusing. Why didn't he just hit me over the head with a club and drag me wherever it was he wanted to take me? Why pretend to be civilized? "We're all going," he said, pointing to the twenty or so boys and girls who made up the Glorieta set. I checked to see if Miss Psycho was among them. She was not, to my immense satisfaction. He was free, then! But not for long, I thought. I was feeling rather smug, I admit.

Breakfast was across the road, at the gas station. It's trendy to end the night at the YPF (the local Esso). There was soccer on the TV. What else would there be on the TV? Marcelo and every other guy in the place kept one eye glued to the screen at all times. The score was nil–nil. While keeping his eye firmly on the ball, he started to play a different kind of football, using my foot as the ball. I normally hate footsie because you always end up playing footsie with the wrong guy: the one sitting next to the one you really want to be playing footsie with. But in this instance, I didn't mind at all—even if I did have to throw away my brand-new fishnets afterward because he had made a huge hole in them. As the match got tense—I think there was a penalty at stake, or something—Marcelo started to grope my thigh. He'd inadvertently found my point of least resistance.

Even though I had decided that tonight would be the night, I did not want to give the game away too fast. Not in front of the others. I was afraid that if I appeared to favor Marcelo, I would sabotage future dances with them—and I wanted to keep my options open. So I pulled away, which had the effect of turning Marcelo on more, not less. He had shifted toward me on the banquette and was now sitting in my lap. Okay, you win, I thought as I chatted with Valeria across the table.

When it came time to leave, I offered Valeria a lift home. I did not want the others to see me and Marcelo take a cab alone. Once we were rid of our alibi, the taxi headed toward my place. He was reciting *"Naranja en Flor"* as he played with my hair and stroked the nape of my neck. It felt just as tingly as it does when you get your hair washed at the hairdresser's. I was preoccupied, though. What was Salvatore, the night porter, going to think? My mind raced to find a way of sneaking Marcelo into the building, thus avoiding Salvatore altogether. But I'm not very good at thinking when my hair, among other things, is being fondled. Unable to come up with a plan, I gave up on looking for one.

We'll have to wing it, I thought.

The taxi pulled up in front of my building. We both got out of the cab, but instead of paying the fare and letting the cab go, Marcelo took me in his arms and said, *"Buenas noches, linda."*

I did a double take. Had I developed sudden hearing problems? He couldn't *possibly* be saying good night!

"I wanted so much to make love to you tonight," he sighed.

So far, I didn't see where the problem lay. (Apparently he *was* saying good night.)

"But it is impossible, *mi amor,*" he said bittersweetly. He could have left out the sweet bit, if you ask me.

"May I ask why?" I admit it was not the most ladylike question. But it was better than bursting into tears, which is what I felt like doing.

"There is someone else," he said, looking at the ground with new-found interest.

"It's that girl, isn't it?" I said. I didn't know Miss Psycho's name.

"Yes, that girl," he mumbled.

"Is she your girlfriend?" I asked.

"No, no, no! *Estas loca!* You must be crazy! Never! But . . ."

"And where is this girl who is not your girlfriend?"

"She's at home . . . waiting for me. I've got to go—I'm sorry."

"Don't worry . . . I quite understand," I said, even though I didn't.

"I'll call you *después*," he said as he made his hasty retreat into the cab. *"Después"* meant "after," that much I did understand. But after *what?*

Five minutes later, as I stood under an ice-cold shower trying to recover my composure, I realized that this had been a long time in coming to me: You have teased your fair share of pricks. For once, a prick has teased you. Now you know what it feels like. Let this be a lesson: never, ever tease a prick again . . .

When I got out of the shower, I was still dripping wet. I was going to have to do something about it—but without Marcelo's help.

May 27, 1999

I went to Refasi last night, which is like saying I went to the cathedral to hear mass. This is where the hardest of hard-core tango dancers start off their week. The congregation is as devoted to the dance as it is to the cocaine that it sneaks off at regular intervals to snort in the not terribly clean loos by the bar.

I was taking a short break, after having danced for three hours without respite, when I noticed a woman sitting alone. She was at a table at the rear of the room. All I could see at first was her head. It glowed like a beacon in the dark and smoky atmosphere. She had shaved her hair and what had grown back was dyed peroxide blond. She looked to be in her early seventies, judging by the deeply furrowed, not to say ravaged, face. When I got a closer look at her, the black eye shadow around the eyes turned the beacon into a skull. More macabre still was the bright red lipstick, which had run to create fine rivulets of blood in the creases on each side of her mouth, carried there by the flow of drool that had escaped it on the couple of occasions she had nodded off to sleep.

I noticed that she had a little sign on her table that read "Tarot," but nobody, it appeared, was interested in his or her long-term destiny. They were far more interested in the short-term question of who would ask them to dance (if they were female) or whether they would get lucky tonight (if they were male). As the evening progressed, my pity for her escalated until it became intolerable. I couldn't bear the sight of her any-more, which is why I had to go and ask her for a consultation. Even if it did mean missing out on a potentially life-altering dance.

My Spanish is still not good enough to go into the finer points of my future, of which I was sure there would be many, so I asked her if she spoke any English. She did not, but as it turned out, she spoke French. I wondered if she was in any way related to Madame Yvonne—the sad ingenue-turned-slut in the tango that I had danced with Marcelo. Per-haps she *was* Madame Yvonne! We got straight down to business. She told me to mix the cards and make them "mine." I normally shuffle as if I've worked in a casino all my life, but I must have been nervous because as I did my collapsing-bridge trick, the cards flew all over the place and I had to get down on all fours to pick them up from under the neighbor's table.

"Promise you won't tell me anything *really* bad?" I said after I had collected myself and all the cards. It was an uncharacteristic attack of caution on my part.

"I only repeat what the cards say, *ma chérie.*"

"Yes, but I don't necessarily want to know *everything* the cards have to say. I'm quite happy to keep the bad stuff as a surprise pudding, if you see what I mean." I don't know why I was so nervous.

"As you wish," she said. She placed the cards face upward, one at a time, in a mysterious pattern. Then she didn't say anything for a while, which made me impatient.

"Well? Do you see anything?" I asked.

"Your hands, please. Let me look at them." I brought my palms up to her. She inspected them carefully. She brought them closer to the light and turned them this way and that. Finally she said: "You will live a long and healthy life." She pointed it out to me. "See? There. That's your lifeline." That was a relief.

"And . . . ?" I said, hungry for more news along those reassuring lines.

"That's all, *ma petite* . . . That will be ten pesos," she said, picking up her cards.

(Help! I'm doomed to a long and healthy life of loneliness, failure, and misery.)

"That bad, hey?" I said casually, fishing for a fish I did not want to catch.

"I didn't say that," she said in a tone that made it impossible to believe her. That's when I panicked and started asking random people if they knew of a tarot reader who would be able to give me a second opinion at four in the morning. But nobody did.

June 3, 1999

I've been warned about the taxis outside the tango clubs. I've been told never to take them because they are a mafia. But I can't be bothered to walk the few yards it would take to stop a regular one. Especially at five in the morning when I'm wearing stilettos and I've danced with fifteen guys for five hours nonstop.

So last night, I got into a cab outside Refasi, a complete wreck (I meant the cab, but I was a wreck too), behind an absolutely enormous cabbie. Osvaldo, one of the regular "doormen" (read: homeless beggars) who moves with the tango circuit from one *milonga* to the next, opened the door to the cab and gently placed me inside before thrusting his hand through the window and into my face, thus indicating that he'd like a tip, please. I magnanimously handed him a peso, which he accepted with a "God bless you, darling" and off we went. I was already dreaming of my bed when we arrived outside my apartment building.

"That's two pesos." I handed the driver a bill. "Sorry, I can't take this. It's torn." Sure enough, I looked at the bill he had returned to me and noticed that the corner was torn off.

"I'm sorry about that," I said as I looked in my purse for another bill. I handed him what I thought was a ten, hoping for some change.

"Nope. Can't take that one. It's A series, you see." I inspected the $2 bill he had handed back to me and sure enough, there was a serial number on it—how interesting. I had never noticed that bills had serial numbers on them.

"Oh, so it is. Sorry about that." I apologized, though I was not clear why an A was bad. I briefly remembered that I thought I had given him a ten. I assumed that I must have been mistaken and that my exhausted mind was playing tricks on me.

I rummaged around in my wallet for another bill. Again, I handed him what I thought was a ten, which was immediately returned to me as a two, this time being unacceptable because it started with a B. Again, I thought, I must be really tired because I was sure that that was a ten I had handed over to him. My mistake again. I was as unclear about why B was bad as I had been about A. But I thought that if I started a conversation on the subject, it would delay me further from getting to my bed. Plus, as I searched for another bill I was embarrassed for having caused so much trouble. This time I checked it thoroughly before handing it over. No, it was not torn. It was definitely a ten and it was a C series. Perhaps it would pass the test this time? I handed it over and waited for him to hand me my change. When he said thank you and good night and didn't look as if he was going to produce any change, I felt the time had come to say something:

"Didn't I just give you a ten? I'd like my change please." I made sure to remain polite. Luckily, we have covered the conditional in my lessons with Marta. I even think I got it right this time.

"No, you gave me a two," he said matter-of-factly.

"I didn't. I gave you a ten. Now give me my change." Present imperative.

"No, miss. You're a foreigner, see, so you don't know what's what when it comes to our money. But I won't hold it against you," said the swine.

I may not know much, but I do know that last night, when I left Refasi, I had $50 in tens in my wallet. This morning, I wake up and I look inside and all I see are a couple of twos, one of which is torn. And I am torn between hate and admiration. After all, it's not every day that you meet a magician.

June 4, 1999

Feeling slightly wary of cabs after yesterday's incident, the price of which, I felt, had outweighed the entertainment value, I decided the time had come to hop on a bus. And also, I reasoned, the only way to avoid being fumigated as they rumble past you and blow out their disgusting black exhaust is to be inside one of them.

I spotted a bus stop around the corner from my apartment, at which a line had formed. To nobody in particular, I said, *"Calle Florida?"* as I tilted my head toward my right shoulder, which provoked a reassuring domino effect of nodding heads and raised thumbs. So I joined the line and waited. The good news was that I didn't have to wait long at all. Buses are extremely frequent and abundant here, putting an end to the bus prejudice I acquired growing up in London, where you are lucky if a bus shows up in your lifetime. Also, I was amazed by how polite the men were at the bus stop. They insisted on letting all the ladies on first. The order of hierarchy at a bus stop seems to be old ladies first, followed by pregnant women with children, followed by remaining females of all shapes and sizes, followed by the blind and the infirm, followed by old men, and finally by remaining males of all shapes and sizes. Did I mention that I like this country? I also noticed that their politeness was not limited to the bus stop itself. Once inside the bus, the same hierarchy prevailed. Which meant that as soon as he saw me, a man who looked to be at least in his eighties and who looked wobbly even when sitting down, sprang out of his seat and offered it to me. I couldn't possibly accept, so I invented some excuse about needing to stand because of poor circulation (this required some creative body language) before moving toward the back of the bus through the thicket of passengers.

In retrospect, I don't know why I was in such a hurry to get on the bleeding bus. Our driver did not believe in using his brakes unless absolutely necessary. He did not have this qualm, however, when it came to the gas pedal. Try as one might to avoid bandying words about too freely, I bandy not when I use the words "reckless" and "lunatic" to describe this man's driving. I could only speculate that the bus company gave bonuses to those drivers who made it to the finish line first. Whatever the cause, the effect was brutal on the passengers' spines—especially on those passengers trying to stay upright. I'm amazed that not more of us did take a tumble as we were plunged headlong toward the front of the bus; tossed this way and that; jiggled from side to side; sucked toward the back with every acceleration, shift of gear, and, finally, and only as a last resort . . . sto-o-o-o-o-p! I guess we didn't fall over because there was no place to fall. For once, I was actually happy to be a sardine.

Above the driver's head, I noticed an icon of the Madonna. I tapped my fellow passenger on the shoulder and asked him about it. He told me that she was the Virgen de Lujan, patron saint of bus drivers.

If he used his brakes more, there would be less need for prayer, was my POV, not that anybody asked me.

Finally, the nice man who told me about the Virgen gave me a nudge to let me know that this was my stop. After I got off, I saw a number of passengers waving at me through the window and I waved back. Their friendliness more than compensated for the trauma of the ride. But I was still shaking. To the point that I had forgotten why I had wanted to come to calle Florida, so I strolled over to Havanna in the hope that an *alfajor* would jog my memory.

June 17, 1999

At a party, I never remember anybody's name. I always have to ask ten times, much to my embarrassment and the annoyance of the person who was introduced to me all of five minutes ago. But at a *milonga*, I remember the name of every single guy I have ever danced with. And there have been lots. I've lost count, but it must be over a hundred by now. Of course, it helps that half of them are called Pablo and the other half Juan, Jorge, or Luis. The difference is that a *milonga* is not a party—in spite of what my family and friends back home believe. It really *is* like going to the office. No kidding.

First, it's where you practice your trade. And the more people you practice your trade with, the better you get. Second, it's where you network. It's between two tangos that a guy, if he likes the way you dance (and/or your ass), will ask you if you are available to practice with him, the first stepping-stone to a potential long-term partnership. It's also where you make "friends" with other dancers, find out what is happening on the scene, what companies are auditioning, who is in town teaching a workshop, etc. So beneath the veneer of frivolous fun, the *milonga* is the place where business transactions of a deadly serious nature are performed.

Of course, business does not always preclude pleasure. In fact, I think I may have landed one of the only two jobs in the world where business *is* pleasure—so my parents ought to be relieved that I chose tango and not the other one.

Last night, as it so happens, business was even more pleasant than usual. When I noticed the young man at the other end of the crowded dance floor nodding in my direction, I could literally hear the avalanche of coins going clank-clank as they gushed out of the slot machine: I had hit the jackpot! The guy was the spitting image of James Dean—actually, he was even more gorgeous than the prototype. He was so beautiful that it was difficult not to look at him without going a deep shade of red, then white, before fainting on the spot. Once I had recovered my composure and picked myself off the metaphorical floor, knees still trembling, we exchanged a few introductory words. His name was Guillermo and he was studying fashion. I misunderstood at first and thought he was studying to be a model—an understandable mistake that anybody with two eyes in their head would have made—but as it turned out, he was an aspiring designer.

When I looked into his eyes for the first time, I thought what a pity that I hadn't brought a bathing suit with me. They were two gigantic pools of deep blue-green water and I even thought I saw a couple of water lilies floating about in them.

As we stood there, waiting for the music to start, I planned the next five years of our life together. Guillermo and I would become partner-lovers immediately, thus fulfilling my dream of reconciling tango with romance once and for all. He would move in with me and within a year or two—i.e., in record time—we would travel the world, teaching sold-out workshops during the day and performing in *Una Noche de Tango* by night. None of this, however, would interfere with our starting a family. I'd give birth to the most beautiful blond children you ever saw: they'd have a combination of his eyes and mine—since mine aren't bad either, so they say—a boy and a girl, who'd dance together before they could walk. It would be just perfect.

The music started, and in a flash, I made the journey back from the future. I bypassed the present entirely as the tango flew me back on its magic carpet to a time that is remote and yet that I experience with such nostalgia, as if it had once been my own. The combined strands of the violin and the *bandoneón* cast their spell on me and I was falling fast . . . when I was forced to recognize that there was a glitch in the plan: Guillermo could barely dance. Okay, that's a slight exaggeration: He wasn't absolutely *terrible*. Objectively speaking, his dancing was quite adequate. But after having just been on a world tour of Europe, Japan, and the States with him, while giving birth to his children, the rude intrusion of reality was more than I could bear. Of course, I mused, as I picked up the pieces of my shattered expectations, with a bit of practice—three to five years' worth—he might reach an acceptable level. But, the inner dialogue continued, by then I'll need a Zimmer frame. I shook my head sadly as I came to the conclusion that I simply couldn't wait for Guillermo to get his act together dancewise. Even if everybody else thinks I am twenty-one, I am only too aware of how mistaken they are.

By the third tango of the set, I had come to terms with the tragedy. In truth, it wasn't too difficult to forgive Guillermo for the crime of being mediocre. I hate it that people get away with murder just because they are good looking, but whoever said that life was fair? And then I thought, Heck, you work so hard, you're entitled to a break every now and then. So I decided to take the day off from the office as I accepted his invitation to dance a second set.

June 29, 1999

I couldn't believe my luck as I audited Guillermo's inventory and thus discovered that his eyes are *not* his best feature. His body is made of concrete: it is rock hard, every inch of it, and I mean *every* inch. I could have spent all night gazing at it—in retrospect, I *should* have. Because what I had forgotten was how painful the impact with concrete can be. I once broke my collarbone when I fell out of a bunk bed in the middle of the night onto a concrete floor. It had happened on a Greek island. I was eight at the time and had been dancing in my sleep to the music they had played at my aunt's wedding that night. It should have taught me my lesson re avoiding hard surfaces, but I've always had a lousy memory.

Guillermo, as I was about to find out, is a proponent of the equation whereby $P = R + P \times 15$.* To be fair, he is not the only member of this school of thought. In fact, in my experience, most men have not the faintest idea of how the female body works. They have watched far too many good actors in bad pornos, leading them to believe that it is necessary to make all that effort to get results. Why doesn't somebody tell them that "less is more" has never been truer than in the sack? To be fair, I did try. But it is difficult to hold forth when you are in the midst of being rammed and pounded. I decided that the best policy, under the circumstances, was to breathe deeply so as to relax the muscles, thereby diminishing the force of impact with the hard surface, which in turn would hopefully result in softening the blow.

The policy was effective to a certain degree in that today I might have ended up entirely crippled versus semicrippled. My main concern is that I'll never be able to close my knees again, which is problematic for a tango dancer, since the number one rule for a woman is "Thou shalt dance with thy knees firmly together at all times." In fact, at Pavadita today, a regular partner of mine asked me if I had gone horseback riding yesterday. I said yes, since I couldn't come up with any other explanation for my bowlegged state. What he doesn't realize is that my

---

*Passion = Ramming + Pounding × 15 minutes

head hurts more than my "inner thighs" (crotch) from all that banging against the wall. I wonder if a headboard would help?

In spite of it all, I must say I like him, and this is not only my masochistic side speaking. He's funny and smart and he's got flair—for example, he borrowed my bright orange latex shirt and it suits him better than it suits me, which is rather annoying, but then again, anything would suit him. He could wear a trash bag and still he'd look beautiful. When somebody is that beautiful, who cares if they are not the world's best dancer/lover? And who knows? Perhaps with a bit of time and practice, we'll be able to soften his edges . . .

July 10, 1999

What a fool I was! Why couldn't I have left his hard edges alone? I should have kept my big mouth shut is what I should have done. Even if it did mean sore "inner thighs" and huge bumps on my head the next day. I'm such a klutz and I have only myself to blame.

It was about five-thirty A.M. and he had come back to my place after La Viruta. I had spent all evening stroking his ego on the dance floor, telling him how well he was dancing when in fact I would much rather have been dancing with Pablo, Ezequiel, Juan, or Pancho, to name but a few of the partners who were so tantalizingly near and yet so far. I displayed incredible stoicism in the face of such self-deprivation, if I do say so myself. By the end of the evening, I had sacrificed three whole sets to Guillermo. That's a lot.

By the time we got home, I was no longer able to keep up the Little Miss Demure act. As he made to kiss me, my mind raced ahead to the pain I was about to endure and, in response, I'm afraid I became all about damage control. No sooner had he stuck it in than I found myself barking instructions at him like a drillmaster at North Point Academy.

"Gently! Slowly! Softly! Does the word 'clitoris' ring any bells? Not there! There! Stay there! In! Out! In! Out! Now! Yes! Yes! No! No! Not now! Damnit!"

What can I say? It was the fear talking. It will come as no surprise that the poor guy was not able to keep up the performance for long with all that backseat driving. After having screwed it up by saying all the wrong things, I tried to make up for it by saying all the right things:

"No, of course it's not your fault. Don't worry. These things happen. It's not you, it's me . . . ," and so forth and so on.

I have to be honest with myself and say that when it comes to sex—and now that I think of it, the same applies to tango—I'm only as good as my partner. I can be great one moment and lousy the next; it all depends on who I am following. But don't ask me to lead them or instruct them in any way, shape, or form. I simply can't. Or won't. I don't know if it's because I lack the self-confidence—I'm not sure I know the steps/erotic moves myself—or if it's out of laziness. More likely, it is my deep-seated desire to be dominated that does not take kindly to telling a novice what to do. As we just saw, put me in that unfortunate position and it's a disaster waiting to happen.

I do wish, though, I could be more like those women who are willing and able to show men the way, both on the floor and in bed, while keeping it feminine at the same time. The question is, how do they do that? How do they lead effectively without falling into the bossiness trap? How do they take charge without immediately turning into mini-Hitlers? Because turning into a mini-Hitler feels even less attractive on the inside than it looks on the outside, let me tell you.

What all this boils down to is that I'm going to have to find another way to make it work with Guillermo. I wonder where I left my copy of *Memoirs of a Geisha?*

July 17, 1999

The last time Guillermo came around to my place, I made sure to sweep the military-drill-cum-sex fiasco under the carpet and switched to my new tactic: Hope for the Best. I had already positioned a soft pillow strategically between head and wall and was deeply inhaling and exhaling Lamaze style in preparation for the onslaught.

But the onslaught didn't come. There wasn't even a raid or a skirmish for that matter. Nothing. It just lay there. Limp. This could be no accident, coincidence, bad luck, or whatever else you want to call it. It could only mean one thing. I am repulsive, I told myself as I tried all the tricks in the trade to revive it. But it hadn't gone to sleep, it was in a coma and it wasn't going to wake up anytime soon. There was nothing I could do to persuade it to come out and play. When it happened the first time, I thought it was him. When it happened the second time, I knew it had to be me.

All I could do was lie limply beside it in sympathy and berate myself for being a castrating bitch—a repulsive one, at that:

It's your fault. No wonder he can't get it up. Look at you: you're the world's most unattractive woman. Let's face it: you've got a fat ass. And it's full of cellulite . . . and more along those lines.

It's never happened to me before. Impotence, I mean. And yes, I'm going to take it personally. Because it did happen to *me*. Or rather it *didn't* happen to me. Guys think it's *their* problem, but it's not: it's we girls who are the victims of their failure in bed. I have never felt so non-plussed in my life. Or is it shame, frustration, and rage, swept under a carpet of nonplusment? The word "anticlimax" doesn't begin to do justice to it because that sounds as if you were on your way to a climax. When the truth is, you never even made it out of the gate.

When I told Valeria what had happened, she said: "It's obvious: he's gay."

Of course! Why didn't I think of it before? This was vastly preferable to my "I'm the world's most unattractive woman" theory. I couldn't believe that my gaydar had let me down so badly. Perhaps it isn't working properly in the Southern Hemisphere. What if it's like the water that drains out of the sink the wrong way? That could spell disaster.

Sure, the explanation satisfied my ego—what straight man could resist me, after all? But it wasn't just an attempt to salvage the old ego. In retrospect, it did seem a bit suspicious that he should look better in my clothes than me.

"There are lots of guys at the *milonga* who use tango as a cover-up, you know," she warned me.

Afterward, I thought about what she had said. And I realized that she was right. What better cover than tango, the epitome of the Macho Man's Dance? A man can put on the biggest swagger, stick out his chest all he wants, play the game of seduction until the cows come home, send you signals across the dance floor as if they were going out of style, but when push comes to shove, he isn't required to take it any further. He can flirt with you all he likes—thus proving to himself and to you how masculine he is—and never deliver the goods. I bet that most of them are not even aware that they are in the closet—that is how taboo it is here. It's hard to exaggerate the influence of the Catholic Church in this country. Italians are a bunch of heathens by comparison.

"Do you think you might . . . um . . . prefer men . . . um . . . to women?" I asked Guillermo after my chat with Valeria. I needed to know.

"What are you saying?! Are you calling me a *maricón*?! Are you crazy? No way!" he exploded. "And besides, I want kids . . . ," he continued, screaming at me at the top of his lungs.

Gay, I said to myself. Definitely gay.

It does upset me, though, that he is no longer talking to me.

July 18, 1999

I consider myself pretty savvy, but apparently I have a lot to learn when it comes to sex (or the lack thereof). I spent most of today on the phone and e-mailing girlfriends to share my humiliation with them, only to discover that I am not alone: dicks are going on strike everywhere. And we're talking dicks that belong to otherwise healthy young men. (It seems that the only dicks *not* going on strike these days belong to the seventy-plus crowd.) Each and every one of my friends had at least one such sob story to relate. This got me thinking, and by the time I was off the phone, I had a number of theories to explain the phenomenon, starting with its local manifestation here in Argentina:

1. The Freudian theory, whereby the Argentine male suffers from a neurosis, namely the "the macho complex." The pressure to live up to the image of Latin Lover is so great that it results in performance anxiety and eventually leads to the Big Shrivel. In technical terms: The Argentine Ego, under pressure from his Latin Lover Superego, can't get his Id up.

2. The Marxist theory says that impotence is a product of the capitalist system. Indeed, it is caused by the current economic recession in Argentina, leading to unemployment, instability in the workplace, and the fear of getting the sack, the result of which is the capitalist woman's inability to get laid. In technical terms, what we are dealing with here is the alienation of the Argentine from his penis. Or is it the alienation of the Argentine penis? Hmm . . . This theory needs more work.

3. According to the feminist theory, there is a conspiracy of the Argentine Phallocracy to put women in their place by keeping them sex starved. In this instance, impotence is a fine example of sexual repression in its most passive-aggressive form.

4. And finally the "They're All Gay" theory. This one needs no further explanation.

No wonder hysteria is so prevalent in Argentina—in both men and women. People are not getting enough sex. At first, I didn't understand why people kept referring to so-and-so as *histérica* or *histérico* or what they meant when they accused so-and-so of *histeriquear*. I have since found out that this means that so-and-so doesn't deliver the goods. (Remember Marcelo?) Since then, I have found out that this applies to everybody, even those who complain most bitterly about it. The Argentine doesn't flirt *in the hope* of getting sex. He or she flirts *in order to withhold* sex. It used to be that only women used this weapon. But now the men have stormed the arsenal and are fighting back, much to the horror of women, who no longer have the monopoly on withholding sex. Everybody is doing it. The question is: how did I get caught in the crossfire?

Making matters worse, it seems that this impotence thing has spread to places like New York, London, and Paris, which is a bummer, because getting on a plane is not going to solve the problem. Only now do I realize how lucky I was with Frank. I can't believe I took IT so much for granted. The fact that I was shacked up for most of my twenties also conspired to keep me blissfully ignorant of the dire state of international sex affairs. Jean . . . ahhhh! Not only was he a wonderful boyfriend (in spite of being French) but an expert lover. How was I to know that it would be virtually impossible to replace him?

So why is it that men all over the globe—not just here in Argentina—no longer lust after women? Did they ever, I wonder, or is this a fiction designed to make today's women feel shitty? Is the problem that sex is no longer taboo and therefore not as exciting to men anymore? Is it that women, now in touch with their sexuality and having read far too many *Cosmopolitan*-type magazines, have turned into insatiable creatures men can no longer satisfy? Is it that men are worn out from the long hours they put in at the office? Is there too much pressure on them to make the dough to pay for the down payment on the house they can't afford or to buy the second car they can't afford either, leaving them too exhausted to perform their marital duties? Is it the fear of AIDS? Is it that women compete directly with and are a threat to men in the workplace? Or is it that there are too many women in the world, resulting in the supply of sex being greater than the demand? Are women taking the wind out of men's sails by not playing hard to get? Are we castrating bitches? Or is it that they are confused and have trouble reading us? They don't know if we want a soft and sensitive type or a hard and dominant type? Resulting in the tragic result: soft in bed/hard out of bed? No wonder they find it easier to masturbate. I don't blame them. So do I.

Wave good-bye to generations X, Y, and Z.

Say hello to the new generation: Gen M.

July 25, 1999

Yesterday, I was made to inhale incense, listen to Indian music, probe people in places I don't normally probe myself (not in public at least), and be probed by them in turn (very much in public). I learned about the existence of a sacrum, which is like the Holy Grail, but I haven't figured out what or where it is yet. Somebody fingered my coccyx—and then I did it back to him. Nobody will be able to call me "tight assed" again. Then I touched my toes with my hands while somebody thumped me on the back and chest as I cried out in an imitation of Tarzan. Then I lay down on the floor and somebody cradled my head in his hands and rocked it from side to side. Then I did it back to him and realized what a heavy thing a head can be. I don't know how we carry it on our shoulders all day long. No wonder we're tired at the end of it. Then my partner pressed my pelvis into the ground as he took hold of my thigh and placed it against his chest while my leg dangled over his shoulder. With his upper body pressing down on one thigh, he drew circles with it and then started all over again with the other. When he was done, he took hold of my feet and shook out my legs, which had become the floppy limbs of a rag doll. In fact, I have never felt this floppy before, not even after half an hour of being beaten by a big, savage Russian with soapy oak branches in the Russian baths on East Tenth Street. Then it was my turn to massage my partner's groin and stroke his thighs. And finally, to finish off, we fondled each other's sternums. By now, I was too relaxed to feel the slightest bit embarrassed.

No, I have not been abducted by some weird sect. It was my first release technique class. I admit that at first I felt rather skeptical and wondered if all this probing and stroking of and by strangers was absolutely necessary. Frankly, it was quite an internal struggle to convince myself not to slap the person who was kneading my gluteus maximus— otherwise known as my big fat ass—so conscientiously. But after a long while—there was lots to knead, after all—the indignation was drained out of me (along with some of the fatty cells, I hope). Indeed, I had lost both the energy and the desire to rebel. Instead, I lay there like a cabbage in my patch and let him proceed to the next task, which involved the fondling of my pectoral muscles—otherwise known as . . .

I do have a good excuse for my behavior. If only I could remember what it was . . . oh yes . . . something about the release of tension in the body leading to a more "organic" dance—apparently cabbages are not the only things to have gone organic these days. The teacher said something about expanding one's range of movement through relaxation. But as far as I'm concerned, I don't need any excuse, good or bad, to go back and behave like an organic cabbage. Just show me my patch, and I'll go and lie in it quite happily, four times a week.

August 2, 1999

Valeria and I were at Almagro when I thought I saw Ben Affleck on the floor. Robert Duvall dances, so why not Ben? Perhaps Bob had initiated Ben, I speculated. Wow! He was amazing! Not only did he dance like an expert but, more important, he had the coziest-looking embrace, which I wanted a piece of as soon as I set eyes on it. I wondered where he found the time to practice between shoots. When I pointed him out to Valeria, she assured me that it was not Ben, but Claudio. I blinked hard and opened my eyes again:

"Are you *sure*, Valeria, that it's not Ben Affleck?"

"Positive. Claudio is one of the top dancers in the world. He's just come back from New York. He was in *Forever Tango*," she said.

If I had wanted to dance with him when I thought he was Ben Affleck, now I wanted to dance with this man who was not Ben Affleck even more. She had said the magic words: *"Forever Tango."* And so I went about making it happen.

We had just danced a set and my eyes were still closed. I was still in that far-off place, that place that is hard to get to but harder still to come back from, when I thought I heard a distant voice calling out to me. I pried open my eyes. It was Claudio. He was talking to me.

"What time is it?" he asked me.

"I don't know. I don't wear a watch," I answered, offended that he was thinking about the time at a time like this. How could he?

He looked at his watch. If he had a watch, why then was he asking *me* the time?

"It's two-thirty," he said.

"Thank you," I replied. I was confused. Had I asked to know the time?

"I'm going to ask you again what time it is," he said.

"Okay," I said, nodding obediently. I had stopped trying to understand.

"What time is it?" he asked me.

"It's two-thirty. Why?" said the good little girl.

"Because I want to remember exactly when it was I fell in love with you," he said.

Coincidentally, I had heard this very same *piropo*—that's what these flirty lines are called—that same afternoon from a guy in the street. I might have let myself feel flattered had I not overheard the guy in question paying the exact same compliment two seconds previously to the girl walking just ahead of me on the sidewalk.

But that had been in the afternoon. Right here and right now (at two-thirty A.M. to be precise), I was in Claudio's arms and the feeling was mutual.

When I floated back to Valeria, she asked me: "So how was it?"

"Divine. Simply divine" was all I could say. One of the many benefits of tango is that it turns me into Helen Keller.

"Did he tell you about Maria?" she asked me.

"No. Who's she?"

"His wife."

And that's when my feet landed back down on the ground with a loud thud.

August 7, 1999

"I can't stand being so near something so far out of my reach," Claudio was saying. If that isn't the definition of tango, I don't know what is. The tango is always about wanting that which you can't have. Either it expresses nostalgia—for your dead mother, for the only girl who ever loved you, for your lost youth, for the old café or street corner where you used to hang out. Or it is about yearning for an impossible and therefore perfect love—for a love that is "out of your reach," to get back to what Claudio was saying.

I giggled coyly, as I do in response to every one of his lines. I will say this for Claudio: he certainly has a wide and varied repertoire of *piropos* up his sleeve.

He doesn't know that I know that he's married. It makes it more interesting that way, I find. It amuses me to see what he'll come up with next. Of course, he only gets away with it because he is the most fabulous dancer ever.

"How about we go to your place for a little *mate?*" was last night's effort.

I didn't know what ruffled my feathers more: that the cheeky boy had invited himself over to my place or what the cheeky boy was suggesting we do at my place, which had very little to do with drinking hot beverages.

Translation: "How about we go to your place for a little *mate?*" = "How about we go to your place so you can give me a blow job?" It's the sucking on the straw that lends to this most Argentine of double entendres.

I didn't know quite how to react. I felt outraged, but I thought that to express outrage would be an overreaction. Besides, he is drop-dead gorgeous and the most divine dancer in the world—and you never know, he might be looking for a partner. Valeria says he is married, but I have yet to see this phantom wife of his. In a nutshell, I couldn't be angry with him, even if I wanted to. So I did what I usually do in these sticky situations: I laughed.

Then, he laughed (to save face?) at his own joke (was it a joke?) before we swept the *mate* under the carpet. They had put *"Vida Mia"* on, by Fresedo, which is *our* song. And once again, we were both touching that which neither of us could have. But now my mind was elsewhere. It was trying very hard to imagine what it might be like. But it didn't get very far. One simply cannot think about blow jobs when dancing to Fresedo. Or at least I can't.

August 10, 1999

"Nice eyes," said Claudio, who was looking at my tits. Then he pinched the right one—it's always the right one for some reason—and went: "Honk Honk."

Although there are at least ten thousand of them to choose from, Claudio has run out of *piropos* and has traded them in for molestation. And I, not wishing to offend his delicate feelings, giggle as coyly as ever, like a schoolgirl at a hilarious joke. I've noticed, though, that my right tit has started to sag. Of course, some people would argue that I get what I deserve, given the see-through tops I wear—without a bra. I would counter that one would expect Claudio to have outgrown the need to touch something to confirm that it is really there.

"I'm looking for a new partner, you know," he said last night as he held me in his irresistible embrace. It really is the best on the circuit—and I should know. It was a good thing he was holding me so tight, otherwise I would have fainted with joy. That's how much I love to dance with him—in spite of the daily mutilation.

"No, I didn't. What happened to . . . Maria?" I gasped out of a combination of shock and asphyxia. This was the first time I let on I knew anything of her existence. Her name had never come up in conversation until that moment.

I have done some of my own investigative work and have found out that she does indeed exist, so much so that she has recently given birth to their second child. That's why they left the show in New York. She's been out of commission for months now, which is why I have never seen her. So when I asked him what had happened to her, I knew very well. But I wanted to see what he would say.

"What's the *bruja* [the witch] got to do with anything?" said Claudio, using this common expression to refer to his wife. He sounded more than a tad annoyed that I had broken the contract and mentioned the unmentionable. How tactless of me. "This is strictly between you and me," he said as he executed a *sanguichito*—a figure that involves the leader trapping your foot between his two, reminiscent of a snack between two slices of bread. "And I want you . . . to be my partner," he said with his tongue dangerously close to my ear. However nice it was to hear these words, it still did not resolve the small problem: that he already had one. And that he was married to her.

Of course, he wasn't My Prince Charming because I don't think My Prince Charming is the type to invite himself over to my place for "*mate*" or to mutilate my right tit. But his words exerted an almost irresistible attraction. They were so powerful, in fact, that I almost forgot, as I said, that he already has a partner and as I also said, is married to her.

"Think about it: dancing with me is a good career move for you," continued My Prince Not So Charming. He *did* have a point.

"I'm listening," I said as I negotiated the *parada*, adroitly stepping over the barrier he had created and resolving my step with a cross. I might have been on the verge of caving, but I still wondered what the catch was.

"We'll have time to talk later. All the time in the world. But first, let's go back to your place to fuck." I wondered no more.

You do have to appreciate his honesty. Few people in this day and age have the balls to put their cards on the table in this way.

"Later, *mi amor*," I said as I stroked his cheek, which is the *porteña* way of saying "No way, José."

Today, I feel doubly relieved with my decision:

    a. I have saved Claudio from infidelity.
    b. I have saved my right tit from Claudio.

August 18, 1999

How could it have slipped my mind? Saying no to a Latin man is the ultimate aphrodisiac. It never fails. How could I have forgotten the Armando episode? It was all coming back to me now, Claudio was seeing to that.

"Have I ever told you that you are the love of my life?" he says.

(Too many times.)

"I would die for you," he says.

(Be my guest.)

"We could give workshops together all over the world. Don't you want to?" he asks.

(Like a hole in the head.)

In brackets are my silent replies. Claudio talks and I listen. I almost wish he would go back to pinching my right tit again. It's less nauseating.

Any sane person would ask me why oh why do you put up with this nonsense? Why don't you just swat the fly once and for all? And I would answer, I've tried, believe me, I've tried. But the bloody fly keeps coming back. Bzzzzz. Bzzzz. Bzzzz. Some call not taking no for an answer persistence. I call it being a pest.

Claudio is in complete denial of the fact that he is a father for the second time. My refrain at each and every one of his attacks is: "And your wife?" But I might as well save my breath because his brain presses the mute button every time I say, "And your wife?"

Claudio may be in denial, but he is not stupid. Not completely. He understands a thing or two about hedging one's bets. While he says: "You'll change your mind, you'll see. And I'll be right here, waiting to drink *mate* with you," he figures it doesn't hurt to stir a couple of other pots in the meantime.

In practice, what this means is that his undying love for me is not incompatible with simultaneous and identical feelings for others.

Yesterday, for example, I overheard him talking to the girl he was dancing with:

"Have I ever told you that you are the love of my life?" he said.

(. . .)

"I would die for you," he said.

(. . .)

"We could give workshops together all over the world. Don't you want to?" he asked.

(. . .)

I couldn't hear her answers, but I didn't need to. I knew exactly what she was thinking. What I didn't expect, however, was my reaction to this little scene. For, mixed in with the relief that the fly had settled elsewhere for the evening, I caught myself feeling peeved. Now how do you explain that?

August 27, 1999

It was four in the morning and all I wanted to do was go to bed but I couldn't because I was waiting up for Claudio. He had told me to leave Tasso first and wait for him at home. He said he would be there in twenty minutes.

It couldn't have happened at a worse time. I was about to get my period. If I was lucky, he was one of those men who found women with periods repulsive. That way I wouldn't have to have sex with him. Because I was suffering from buyer's remorse. I didn't want to go to bed with him anymore. In fact, I never had. But it was too late now. No, I was going to have to put a brave face on it. Now that I had said I would, I had to. One lesson that was still very much on my mind was the one Marcelo had taught me. It was a lesson I wished I could forget.

"If no means no, then yes must mean yes. Always. Out of principal," I said to the self who was trying to find a loophole.

This is how I had gotten myself into the mess. We had been at Tasso, and, as usual, he had been groveling. Up until now, I had done a super job of keeping him on the leash. My balancing act had consisted of flirting with him just enough to make him feel attractive (I don't know how

I ever thought he was. I will never be able to watch another Ben Affleck movie without cringing), while finding all sorts of reasons to not consummate the relationship: "And your wife?," "And your wife?," "And your wife?" But there comes a point when you can't say "And your wife?" anymore: the record-player that is playing the broken record breaks down. That's when you have to start looking elsewhere for excuses: "I like you too much," "I'm scared," "I don't want to lose you," and so on.

Why haven't I sent him to hell? Good question. Because he's too damned good, that's why. And like most men, he will only dance with you if he thinks he has a chance of getting into your pants. And so I have kept him guessing for as long as possible. I think I have broken a world record or two, speaking of broken records. But now, like Ulysses's wife, Penelope, I had run out of delaying tactics. Call it exhaustion due to my premenstrual state, or call it lack of imagination, but I was unable to come up with an excuse for not going to bed with the suitor. So I had said yes.

As soon as I got home, I put on the *Forever Tango* sound track full blast and jumped into the shower, hoping that it might put me in the mood. But it didn't. And to make things messier still, it was while in the shower that I realized I was no longer premenstrual. Poor Claudio! He would be so disappointed (fingers crossed).

I made myself some *mate* to pass the time before I broke the (hopefully) bad news to him. By now, it had been a lot longer than twenty minutes. In fact, it had been forty minutes. I wondered what was keeping him. I imagined that he was crowing to Fabian and Teté about his imminent conquest. He had pretended he wanted to be discreet about it, but what was the point of cheating on your wife if you couldn't brag about it to your friends? I bet that was why he was late.

My *mate* had become "washed out," as they say, i.e., it had lost its flavor, and he still hadn't shown up. I'd had enough of waiting. Tough titties for him! I had given him an opportunity but he hadn't taken it. All fair, all square. I was going to bed.

It was only as I passed the bookcase on the way to my bedroom that

I spotted the battered copy of *Bridget Jones's Diary* on the shelf. And I remembered the scene in which Mark Darcy comes to pick her up on a date but she doesn't hear the doorbell because she is drying her hair.

And I thought: Oh dear.

September 3, 1999

Everywhere you go, it's the same. You get into a cab because you figure you'll get to your destination faster but you end up wishing you had taken the bus or the metro because the price you pay is too high. Not the one on the meter. Taxis in B.A. are cheap. I'm referring to the personal cost, whereby one is subjected to the vitriol that spills out of the driver's mouth and into your psyche, where it burns you for the rest of the day. It has to be the world's most miserable profession. Driving a taxi seems to drive taxi drivers mad. And taxi drivers drive those they are driving mad.

Take today. I was late for my Spanish lesson with Marta, which is why I hopped into a cab in the first place. But we got stuck in traffic, and for an hour, I had to listen to the driver's ranting and raving regarding the state of the economy and listen to his analysis of the situation. *"Que bronca!"* he kept on muttering between loud snorts. He was referring to his emotional state, which was not good. In fact, it was terrible. By repeating *"Que bronca!"* every two seconds, he was communicating the uniquely Argentine mix of rage, resentment, frustration, and bitterness that has built up and blended into one sentiment so deep-seated in the soul of the otherwise gentle Argentine that to eradicate it, you would have to pull out his soul by the roots. You see, an Argentine's *bronca* is the dark side of his generally "lite" moon.

Although the taxi ride was far too long for my liking, it was not long enough for my taxi driver to make the journey back from his dark side. And unfortunately, my Spanish has improved to the point where I couldn't completely block out what he was saying. I sometimes pretend that I still don't speak it, but I've never been a very good liar. I don't mind so much that taxi drivers are angry people. What irritates me is that they regard themselves as belonging to the intellectual elite. Having been privy to the (unoriginal) opinions of other customers in their backseats, they feel the need to share the banal expressions of the zeitgeist as if they were rare pearls of wisdom. According to Enrique Fernandez, today's pundit at the wheel, the country's two-year recession is the fault of the pigs in power, and they should all be executed on the spot. I made sympathetic noises whenever applicable. The crescendo came when he volunteered to be on the firing squad. I hoped he might start with me. At least my headache would go away if I was dead.

You certainly wouldn't guess that the country is in the dire straits that Enrique says it is. The cafés are packed around the clock. Everyone, even the old, who in other countries have the decency to stay out of sight, at home and in front of the TV, is out with friends, living it up, exchanging news and views volubly over *lágrimas* (milk with only a little "teardrop" of coffee) or fake champagne. You can't tell whether it is four in the afternoon or six in the morning, Monday or Friday. It is always a good time to be at the café. So frankly, I don't know what Enrique is going on about. If you ask me, Buenos Aires makes New York look depressed.

September 30, 1999

If you put Julio and José Vargas side by side, Julio is the beautiful one and José is the sexy one. But that's only if you place them side by side. If not—if you happen to catch the one without the other—then it's absolutely impossible to tell which is which. They are not twins but they *are* identical. And this can have unfortunate repercussions, as I found out last night at Refasi.

You want to be able to tell Julio and José apart for one good reason. While the latter is the partner of the legendary Graciela Gómez, aka "La Rosarina," and God's gift to female tango dancers, the former is not (God's gift to women dancers). In fact, the former is quite the opposite. I would even go so far as to say that it is hazardous to one's health to dance with the former.

Not that you could tell by watching him, for Julio looks almost as good as José on the floor. But he has one disadvantage. And I'm not talking about the fact that he doesn't understand the meaning of the word "lead"—which is a pretty unforgivable offense in itself. No. The sticking point is that he is blind. And I don't say this metaphorically. Bats can see better than Julio. Which means that as his follower, you end up doing less following and more guiding, unless you don't mind being trod on, while apologizing to others for treading on them, and bashing into tables, chairs, and other inanimate objects. In short, to compare José with Julio is to compare a dream with a nightmare.

Last night at Refasi, as bad luck would have it, only one of the Vargas brothers was present. The million-dollar question was: which one was it? It became urgent that I decide, given that he, whoever he was, was now signaling for me to dance with him. If it was José, the correct course was to smile (jumping up and down with excitement inside) and join him on the dance floor (refraining from throwing oneself at him, shouting, "I'm yours! I'm yours!" if possible). But if it turned out that he was not José, but Julio, this would be a mistake of incalculable proportions. The correct course of action in scenario B would be to: *"hacerse la boluda."* This is the most useful term you'll ever learn. Roughly translated, it means to "play the idiot," i.e., to pretend you "don't get it." I have become rather versed at being a moron. It is a basic survival skill at the *milonga*. I don't know how many times a night I am forced to pretend that I never saw the guy over there in the corner, desperately seeking my attention.

The dilemma was huge and needed a speedy resolution. I proceeded to calculate the risks, placing the potential reward of dancing with José in the balance with the certain horror if José turned out to be Julio. Usually, when I have to choose between doing and not doing, I do—and pay later. But in this case, I hate to admit that I chickened out. Once again, I was overcome by the fear of injury. And so I deployed strategy B. Suddenly my eyes glazed over and my head turned just a fraction so that it appeared I was looking intently at the empty space to the left of Julio/José.

I've never been lucky when it comes to bets. Out of the corner of my glazed eyeball, I caught the expression of surprise on what could only be José's face. He could not understand why I had turned him down. Nobody ever turns him down, and for good reason, as I think I have made abundantly clear. It's a good thing I had my hair done up in a bun, because otherwise I would have torn it all out, one strand at a time. I'm not overreacting. The consequences of rejecting a man at the *milonga* are often irreversible. They tend to take it personally and never ask you to dance again. The thought is too horrendous to contemplate. Oh Lord, what have I done?

October 14, 1999

Not only has José forgiven me for dissing him, it seems to have worked in my favor. Apparently the mistaken rejection has made me appear less eager and therefore more attractive. But I will mourn the loss of that set we did not dance for the rest of my life. That's how good he is, and he knows it, which makes him even sexier than he already is, which is pretty damned sexy indeed. José is not gorgeous (like his brother) in the classical sense of the word. He has the same Mediterranean olive complexion, dark hair, and goatee. But his skin is pitted from acne that did not heal well. It's funny, but what might be an immediate disqualifier in someone else, you skip merrily over in him. His body, on the other hand, is beautiful, and I say this without the slightest reservation. He is so well chiseled that even Phidias could not have done a better job. He's got *it*, whatever *it* is. And I want *it* like I've never wanted *it* before. Of course, no matter how much I long to be his partner, I cannot delude myself that he is The One. After all, he is already dancing with La Rosarina, and no matter how much I would like to, I know that I will never be able to compete with her—not in a million years. I wish I didn't have this annoying tendency to remain lucid even when I am overcome with uncontrollable desire.

Anyway, imagine how flattered I felt—and my state of panic—when this star, who is from the farthest of far-off galaxies, asked me out last night between two tangos. (This time, I made sure to accept José/Julio, whoever he was. Blindly.) Actually, I was amazed, since guys at a *milonga never* ask you out. They assume that they can pick you up there and go back to your place for a bonk. (Never theirs, because they [1] live in a hovel [2] with their mother, [3] sister, [4] girlfriend, or [5] wife. It hasn't yet occurred to them that this is probably why they are getting less sex than they'd like in an ideal world.) They have yet to discover the existence of the telephone. Either that or it's beneath them to call a woman. Now you see why from amazement, I passed into shock when I heard José's voice on the other end of the line. It sounded somewhat stiff—how could that be? Gods don't get nervous, do they? He was calling to formalize the invitation to go to the theater with him next Tuesday. I could barely string two words together, for I, being a mere mortal, was a lot more nervous than he.

I can't remember when the last time was that I went out on a proper date. I'm so out of practice that I think I've forgotten how.

October 19, 1999

For all intents and purposes, I was on a date with God. God might only have been twenty-one years old (so technically, we're the same age) and his skin might have been pitted, but he was still God. When one is out on a date with God, one is not in the most relaxed of states. Indeed, for the first time ever, one becomes completely and utterly tongue-tied. And when one does finally manage to undo the knot, it is to say such stupid, stupid things that one quickly ties it back up to control the damage and stop oneself from coming out with any further stupidities. The only remedy for one in this instance is to turn to booze.

"Do you always drink this much?" José asked me. I suspect he had never before been on a date with a woman who drank a drop of alcohol. Women don't drink anything more dangerous than sparkling water in Argentina—and even that is considered risqué. They are worried that the bubbles might go to their head—or worse still, to their thighs. And there I was doing my best to imitate a fish.

"Yes . . . I mean no . . . I mean, I don't know." This gives you a feel for the scintillating conversation I treated him to all night.

After the show—he took me to see something, but I can't remember what—we had dinner, and then after dinner we went to Almagro. On the way over there in the cab, we drove by a church and I noticed that both José and the driver made the sign of the cross in unison. It was a touching display of synchronized piety, I thought. And it made me fall even harder for José, whom I hadn't suspected of a spiritual dimension. The guy had a lot more depth than I had given him credit for.

We were at Almagro and they had wheeled out poor old Carmencita Calderón, who was turning one hundred, and forced the old bag to give an exhibition. I hope they let me sit in my wheelchair in peace when I'm a hundred. I'm not sure whether it was absurd or sublime. I'll get back to you on that.

Julio joined us and I started to drink more heavily. Once more, I found myself trapped between heaven and hell. For every set I danced with José, I was forced to suffer the torment of dancing one with Julio. How could I refuse him? He was sitting at our table, for heaven's sake! And the lighting at Almagro, being what it is—extremely dark—only made matters worse. When we collided with a table and sent the champagne bottle on top of it flying and spilling its contents into my favorite black suede heels, I came dangerously close to blurting out the following speech, which I had prepared during the previous tango, which had not been more fortunate:

"Julio, my love [I always find it easier to soften a blow with a verbal caress], I think you are great and I want us to be friends. That's why it is imperative that you stop asking me to dance. And that we put an end to this farce once and for all. Otherwise I'll scream. Thank you for understanding." Of course, I didn't say that. Actually, I didn't have the guts to say anything at all. I held my tongue and limped back to our table, making funny squelching sounds as I did.

Finally José took pity on me and asked me if I wanted to leave.

"Yes!" I cried a little too enthusiastically.

Finally we would be alone, the two of us, I thought as I sighed with relief. The moment I had been waiting for all evening was just around the corner. Even the amount of alcohol my shoes and I had imbibed could not deaden the rush of excitement I felt at the prospect of the first kiss I was about to receive. I'd paid a high price (my shoes were ruined; I was going to have to have a new pair made), but his kiss was bound to make up for everything.

I'm sure it would have, had he given it to me. Instead, he said, "I'll call you tomorrow," and without pausing he told the driver of the taxi that had stopped in front of my building to continue on to Armenia 1366—the address for La Viruta. I looked at the clock on the dashboard of the taxi as I got out of the cab: it was only four A.M. He'd get in another two and a half hours of dancing, if he hurried.

As he disappeared into the night he blew me a kiss from inside the getaway cab. And as he did, I knew that I was the one who had blown it.

If there is a moral to be drawn from this sad tale it is that when on a date with God, drink water only—flat, not sparkling.

November 5, 1999

"Mañana" apparently means "in two weeks." Of course, he rang on the very day I had given up on him. I have said this before: things only happen when you no longer want them to. I had sworn to myself that if he did call, I would give him the cold shoulder. I haven't slept in the last ten days because I have been so busy picturing hundreds of different scenarios. In every single one of them, he is groveling, while I tower above him haughtily, impervious to each and every one of his attempts to regain my favor.

It's funny, though, that no matter how many millions of times one may write and rewrite the script, life never lets you say your lines the way you had planned and so I said yes—before he had even finished asking me out again.

He took me out to dinner at El Palacio de la Papa Frita (French Fry Palace), on Corrientes—it's the thought that counts—and this time I made sure not to drink a drop. I didn't need to: I was drunk with happiness. I couldn't get over it. He had actually called when he'd said he would. Even if it wasn't exactly *when*, but two weeks after he'd said he would. That is still a lot better than not calling at all, which is the case 99.99 percent of the time. I managed to be quite coherent this time around. To be honest, I can't remember the details of our conversation because the real conversation was happening at another level. He spent the whole evening looking deeply into my eyes and making me feel like I was the only person on earth. When you feel that way, it's really hard to register anything else. I was in such an altered state that I couldn't help fantasizing, in spite of all the evidence to the contrary, and in the face of all logic, that he would dump La Rosarina—possibly the world's top female tango dancer—in order to be my partner. I reiterate: I had not had a drop of alcohol. Perhaps I should have.

"I thought you and she were an item," I said, oh so casually.

"We used to be. But not anymore," he said, his hand no longer stroking mine.

"I only ask because I don't want to step on anybody's toes," I said, trying to regain the lost brownie points as quickly as possible. His hand went back to its stroking.

"You aren't stepping on anybody's toes, *mi amor*—and anyway, I'm here with you, aren't I?" he said as he leaned over the table and sealed the end of the conversation with a lingering kiss that tasted of *tuco*—your basic tomato sauce. It tasted a lot better than it sounds.

In the cab afterward, on our way over to the *milonga*, I was once again struck by José's devotion as he crossed himself before kissing the tip of his thumb when we went by a church. Not being religious myself, I am not normally attracted to religiousness in others. But in him, it was so cute! I liked *everything* about him more and more. Even the way he crossed himself.

Then, when we entered *Niño Bien* together, arm in arm, I thought I would faint from pride. I couldn't believe how soon I had made it to the farthest galaxy. I wasn't on top of the world: I was way, way, way beyond it. La Rosarina was already sitting at a table by the floor. I felt slightly uneasy, but I did my best to ignore the feeling. As we made our way over to her table, I kept reminding myself of José's words: there was nothing to worry about. They were no longer an item. He was here with me.

Was that a chilly reception I detected beneath La Rosarina's warm and friendly veneer? Perhaps I was being paranoid, given that I had been plotting only moments ago to steal her partner. Whatever the case may have been, it wasn't the most comfortable of situations sitting between the two of them. It was worse, in fact, than sitting between him and his brother. To make matters more awkward still, José spent all night dancing with me and didn't ask her to dance once. I thought that was a bit much. His lack of chivalry toward her made me feel sorry for her. I almost asked him to dance with her, out of pity. She *was* the soon-to-be-dumpee after all. But I couldn't bring myself to give up even a single dance with him.

We danced and danced until five in the morning. La Rosarina had left way before then, but I was too swept up in José to notice when exactly. Then on came the *"Cumparsita."* Already? I thought. I could have gone on for *hours*.

Cut to my apartment. I was already naked and José was on his way there. As his shirt came off, I couldn't help but notice that God was sprouting hair on his back. In a year or two it would qualify as a hairy back. This would be a bigger test of my love for him than the acne. A much bigger test.

Not even God is perfect, I thought. Try not to look at it too much, I advised myself.

As it turned out, it wasn't as hard as I'd thought it would be, since with José's help, I finally remembered what the big deal was about sex.

"Oh my God!" was all I could repeat. I couldn't believe I was having sex with Him. I felt as privileged as Niobe. She was the first mortal woman to consort with Zeus. It wasn't that he did anything out of this world. It was just one of those blessed instances when it takes very little effort for planets to collide and for meteors to light up the sky. Or putting it another way, we "had skin." In spite of the acne on his.

Our morning of passion ended at around ten. I was spent and was now lying lazily on top of him in a hazy state of satiated desire.

"I need to pee," he said as he shook me off him.

After he was done peeing, I noticed that he didn't come back into the bedroom. What was he up to? I went to inspect matters in the living room, where I found him collecting his belongings, strewn all over the floor.

"What are you doing?" I asked him.

"I'm going," he said as he put his trousers on.

"Going where?" I asked him. Oh no. I recognized that feeling in the pit of my stomach.

"To confession," he said, putting on his socks.

"What?" I said. I thought I had heard every excuse under the sun by now, but this was a good one.

"I'm going to confess my sins," he repeated.

"What do you mean?" And then, "You're joking, right?" in a "Ha! Ha! I get it now!" kind of voice.

"No, I'm not, as a matter of fact," he said, putting on his shirt with his back to me.

"I don't understand." For once, I wasn't pretending to be thick.

"I'm not supposed to have sex before marriage," he said.

"And you only just remembered now?" I asked him. Sometimes I think that the only person who suffers the sting of my scathing remarks is me. He didn't bother to answer. I followed up with: "Do you go to confession every time you have sex?"

"Yup, pretty much," he said.

"Have a good one!" I said, knowing that this was probably not the appropriate thing to say.

It appears that guilt is a turn-on for some. Not for me, though. It has turned me off altogether. As far as I'm concerned, José can confess as much as he likes, he's still going to hell. I don't fancy the idea of a priest enjoying the lurid details of *my* sex life. They are *my* lurid details, and I would very much like to keep them that way.

December 10, 1999

Today is a happy day for Argentina. Menem is out! The crowd is celebrating outside my window and the gentle breeze is carrying the sound
of their hope into my living room. They have elected a new president.
His name is Fernando de la Rúa. Apparently he is so dull, it is reassuring. Surely nothing bad can happen under the care of someone so boring, everybody is saying. Not like the flamboyant Menem. You can hear
the collective sigh of relief.

"The *chanta*'s gone!" they chant outside.

That's an important word if you want to understand anything about
Argentina. To be a *chanta* is to be cheating/lying/corrupt/deceitful—
you get the picture. If you live in this country, you hear the word a lot.

And yet, cheating is a necessary by-product of Catholic culture, if
my experience with José has taught me anything. When pleasure is considered a sin, it's only natural to try to indulge in it behind the church's
back. Then, to feel guilty about it. And finally, to confess to it when it is
rather conveniently too late to undo it. In a culture in which it is viewed
as sinful, there is no pleasure without cheating and no cheating without
pleasure.

This explains why the most common refrain I hear among the guys I
dance with is: "Who have you been cheating on me with lately?" The
fact that we haven't actually had sex is neither here nor there.

Thus, the tango would appear to be a perfect vehicle for Catholic
pleasure since you can experience the guilt associated with thoughts of
sex without actually going the whole nine yards and going to hell as a
result—unless you sprint rather rapidly out of people's apartments to
confess straight afterward. But. There does come a point where the sexual urges that have been brought to a boiling point by all this guilt can
no longer be repressed. Which inevitably leads to the leap into the
flames, followed by the leap out of bed and straight into the confes-
sional. Making the tango not such a perfect vehicle of Catholic pleasure
after all—as priests all over Buenos Aires will tell you.

Back to Argentina today. What is true of sex is true of politics, hence the long tradition of corruption in this country. The temptation to cheat is simply too great. But there is a positive side to sin.

Namely, that it precedes redemption. I think this is how many Argentines view the outcome of these elections. It's as if, after years of living with a husband who has cheated on them right, left, and center, thereby shattering their self-esteem as well as their faith in the system, the divorce has come through and they are finally going to be able to start from scratch. I hope they are right. I may not be a good Catholic—or a bad one, for that matter—but it won't stop me from joining them in their prayers. Amen.

December 31, 1999

To think that this time last year I was lying down on Beth's couch, feeling miserable—and cold. Has a whole year really passed since then? And has it really been nine months since I moved to Buenos Aires? Why does it always come as a huge shock when you realize how "quickly time has flown"? It's one of those clichés that never fails to astonish. While we're at it, now is as good a time as any to reflect on the past year and to set goals for the next. So here goes:

1. I have swapped New York for Buenos Aires. This was the best decision I ever made. I love everything about this city—even the smelly diesel buses.

2. I have moved from a one-bedroom apartment in a doorman building on the Upper East Side to a one-bedroom apartment in a doorman building on Plaza Congreso. I love my balcony, I love my doormen. And my parents love that it's a quarter of the price. Or so they should.

3. I've picked up a new language. Granted, I still get the question: "Where are you from?" all the time, but in spite of my accent, I'm pretty fluent already. I've even made progress on my *lumfardo*—which means that, sadly, I now understand the tango lyrics without the help of Marcelo and his ticklish whiskers.

4. I've made more new friends in nine months than I have all over the world in my entire lifetime. Starting with my best friend, Valeria. I don't know what I would do without her. Looking back on it, I was silly to worry that they would send me packing. In fact, I sometimes say—if the person who asked the dreaded question has enough time to listen to the long version—"I'm Greek and American by birth. English and French by education. And *porteña* by adoption."

5. Indeed, I am often mistaken for a *porteña* these days—until I open my mouth. My sexy new look has a lot to do with it. I have accumulated an impressive collection of tops that barely cover my anatomy and dangle precariously thanks to threads that zigzag across my back. As for my pants and skirts, they barely make it above my pubic line. But this is accidental (see below). As for my heels, I now wear only black suede. Long gone are the patent leather T-straps that scream "Tourist!" As a result, the stock price of "Ba-se-leena" has taken a dramatic plunge.

6. I drink *mate* and nibble on *alfajores* all day long. I'm not sure if this is an accomplishment, though.

7. I have danced with most of the Pablos, every Luis, and all the Jorges at the *milonga*. In other words, I have networked, networked, networked! This is also proof of how popular, popular, popular I am! I'm not sure Claudio would agree with me, though.

8. I have lost so much weight as a result of dancing all day and all night that I now float in the pants that were tight on me last year—in spite of all the *alfajores*. Hence my problem keeping them and the skirts I wear above my pubic line (see above). This is probably the achievement I am most proud of!

9. I haven't only shed pounds: I have shed years. Ten to be precise. Just ask anyone at La Glorieta how old I am and they'll tell you: Twenty-one!

10. My ballet and release classes have improved my posture,

flexibility, range, and quality of movement. Most important, I feel *taller* and *leaner*! I don't know if I have really grown, but it certainly feels that way. The fact that I'm never seen out of my heels is only part of the explanation.

So in summary, it's been a good year. I have the right clothes, the right shoes, and the right body (sort of). I look the part, though I don't exactly sound it. My tango is getting better by the day and the guys are taking notice. I barely ever sit down at a *milonga*. Which brings us to:

11. I haven't found my partner. Why the hell not?! And where the hell is he?! Well, at least it's pretty clear what my goal needs to be for next year. Though they do say—"they" being taxi drivers—that things happen when you least expect them. So really, my goal for next year ought to be *not* to expect him—since if I do, he won't show up. But how do you *not* expect the one thing you want above all others? The one thing you obsess about day and night? And the only thing that is missing from your life?

    I will try very hard not to expect him. Wouldn't it be amazing, though, if I met him tonight at Niño Bien? That would be a happy start to the New Year! Speaking of which, I'd better get ready, because Valeria is expecting me. And *unlike* my partner, I show up when expected.

Enrosque

1. In tango, the corkscrew motion of the leader's upper body that winds and unwinds as he leads the follower into a *"giro"*—a turn.

See adjective:

Enroscado/a

1. Of a person: emotionally screwed up/twisted. Normally used in the masculine.

2. Of a situation: complicated, tangled, knotty—i.e. a headache. And very common in Buenos Aires.

January 4, 2000

On Sunday, I went to Parakultural. To get there, you have to climb a steep and unlit flight of stairs, which, I suppose, adds to the illicit charm of the thing. From the shadows, a dark figure jumps out at you.

"That'll be five pesos," he says.

You pay, and Open, Sesame! You step into a dark cavern, decorated with the lights left over from Christmas still dangling from the damp walls, along which are lined some rusty metallic tables and chairs retrieved from a Dumpster. If you don't get there early, i.e., by two A.M., you won't find a seat because it gets packed. In which case you climb up onto the stage and sit there. It is a scruffy *milonga*, unlike the glamorous Almagro or Niño Bien, where it would be a criminal offense to place your bottom on anything other than a chair. As much as I like the casual ambience of the place, I hate the floor. It is rough and uneven, coming apart at the seams and a minefield of sharp nails. You can forget about gliding smoothly across the floor. In fact, you'll consider yourself lucky if you only trip half a dozen times. Or if you don't contract tetanus. And it's torture on the knees because you can't pivot. Try executing an *ocho* (a figure eight) without pivoting and you'll see what I mean. Help! I'm turning into a fusspot. Somebody shoot me.

I immediately spotted the best dancer in the room. I couldn't make him out too well in the dark, but he had the high cheekbones and dark

features of a Native American and his glistening black mane looked blue
under the Christmas lights. He was damn sexy—from what I could tell.
It was the way he moved: his self-assured, deliberate, and giant steps
took up the whole room. Every one else shrank next to him.

"Who's *that*?" I asked Valeria.

"*That* is el Chino," she said, raising an eyebrow and holding it at
what looked like a deprecating angle from where I was sitting.

Argentines call anyone who looks vaguely Native American
"Chino." In their eyes, Native American looking = Asian looking. And
all Asians, including Japanese, are lumped together as Chinese. (Political correctness has not made it this far south yet.) As you might expect,
there are lots of Chinos in Argentina. Especially up north where far
fewer Europeans went to settle. This particular Chino is from the
province of Jujuy, a stone's throw from the Bolivian border.

In spite of Valeria's apparent disdain for him, I made a mental note:
must dance with that man. One thing I have learned in tango is that one
needs to help one's luck, something I am completely incapable of doing
in the real world. But here in the relative safety of the tango salon, I have
become shameless. It helps being so obsessed that you won't take no for
an answer. And so, in the short breaks between sets, I stared at him. As
much as it is possible to stare at someone when it is pitch black. It's like
fishing in the dark, really.

But lo and behold, his radar was on high frequency. He picked up the
signal and nodded at me from his end of the room. I nodded back, and
as he made his way over to the table to collect me, I got up to meet him
halfway. But when I arrived, he kept walking toward the table, where
Valeria sat, cool as a cat. They exchanged a few words and finally she got
up and followed him to the floor. I went back to my seat with my tail between my legs and my cheeks burning like red-hot coals. Mortified
doesn't even begin to describe how I felt. Luckily it was so dark in there
that nobody noticed. And when Valeria came back to the table afterward, we made a silent pact not to broach the prickly subject, erecting a
wall of silence between us instead.

January 11, 2000

I went back to Parakultural last night—on a fishing expedition, this time. I was hoping to catch el Chino. I'll tell you, it's not easy reeling in these 150-pounders!

I made sure to get there early so that I would be in prime position when the big fish arrived. I had prepared the bait in the form of a brand-new silver backless number that had very little holding it up in front either. I don't know how I managed not to lose the dress on the floor, but by some miracle, I managed to keep it on my back (or not on my back, in this case). Anyway, I looked pretty stunning, if I say so myself. I also looked completely out of place—way too overdressed for this grungy *milonga*. Luckily, it was so dark that nobody could see what I was wearing. But it served a purpose: it made me feel sexy and gave me the requisite confidence to fish with a vengeance after last week's humiliation.

And it worked! Perhaps it had something to do with the fact that I was not with Valeria for once. If I had been, I'm sure he wouldn't have wanted to dance with me at all. He wouldn't have seen me because he'd have been so busy making a beeline for her. I won't deny that she does get on my nerves sometimes. Anyway, this time, when I saw him doing the *cabeʒeo* in what looked like my direction, I made sure to stay glued to my seat. He did it a number of times and I sat there. I wasn't going to risk it, not after last week's fiasco. Finally, he had to come and yank me out of my seat, physically. But I still was not going to take any chances. I did a 180-degree scan of the room, to make 100 percent sure he didn't really want to dance with somebody else. But apparently it *was* me he wanted to dance with, so I got up and followed him to the floor.

As we stood there, waiting for the music to start, he introduced himself. I didn't tell him I already knew who he was—nor did I tell him that I had come to Parakultural tonight for him and him alone. Instead, I let myself fall under the spell of his deep, melodious voice. Then, the music gave us the signal to start dancing. Except that we didn't dance: we floated on air. I swear that last night, I levitated. I am convinced that el Chino was practicing some form of ancient magic on me. The proof is that I didn't trip—not once—when I executed my *ochos* on the lousy, nail-infested floor.

January 20, 2000

He is Fred and I am Ginger, and together we are dancing cheek to cheek in that scene from *Top Hat*. I am wearing the white dress with the ostrich feathers that fly about as he whooshes me all over the place. He looks dashing as always in his white tie. And "I'm in heaven!"

Dancing with Chino is absolutely effortless, and that's because our bodies fit together like two pieces of a jigsaw puzzle. There is never any need to adjust or readjust positions. We are both as comfortable in each other's arms as one can only be at home, my head nestling between his neck and shoulder, his arm molding the contours of my back. My body has found its brother. His body has found its sister. And you know what they say about incest.

And then, there is everything else: his musicality, his inventiveness, his technique—everything is right. I have found my match. He is The One. If it feels this good for me, then surely it must feel this good for him. I simply can't believe that the feeling is not mutual. It just *has* to be. It's not every day that you dance with someone who doesn't *know* your heart, he *shares* it. The question is: when is my match going to see the light?

When is he going to ask me to practice with him? is the obsessive thought spinning around in my mind as he spins me around the floor night after night. All that remains for me to do is to wait. (Apparently I was put on this earth to bide my time in waiting rooms.) I know he's available. He's even told me that he is looking for a partner. There is nothing I hate more than when they dangle carrots in front of you like that!

Last night, my intuition told me that the moment I had been waiting for had come. The set had just ended, the feathers on Ginger's boa had not yet settled, and he was escorting me back to my table. And that's when he said it:

"*Che*, do you know where Valeria is?"

When, after a pause and in barely audible tones, I told him that I did not, he asked me: "Do you have her number?"

"Sure," I said, forcing my mouth into a rictus.

I gave him her number without asking him why he wanted it because I didn't want to know what I knew already.

January 25, 2000

"You win some, you lose some," I tell my pillow night after night. I still can't sleep, though. Crushing disappointment has turned me into an insomniac, just as my first rush of passion for the tango once did. I am trying very hard not to hold a grudge against Valeria. It's not easy. But I tell myself that it's only right that the better dancer of the night win.

I hope that if I don the appearance of a gracious loser, I will eventually feel like one.

February 1, 2000

Valeria and I were sitting together at Almagro. We are back to being partners in crime. I am proud to say that I have put the whole episode behind me. We avoid talking about him, though, just for safety's sake. I don't ask her how things are going with him and she doesn't volunteer the information either.

Of course, we see him at the *milonga* almost every day. He is very diplomatic, I must say. He makes sure to ask us both to dance in strictly alternating fashion. I've even noticed that if, say, on one night he asks her first, then he'll make sure to ask me first on the following night.

After one of us has danced a set with him, we come back to the table and chat about something unrelated as we fan ourselves or wipe our pearly brows with handkerchieves. As if we hadn't danced with him at all.

Imagine my shock, then, when last night, during a break between two tangos, he said: "I've been asked to give an exhibition at La Pavadita. Do you want to do it with me?"

"What about Valeria?" I asked him, flabbergasted.

"What about her?" he said, sounding genuinely confused.

"It's just that well . . . with you two practicing together, I don't—"

"What? Did she tell you we were practicing?" he asked me. He didn't sound happy.

"Um . . . no, actually, come to think of it. But I just assumed—"

"Well, you assumed wrong," he said bluntly.

"Oh," I said. I couldn't believe what a moron I was! Why had he asked me for her number, then? But I didn't probe. I wanted to savor the moment of victory. "I'd love to do the exhibition with you, Chino," I said once I had recovered the faculty of speech. There *is* a God, after all, I thought.

I literally ran back to the table to share the news with Valeria.

"Isn't that great?!" I cried excitedly.

"Yes, it is." But it came out of her mouth sounding more like "No, it's not." Why was she being such a sourpuss? She wasn't jealous, was she?

"There's something I need to tell you," she said.

"Are you in to him? Because if you are—"

"What?! *Chino?* You must be kidding!"

"It's just that I thought . . . Well, he asked me for your number and I thought he was going to ask you to prac—"

"He did. But I turned him down," she said.

"What?!" It was my turn to exclaim. "Why? I don't understand." How could anyone turn him down? Did she have a screw loose?

"Listen, I didn't want to tell you at first, because I hate spreading rumors, but . . ."

"What? Tell me! What is it?"

"You don't want to get involved with Chino. Dance with him at the *milonga* all you like, but you don't want to be his partner. Trust me," she said.

"But I *do*! I *do* want to dance with him!" I cried.

"No you don't: the man is . . . well, he's a . . . thief. There. I've said it. He is in and out of jail constantly. He's done time for armed robbery," she said. "Ask anybody—it's common knowledge," she added.

That explains why, when I got up to dance with him the other day, a woman I didn't know was tapping the skin beneath her eye with her index finger: sign language for *"Ojo!"* ("Careful!") At the time, I thought she was saying to be careful not to mess up because he was such a good dancer.

"You win, Vale. I'll leave my wallet at home when I practice with him," I said.

The answer did not satisfy her. She didn't smile at my attempt at humor. She scowled, in fact. But she can scowl as much as she likes. Nothing, and I mean nothing, is going to stop me from giving my very first exhibition with el Chino. It's my dream come true. A partner— and when I least expected it! Just as all those clever taxi drivers keep on saying.

February 10, 2000

What the hell was I thinking?

Before anyone panics, he hasn't robbed me. I hardly bring any cash to our practice sessions and the little that I do bring, I make sure to stuff down my bra. Given the tendency of his hands to wander, though, I'm not sure that's the best hiding place.

No, that's not why I'm having second thoughts about the whole thing. I must have been crazy to think that I could show the Argentines how to dance the tango. I can't believe how arrogant I am at times! And we're talking about the most vicious kind of Argentine: tango dancers. They are going to be rooting for the *"gringa"* to fuck up. I know it. One wrong step and they'll feed me to the lions. I've seen enough exhibitions so that I can hear the nasty comments they will make. What's more, they won't even bother to wait to make them behind my back.

"Did you see that sloppy footwork?" they'll whisper to one another.

"What was el Chino thinking when he asked her to do the exhibition?" they'll snicker, while I am still dancing.

"If she had any technique, it would suck, so it's a good thing she doesn't," is what they will say to finish me off.

Now I know what performance anxiety feels like. And I swear that from now on, I will have nothing but compassion for the guys who suffer from it!

February 21, 2000

At least my new, snazzy purple suede shoes would inspire the admiration my technique would not, was my one consoling thought before the exhibition.

Before going on, I asked Chino if he was nervous.

"Course not," he said.

I have never felt so alone.

The MC asked the dancers to clear the floor. He had the pleasure of announcing that el Chino was going to honor them with an exhibition tonight (heated applause) . . . And that he was dancing with a charming new partner. Could he please hear a warm welcome for La Griega? (Polite applause.)

In the end, I decided to be Greek, because I thought they might be kinder to me and my technique if I were Greek rather than "Gringa" or the variant "Yanki." To be Inglesa was out of the question, not because of the Falklands, but because I can't think of anything less sexy than an English tango dancer—if the words "English" and "tango dancer" are not an oxymoron, they should be. With the exception of Sally Potter, who in spite of her ethnic disadvantage did a good job in *The Tango Lesson.* Of course, anyone would look good dancing with Pablo Verón—even me . . . Where were we? Oh yes, now I remember:

I badly needed to go to the loo. I also needed a stretcher. My legs had gone numb. This was not the most convenient time to become a paraplegic, I thought. But by some miracle, I found myself in the middle of the dance floor with Chino. There was a hush of anticipation. I was standing a couple of inches away from him, but I couldn't see him clearly, the spotlight was so blinding. And it was damned hot. It was a good thing my dress was so skimpy.

It was when he took me in his arms that I noticed he was shaking. Or was it me? Whoever it was, it was contagious. Now we were like two leaves in the autumn wind. If he wasn't nervous, I wondered what it was like when he *was*. Did he shake like this when he held a gun to people's heads? I doubted it. Armed robbery is much less scary than a tango exhibition, and the risks far smaller.

The music began, and it didn't sound anything like the tango we had practiced. Perhaps that was because it wasn't the tango we had practiced. But we got through it somehow—at any rate, that's the way it looked from up there. My mind had floated off like a balloon and was watching the performance from a safe distance. But as we approached the finish line, it stopped being such a spoil sport and came back down to join us. This coincided with the moment I started to enjoy myself—which also coincided with the moment the tango ended. The crowd was cheering and I found myself sitting on Chino's lap in a *sentada,* my legs wrapped around his thigh.

All things considered, it could have been worse. Chino was so happy, he stopped shaking. And then he asked me if I wanted to do another with him. You'd have thought that I'd learned my lesson by now. But I said yes!

February 25, 2000

Chino and I were going to meet at the studio to practice. We don't practice at my place because I don't want him to know where I live. It's not that I don't trust him. It's that . . . I don't trust him. What I'm worried about is that while I'd like to think of us as Bonnie and Clyde, I'm not sure he sees us in that way. I think he might see himself as Butch Cassidy and me as the bank. Not that I have much to steal, but I'd rather not tempt the devil . . . Of course, this doesn't stop me from fantasizing about tempting the devil. All the time, day and night. He is such a sexy thing. Actually, the reason he is so attractive to me—apart from the fact that he is a dangerous criminal—is that he is the only guy so far not to have hit on me. Bar the odd grope here and there.

I wonder why not?

Before leaving home to go practice for the upcoming exhibition at Confitería Ideal, I went through all the usual preparations, emptying my wallet of most of its contents, leaving only a few tokens for the Metro and a five peso bill to cover my share of the studio rental.

I was first to arrive. There was nothing unusual about that. He's always late. They all are—it's something in the water. I did some stretching to pass the time. He still didn't show up. I got to chatting with the receptionist at the dance studio. He still didn't show up. I thought about calling him but remembered I couldn't, for one simple reason: I don't have his number. You see, he doesn't have a fixed address. And since I haven't given him my number (I gave him some bullshit excuse, but the real reason is that I didn't want him to find out where I live), he has no way of getting in touch with me if he needs to reschedule.

As I left the studio, I thought the time had arrived to stop all this nonsense and give him my number, already! After all, he *is* my partner, robber or no robber. And we need to be able to get in touch with each other in case of emergency.

What if something has happened to him? I worried.

And my worrying escalated last night when he didn't appear at Refasi. Where on earth is he?

March 12, 2000

I have gone to every *milonga* in town and Chino is nowhere to be found. It's been two whole weeks since he disappeared without a trace, leaving me with nothing to do but sip sadly on my champagne.

Rumor has it he's in jail again. Apparently, he was caught red-handed stealing a shipment of electrical items from a warehouse. Valeria had one of those I-told-you-so expressions on her face when she told me so.

But as far as I'm concerned, he got away scot-free with stealing something much more valuable than a stupid shipment of washing machines and tumble dryers.

And it's not even insured.

March 15, 2000

Yesterday was my birthday, but I didn't feel like celebrating. I was still feeling sad about Chino. All I wanted to do was have an early night— i.e., go to bed before seven A.M. And so by about two o'clock, I was snoring away happily (of course I don't snore), earplugs in place, enjoying some much-needed repair to my body. When suddenly, I realized I was having a nightmare. I was dreaming that someone was ringing the bell persistently, trying to wake me up.

It was not a nightmare. It was five in the morning and the intercom was buzzing like nobody's business. Needless to say, I was not feeling at my most social.

"I'm gonna sue the earplug company," I grumbled as I staggered to the intercom.

"Who is it?" I asked without making the least effort to sound welcoming.

"It's me!" answered an unbearably cheerful voice.

"Who's 'me'?" I hate it when people say "It's me" and expect you to know who "me" is.

"Guillermo!" he exclaimed, sounding wounded that I hadn't recognized his voice.

Can somebody please explain why it is that as soon as they become exes, boyfriends who, when you were going out with them, avoided you like the plague suddenly want to see you at all hours? Don't get me wrong: I'm thrilled that Guille and I are back on speaking terms. We've both decided to pretend that I never said what I said. It's an arrangement that works well for both of us. But I just wished we didn't have to be on speaking terms right now, at five in the morning, when I was trying to get some sleep.

"Guille, my love, can you come back another time?" (Another lifetime?)

"I have a surprise. It can't wait! Let me in!" He sounded like a kid. And I can't be cruel to kids no matter how much I want to be.

"Of course, sweetie pie." I was too despondent to think of any witty asides. Guillermo was already in the door and dragging me to the balcony.

"Look!" he cried enthusiastically as he pointed to the skies. "It's a full moon tonight! Isn't it beautiful?"

"Guille, don't tell me you've come to give me the moon at five in the morning, on the one day of the year I was going to get a full night's sleep," I said, holding back tears of frustration.

If I pushed him off the balcony, nobody would be any the wiser. The street was deserted. It could easily look like a suicide/accident. I was looking down over the ledge, to estimate the mess the impact of his body would make on the asphalt, when I saw it. He had spray-painted a vacant parking spot right beneath my apartment with the words *"Feliz Cumple!"* (Happy Birthday) and he had drawn a silly cartoon around his name. It was with a tear in my eye and a smile on my face that I spared his life.

Another thing: why is it that exes give better presents than they did before you exed them?

March 20, 2000

Javier, Pancho, and Jorge are not Siamese triplets in the scientific sense—but they might as well be. The only times I ever see them severed from each other is when they are dancing. Then their hips become temporarily unglued as they go off and conjoin with a twin of the female variety. The triplets are not joined at the head or the spine, nor do they share a heart. They share an organ in the broader sense of the word "share." And it looks more and more as if this organ is pointed in my direction. I'm not quite sure what to make of being in this triple line of fire. Of course, I realize I'm just a pawn in their friendly (fiercely competitive) game (war). And I'll bet a peso or two that they have bet more than that on who can get me into bed first. What they don't realize is that the race has been rigged.

Having said that, it's going to be a close one. In fact, I haven't decided yet who the winner is or what the placement. They are all three divine dancers, as well as being medium, dark, and handsome—which is better than tall, dark, and handsome since tall is not good when it comes to tango. (As we know from bitter experience, tall men invariably want to dance with giant stick insects.)

I'll admit I was more than a little surprised when Pancho called me the other day to invite me to see *Forever Tango*. The show has come back to Buenos Aires for the season. It features many top couples, including Claudio and Maria (who is no longer breast-feeding). Claudio is pretending he doesn't know me, which is a mixed blessing. As much as I hate it that he doesn't dance with me anymore, it's a relief that I don't have to keep saying "And your wife?" all the time. Not to mention how relieved my right tit feels.

Anyway, back to Pancho. I would never have bet on him as the first triplet out of the gate because, to be blunt, he is what the Argentines call a *flan*, i.e., a wet blanket. Note how the Spanish version is sweeter than the English. But as much as I love crème caramel, this would normally disqualify a candidate from the running. I never know what to say to these people, and there is nothing I hate more than not knowing what to say. In fact, I would rather go out with a serial killer than with a wet blanket. At least there isn't the danger of getting bored. *Normally*. Out there "in the real world." But in here, the value system is quite different. In here, it's not wet blanket versus serial killer. It's Partner Material versus Not Partner Material.

And Pancho is definitely Partner Material, which is why it was immediately clear to me that I wasn't going to dismiss him on the grounds of his flanhood. In fact, of the three triplets, he is possibly the best dancer. Dancing with him is an otherworldly experience. It's like going for a walk on the moon, except that you don't have to wear those ugly moon boots. It's a funny thing, but his weakness of character turns into a strength on the dance floor, where his presence is *so* weak that you can't feel it at all. It is like dancing with thin air. And in order to dance with thin air successfully, you must turn yourself into a feather, floating this way and that in the gentle breeze. There is nothing nicer. The only snag is when you stop dancing and you remember that you weigh substantially more than a feather.

It was quite a surprise, then, when Pancho called to invite me to the theater. We agreed to meet in front of it ten minutes before the start of the show. I was there at ten to eight. He wasn't. There was nothing unusual about that: I am convinced that Argentines have an L-chromosome (where *L* stands for Late). I waited patiently, confident that he would eventually show up. When they rang the gong, I continued to wait, still optimistic that Pancho would overcome the chromosomal challenge. I witnessed the happy endings of fellow waiters' suffering when other latecomers drifted inside the lobby as if they had all the time in the world. I visualized the moment when my latecomer would come drifting to me.

The final gong went and, along with it, all hope. I threw up my arms in despair before dashing to the box office to buy myself a ticket. Lucky there was one.

"Why me? Why does it always bloody happen to me?" I shook my finger at God as I ran up the stairs two by two to get to my seat before the curtain went up. And then I wondered "Why me?" throughout the entire show. I was fuming so much that I couldn't see a thing. Not the dancers (though Maria did look a bit chubby still), not the sets, not the costumes, not the music. The entire production went on behind the thick veil of my persecution complex. I could vaguely hear the din of the distant applause coming from the man in the seat next to me—I think I even went through the motions of clapping when it looked as if clapping was in order—all the while punishing myself with thoughts of curses and bad karma. I came to the usual conclusion: I must have been a really horrible person in my previous life.

When the telephone rang this morning, I didn't feel like talking to anyone. I was in one of my social-pariah moods. But I changed my mind at the last minute and picked up.

"What happened to you yesterday?" said Pancho. It sounded almost as if he was accusing me, which I thought was a bit rich.

"What a coincidence. I was going to ask you the same thing," said I, speaking in a lower and slower voice than usual. Not a good sign. When I speak low and slow, it is usually an indication that I am about to chop off the head of the person I am speaking low and slow to before throwing it into a vat of boiling oil and cooking it for dinner.

"I waited for you for half an hour. I even missed the opening number, which everyone says is the best bit. You didn't show, so I gave up and went in. I wasn't even able to get rid of the extra ticket," went his story. It wasn't a bad story, I had to grant him.

"Well, I was there, right where you told me to be. And you weren't." If he thought I was going to be a pushover, he could think again. (Though the revelation that he had waited for half an hour did make me feel better. Even if it *was* a lie.) I continued: "*When you didn't show up*, I bought myself a ticket and went to see the show *alone*. And yes, the opening number *is* the best bit. Claudio and Maria do a fabulous job, I must say." I couldn't help being a bitch, even though being a bitch is counterproductive.

After another few rounds of "Oh no, you weren't" and "Oh yes, I was," where each of us took it in turn to play prosecutor/defendant, the mystery was finally solved. We retraced our movements, and thus untangled the knot of our *desencuentro*. I think it's telling that Argentines have a word for "failed encounter," where Anglo-Saxons do not. As it turned out, he had been waiting for me at the entrance of the theater at approximately twenty minutes before four P.M., while my wait had ended with the throwing up of the arms in despair at thirty seconds before eight P.M. The word "matinée" never having been mentioned, I had assumed that he meant the evening performance, being totally unaware, as I was, of the existence of a matinée.

This will never work. How can I be partners with someone who can't even set a date? I can already see what a nightmare it will be trying to get together with him to practice. He at one studio at ten in the morning and I at another at ten at night. No, no, no, it won't do. Which means, I'm afraid, that Pancho is out of the running and that we're down to twins.

Beyond the disappointment, I am relieved that I am not cursed. This calls for a celebration dinner! But not with him. It would be far too awkward to eat dinner with someone I have fantasized about as an appetizer.

March 29, 2000

I was dancing with somebody or other (I can't remember, so he can't have been spectacular) at Salon Canning when I spotted Jorge as he walked in. Triplet number two also spotted me. It wasn't hard since my face lit up like a halogen lamp the moment I saw him. Not because he is my favorite dancer. To be honest, of the three, he is the least experienced. Having said that, he is still very good, and with some work, I'm sure it will be possible to fix his bad habit of looking down at the floor all the time. Given his stature, which is not the tallest—though perfectly acceptable—this invariably means that dancing with him turns into a head-butting session. I have hinted at the problem several times and even gone so far as to mention a headache, but my hints have fallen on deaf ears. Now that he's a serious candidate—what with

Pancho out of the running and Javier otherwise occupied (I can't figure out if he's occupied with Silvia, his girlfriend, or with Romina, who he is always dancing with)—I'm going to have to be less subtle, I think. It's his only shortcoming, really. Other than that, he is wonderfully inventive and extremely musical. He also has another advantage: he's gorgeous.

Actually, I have had a crush on him since I first saw him—even though he looks like he's only twelve years old. Probably *because* he looks like he's only twelve years old. I wish I could say he brought out only my maternal instincts, but that would be lying. I go all soft and gooey every time I look into those big brown eyes of his. What I see in them can only be the reflection of my own tender feelings toward him, because, judging by his jaw, which he keeps clenched in a tough-guy attitude that says "Leave me alone" and makes me want to do quite the opposite, he doesn't appear to share those tender feelings. He has the soft, milky skin of a virgin, and the dark, unruly hair of a nineteenth-century romantic hero, which I have to physically restrain myself from ruffling each time I get close to him. And if I haven't mentioned it already: he is twenty-three years old. So I am not *quite* old enough to be his mother, but that's basically why I haven't rushed in. Truth be told, I have done everything in my power to curb my pedophile instincts, and I've been so good up until now. But I'm afraid I'm not going to be good for much longer and it's all Valeria's fault.

"He is such a *bonbón* [I have since discovered that the metaphorical meaning of this candy = a cutie]. Is there anything going on between you two?" she asked me at La Glorieta the other day, after Jorge and I had finished dancing a set.

"No," I said. For some reason, I didn't want to tell her that he was my latest candidate. Partly because I feel embarrassed every time I get excited about someone and then it doesn't work out. And partly out of the superstitious belief that talking about things precludes them from happening. I wanted to wait until it was a fait accompli before announcing it to the world or even to my best friend.

"Why not?" she inquired.

"No particular reason. Only that he's almost ten years younger than me," I said. In fact, this is going to be the real snag if ever we do become partners. But I guess we'll have to cross that bridge when we come to it.

"That hasn't stopped you in the past," she reminded me.

"Yes, I know. But it's time I grew up. And anyway, going out with younger men doesn't lead anywhere," I said. It doesn't. So why am I even thinking about Jorge as a partner? There are hardly any guys my age on the circuit—they're all either eighty-one or twenty-one—that's why.

"Where do you want it to lead?" she asked. "What do you want from a guy?"

Everything: that's what. I want it *all!* And I want it now! And I won't take an iota less. But you can't go around telling people this because they'll lock you up in the loony bin. It's hard enough admitting it to yourself. Which is why I wasn't able to answer Valeria's question.

"I don't know," I replied.

"Well, if you don't want him, I'll have him," she said.

Not so fast, I thought.

Now we were lost in *"Oblivion."* Los Cosos de al Lao were playing live. I'm sure that Piazzolla would have turned over in his grave if he knew that people were committing the sacrilege of dancing to his music. If only he knew how good it felt, maybe he'd change his mind. As Jorge steered me past the band, I opened my eyes for a second and smiled at the pianist, who is going out with my new friend Monica.

I met her in one of Miguel Angel's classes. When he teased me as usual about my bottom in front of the whole class (he's one of those fairies who believes that all girls should be anorexic), she immediately came to my defense, saying it wasn't so fat and what was he talking about? After class, we went for a coffee, and, stuffing ourselves with three *medialunas* each to spite him, we struck up an instant friendship. She is hysterically funny and does a perfect imitation of him: " 'Is that what you call a plié?! That is what *I* call a woman giving birth in a rice paddy! No! No! No!' "

She told me how she had originally trained in the Graham technique, but like many professional dancers, she is focusing on tango these days because that's where the money is. She certainly has the looks, with her cascade of shiny black hair, her alabaster skin, her rosebud for a mouth, and her nose that is ever so slightly upturned at the tip.

I am really happy for her: She couldn't have landed a nicer guy than Martin, whose hands were currently running up and down the keyboard as he swayed back and forth on his stool in deep concentration. And then Gabriel, the bass player, stuck out his tongue, which was his way of reserving a dance with me. The expression "He that plays doesn't dance" certainly doesn't apply to him. I accepted by sticking mine out back at him.

I closed my eyes and the music sucked me up once more into its vacuum. Jorge even managed to avoid head-butting me, which made it all the more irresistible. When the tango ended at last, our feet had stopped moving but we did not part. Standing as still as a statue, I listened to his heart. I felt the pressure of his palm on my bare back, while with my arm draped lightly around his neck, my hand exerted its pressure on his shoulder before it wandered down to his bicep. There is no getting away from it: younger men do have fabulous biceps and I am doomed to be a pedophile forever.

Apparently, there was a problem with the sound system. The band members were scuttling around as they tried to sort it out as quickly as possible.

"I dare you to ask me out on a date!" I whispered in his ear. This wasn't exactly a subtle signal for him to take the initiative, but he got the message.

As his head bounced up from off the ground in a spasm, I saw on his face an expression I recognized at once: terror. Now he was grabbing his curly locks, about to pull a clump out of his scalp.

"Ahhhhhhhh" was the sound that came out of his mouth. I think what he was trying to scream was: *"Ayuda!!!!!"* (Help!!!!!)

I wish I didn't have to resort to these strong-arm tactics. But I don't have a choice. Since apparently I scare the living daylights out of men—I really don't know why—this leaves me with no other option than to pretend that I am not scared of them. If only they knew the truth: I am ten times more scared of them than they are of me. But I am also ten times more desperate (For sex? For love? Is there a difference?). That is what gets me over the hurdle that they stumble against time and time again.

Finally, the problems with the sound system were fixed, much to the relief of the dancers, who had started to clap their hands and stomp their feet with impatience. The music started again, and we took up our dancing where we had left off. By the end of the tango, he had recovered his composure

"There's a Miró exhibition at the Museum of Fine Arts. Do you like Miró?" he asked me.

"Yes, I love Miró." To be honest, I am completely indifferent to painting in general and to Miró in particular. It has only taken me thirty years of traipsing through countless museums, of standing for hundreds of hours in front of masterpieces of all shapes and sizes, and of feeling nothing at all to realize it.

"Do you want to go tomorrow afternoon?" His voice was still trembling.

After a pause to indicate that I was checking my mental calendar for appointments with other barely legal tango dancers, I looked into his big brown (terrified) eyes and said: "Tomorrow afternoon would be perfect."

March 31, 2000

Jorge and I met outside the museum. I can't say that he looked all that pleased to see me. He still had that "I've been kidnapped" expression on his face that he had not managed to wipe off since the previous night. But he was there—a definite improvement on my previous attempt to meet his twin.

We went inside the museum, where he made the gesture of buying our tickets. This is perfectly natural behavior for Argentine men, who as

I have already pointed out are gallant *caballeros*, but I have not come to expect normal behavior from the subspecies otherwise known as the Argentine Tango Dancer. So it was a pleasant surprise that he actually reached into his pocket and went through the ritual, symbolizing that we were on a date (whether he liked it or not).

As soon as we entered the first room of the exhibition, it became apparent that he had even less interest in Miró than I. The object of our visit now became to leave the building as soon as it was decent to do so. Fifteen minutes later, we got to the finish line, having sprinted by a number of large blue canvases with red, yellow, and black amoebas on them.

Outside the museum once more, we got some soft ice cream from a van (he paid) and wandered into the square across the road, where we found a bench under an *ombu*. There is nothing nicer than sitting in the fresh shade of these great, big, tropical shrubs (apparently they are not trees, though they could have fooled me) with their sprawling, tarantula-like roots and their glossy, dark, rubbery leaves. As I was saying, there is nothing nicer than sitting under an *ombu* apart from kissing under an *ombu*. Which is what Jorge proceeded to do without further ado.

To be more precise, his mouth vacuumed mine with such ardor that I was taken aback. Perhaps he wanted some of my chocolate ice cream since he'd already finished his vanilla. He certainly did a good job of licking the pot clean. I wondered when the last time was that he had kissed somebody. I know I'm sexy, but not *that* sexy!

There are two possible reactions to this kind of sensory overload. In some cases, your best defense can be to attack, i.e., give as good as you get, much to the distress of any involuntary witnesses of this PDA (Public Display of Affection). The alternative is to try to guide the proceedings toward more sensuality and less saliva. Though I have nothing against saliva per se, this was the option I chose. It was all starting to go quite nicely when he interrupted the program to bring me a news update:

"I don't want a relationship," he said.

I still had his saliva in my mouth and he still had my chocolate ice cream in his. Doesn't he know it is rude to talk with one's mouth full? And while we're on the subject: why do people think they can get away with being rude by using "honesty" as an excuse? If ever there was an overrated virtue . . . What happened to the good old-fashioned lie? At least when they omit to tell the truth, the whole truth, and nothing but the truth, a girl can take off into a flight of fantasy—even if only for a split second before she crash-lands back down to earth. But when every-body goes around being "honest" all the time, how is she ever going to get off the ground?

The lyrics of one of my favorite tangos came to mind: "Keep on ly-ing to me. I like it better when you do." I had never really understood these enigmatic lines. Now I knew exactly what they meant.

"You know I'm moving to Europe, right?" he continued. Did I? It must have slipped my mind.

"When?" I asked in my casual-inquiry voice.

"In a couple of months," he said.

If I didn't block it out, the pain of the disappointment would be so overwhelming that I was liable to do or say something foolish.

Okay, so you have lost a potential tango partner. Find some alterna-tive use for him, I rationalized.

To him I said: "Well, then . . . let's enjoy the time we have together. Just because things don't last, it doesn't mean that they aren't worth living."

"Right," said he. "Wrong," said his eyes. Deep down, he knew as well as I that this was BS.

In the meantime, I told myself that if I went back to kissing him, it might make me feel better. And also, I thought that if I went back to kissing him, he would shut up instead of saying hurtful things. And when we went back to his place afterward, I thought that if I switched off the light, I wouldn't have to look into those big, brown, hurtful eyes of his. But it was a useless precaution: I could see them anyway, even in the dark and with my eyes shut.

April 9, 2000

Romina is only nineteen years old, and in my book, she's the most talented dancer on the circuit, which makes me want to shoot myself every time I see her on the floor. She is also the most determined. She set out to be Javier's partner (triplet number three), and by Jove she got him! After a year of playing the role of Other Woman, she has finally managed to wrest him away from Silvia and is now starring as Official Girlfriend and Partner.

Of course, this does not mean that Javier has changed his sexually incontinent ways. I don't know how she puts up with it. He sleeps around, left, right, and center. And he doesn't even go to the trouble of hiding it. She caught him with somebody the other day. But she is so sure that they are meant to dance together that put up with it she does. I don't think I could. In fact, I know for certain that I could not. Which makes me wonder why I don't give up. Because if that's what it takes, I ain't got it.

Anyway, imagine my surprise when the other day at La Glorieta, she asked me: "Do you want to borrow my boyfriend?"

I asked her to repeat herself, please. When she said again what I thought she had, I exclaimed while simultaneously trying not to sound *too* enthusiastic lest she withdraw her offer, "I'd love to."

"I need to go home to Cordoba for a while—I don't know how long exactly. It might be a month or two. My father is ill—" Here she choked up and wasn't able to finish her sentence. I took her hand and stroked it. Then she went on: "I need to spend some time with him. Here's the thing: I need someone to look after Javier while I'm away. I thought of you. I can't trust him with anybody else," she said.

That was a double-edged compliment, if ever I heard one! Did she think I was so repulsive that I was the only woman on earth Javier could resist? Maybe she thought that since I am going out with Jorge—though technically, we're not going out (his words, not mine)—that Javier would be safe in the hands of his best friend's non-girlfriend. But what she has failed to notice is that Javier's organ, the one he shares with Jorge and Pancho, continues to be pointed in my direction. Which isn't saying much, given that Javier's organ is pointed *in all directions, at all times*. You certainly can't count on it to tell you which way is north.

Nonetheless, it *is* flattering that (a) she thinks I'm good enough to train with her boyfriend, and (b) she trusts me. It's a good thing she doesn't know my history. If she did, I doubt she'd be so quick to entrust him me to. She's lucky that the one and only time I ever tried to steal an OPB (Other Person's Boyfriend) was so disastrous that I have learned my lesson once and for all. I would prefer not to recall my humiliation at being caught in the act, nor the girl's ensuing attempt at suicide (pills) nor the subsequent devastation when he chose her over me. I spent a long, long time recovering in the burn unit afterward. The scars eventually healed—but only the ones on the surface; the ones beneath my skin will never heal. No. I have no intention of making the same mistake twice. There are far too many other mistakes to make before I make the same one again.

"I promise to look after him well for you," I said.

"Not *too* well," laughed Romina nervously.

"No, not *too* well," I laughed even more nervously.

April 17, 2000

The triplets and I played *truco* last night. It's hard to believe that the Argentines didn't invent the card game that is the epitome of their culture. But they didn't. It was imported by the Spaniards.

Javier and I were playing against Jorge and Pancho. Jorge had just dealt the cards. I inspected mine: I had no points. So I closed my eyes, to indicate that I was "blind," as the expression goes. Javier raised his eyebrows at me, which meant that he had the highest card in the deck: the ace of swords. You see, you are encouraged to cheat by signaling to your partner which cards you hold in your hand. As I said, it doesn't get more Argentine. Javier wrinkled his nose. Was it a signal or was he about to sneeze? If it was a signal, I couldn't remember what it meant.

Oh well, I'd have to let that one pass. I responded with what was supposed to be a twitch of the right side of my mouth, an indication that I held the seven of swords.

Javier looked perplexed: He had no idea what I was trying to say. Apparently, I still have not mastered that one. I haven't played *truco* in a while, and so I'm out of practice when it comes to my facial ticks. I tried again. But I wasn't any more successful. I couldn't twitch one side of my mouth without twitching the other. I think Javier was starting to rue the day he had asked me if I played and I had said, *"Màs o menos,"* meaning "sort of."

I moved on to the next signal: I pursed my lips and blew him a kiss. He blew me a kiss back. Did he have a two, as well? Or was he teasing? Or was he bluffing for the benefit of Jorge and Pancho? The thing is, I didn't really have a two either, but I thought a bluff was in order since I felt Jorge's eyes on me. And anyway, it's one of the only signals I can get right.

After everybody had finished flashing signals at each other, while trying to intercept those going back and forth between the opponents, it was time to start the bidding. If you think this is one of those quiet games like bridge or poker, it's not. As I think I might have mentioned, it's the most Argentine of games. As such, it is an excuse to talk nonstop, whether in prose or in the traditional *versos* that one recites during the bidding and the cardplay. *Truco* is the perfect outlet for the Argentine's need to chatter at all costs. It may not be of substance, it may be all air, it may not be true—but he'll say it anyway.

I've said this before: I'm not a confident liar. That's because I'm convinced I'm see-through. So when I said, *"Envido"* (the opening bid), without having the necessary points in my hand, I was sure I would be caught out. But I wasn't. We played the round and won it. Jorge and Pancho couldn't believe it when they discovered that La Griega had bluffed!

By the end of the evening, practice had made perfect. I could execute a perfect twitch with both the left and the right side of my mouth, while my lower lip was red from having been bitten so many times (the signal that you hold a three). I played recklessly, saying *"Truco"* and *"Quiero vale quatro"* and a whole lot of other bids without really knowing what I was saying. And we won!

The funny thing is that I always win at this game—I'm not sure I like what that says about me. Perhaps I ought to consider a career switch. I bet I'd have less trouble finding a partner if I turned professional *truco* player.

April 25, 2000

You know how difficult it is to resist a forbidden fruit? Well, imagine how difficult it is to resist a fruit that is forbidden not once, but four times over.

To make things even more difficult, we're not talking about a fruit that is sitting quietly on its tree, minding its own business. We're talking about a fruit that is begging to be plucked, a fruit that is literally crying out: "Eat me! Eat me!" A fruit that uses every trick in the book to tempt the weak girl that I am: breathing into my ear and down my neck, when it is not moaning; squeezing me so tight that my tits hurt; and generally oozing testosterone from every pore as it presses its groin against mine. Yesterday, it even kissed me on the lips as it left my apartment after our practice session.

When Romina asked me to "babysit" Javier, and I said yes, I didn't realize what a handful this baby would prove to be. Of course, I knew I was playing with fire, but I really and truly thought I would be able to handle him. Or maybe it's just that I like playing with fire.

Anyway, I underwent a particularly hard test of my virtue yesterday. If I am honest, it was not the test that was hard but my virtue that is easy.

I must constantly remind myself why it is I MUST NOT have sex with him.

1. I am *not* in a relationship and the person I am *not* in a relationship with is Jorge.

2. Jorge is Javier's best friend. In fact, they are attached at the hip—apart from when Jorge feels like having sex with me. (I wonder how real Siamese twins manage it?)
3. Javier is going out with someone.
4. That someone is my good friend Romina.
5. That someone has entrusted him to me with the specific, though perhaps not fully verbalized, though pretty clear understanding that I would not have sex with him while she was away looking after her dying father in Cordoba.

So, in fact, that makes five reasons—not four—for not going to bed with him, which makes the temptation to eat the fruit five—not four—times greater.

April 30, 2000

It was five in the morning and we were getting ready to leave La Catedral. We being Jorge, Pancho, and I. Javier was MIA. He must have been shagging somebody.

The three of us left together and strolled for a while through Buenos Aires at dawn. I felt something in the air as I played piggy-in-the-middle, my arms linked through theirs. We were headed in a direction I wasn't sure I wanted to be heading in. I could see the conniving looks going back and forth between Jorge and Pancho, the smirks on their faces.

It was like having one of those dreams where you are at the wheel of a racing car, but you've never passed your driver's-license test. And to make matters worse, your leg is too short to reach the brake pedal. The car is swerving all over the place and any minute now it is going to skid and crash. But in retrospect, I needn't have felt so anxious. What I hadn't foreseen was how much fun it is to drive when (a) you don't know how, and (b) your legs are too short.

"Let's go down to the river!" said Jorge.

"Okay!" I said. I had no brakes, remember?

"Okay!" said the flan.

When Jorge suggested going down to the river, the suggestion had conjured up a tranquil scene of trees, stars, and dewy grass. My mental picture of rivers did not include sooty factories, abandoned warehouses, curious kids, and even more curious cops. "Tranquil" was a relative term when it came to describing the spot we picked. But it was ours.

I don't know what came over me, but I stopped being nervous (was it the joint? Jorge had gotten his hands on some first-rate stuff thanks to a cousin of his who is a cop). I lay back and gazed up at the stars, which were only three-quarters obstructed by the factory chimneys. I exhaled deeply and the anxiety wafted away with the smoke. The next drag filled me with serenity: I knew that everything was going to be all right.

The universe must have heard me because a hand started to caress me over my dress. It drew large, deliberate circles. Did the hand belong to Jorge? Did it belong to Pancho? Did it matter? And then another hand joined in, caressing me with a firmness that bordered on roughness. It was an impatient hand that wanted to explore beneath the dress, probing for skin. When it had found what it was looking for, it roamed about freely as it expanded its circular motion with each stroke, until it completely covered the great expanse, otherwise known as my stomach. A third hand appeared on the scene—well, more precisely, on my thigh. This was getting interesting! The pressure mounted. And then the fourth hand, not wishing to miss out on the fun, joined the task force to concentrate on my breasts: fondling, pinching, flicking, squeezing, teasing, pulling, tickling, and generally getting up to no good at all.

Now a mouth joined in. And then another. The kisses were so well coordinated that I wondered if they did this sort of thing on a regular basis. Finally, I understood the term "brothers in arms." And then I lost track of which hand was where. And whose mouth was whose.

I'm not usually one for much foreplay and have even been known to skip it altogether. The reason being that I'm far too impatient to get to the main course. But threeplay, I discovered, was a different story . . . I didn't mind at all that it went on all night long. Because it was true: many hands did make light work!

May 4, 2000

"I can't do this," said Jorge as he removed the used condom—empty, as usual. This was on Thursday.

"Do what?" I said, pretending I didn't know.

"Umm . . . see you," he said.

"But you're *not* seeing me. Remember?" I said. I couldn't help being sarcastic.

"You know what I mean," he said.

"No, actually, I don't." I was going to make this as difficult for him as possible.

"I don't want to fuck anymore," he said, an ash from his cigarette burning a hole in my sheet.

"Oh." On second thought.

It figures. The other night's tryst was bound to ruin everything. I should have listened to my nerves instead of the pot. Although frankly, it isn't the fucking I am going to miss, since I have been known to have a better time at my gynecologist's.

It's hard to enjoy sex when your partner isn't. I recently discovered that the technical term for when a guy doesn't come after hours of trying is SRD (Semen Retention Disorder). This is not the first time I have come face-to-face with this "disorder." The way I see it, it's not a disorder at all: it's a power kick—where more often than not, the person who has the power ends up kicking himself in the butt. Granted, by retaining their semen, they are keeping control. But at the end of the day, you really have to feel sorry for these guys who get off on not getting off.

Nobody talks about men's inability to enjoy sex because they are too busy talking about how women are frigid. Baloney! When will people stop repeating the same tired old discourse about how men are the more sexually motivated gender? Sure they are! In their fantasies, when there is no immediate danger of having to go to bed with anyone. But what happens when a girl stops saying no and starts saying yes? Suddenly, he's not so gung-ho, is what. Of course, he'll explain his sudden loss of appetite by saying she wasn't so hot close up. But it's he who was never really as hot for sex as he liked to think. He can talk all he wants, but when the time comes to PERFORM, you realize that's all it was: TALK. Luckily there are the exceptions to the rule—"Oh, Frank, Frank, where art thou, Frank?"—but for the most part, women today must contend with men who can't get it up, or if they can, they can't give it up, or if they can, it's premature. Or is it me?

They do come up with the most creative excuses for holding back, though. Jorge claimed once during pillow talk that he was controlling his ejaculation so as to keep his essence intact. It was part of his "Taoist" philosophy. The words "yin" and "yang" came up frequently in the conversation, as did the notion of his seed and its relation to his power. And since I am fascinated by Chinese philosophy, I didn't hear the alarm bells ringing madly in my head. I had just had an orgasm—*I* wasn't going to deprive myself—so my brain wasn't working 100 percent. But now that my synapses are up and running again, the bottom line is that he didn't have an O!

My point is that men are just as vulnerable in the sack as women. Jorge is no different than a woman who blocks her own orgasm until she feels safe in the relationship. The only difference between men and women is that men won't admit to it. They claim they can have sex without feeling anything at all, and I claim they are lying. I had hoped he might eventually let go. The question is why, then, did I have to go and fool around with his best friend—in front of him, no less? In hindsight, this wasn't exactly conducive to his relaxing in the sack. And I ought to have my synapses checked.

May 6, 2000

It has finally hit me that it's over.

The devastation I feel is nowhere nearly proportionate to the event, and yet there is nothing I can do to lessen it. I remember once visiting the London Dungeons, a waxworks museum where they exhibit every torture and form of execution under the sun. It's extraordinary what imagination people have when it comes to doing away with each other. Anyway, one particularly clever one has stuck in my mind. It's the one where they open you up, remove all your entrails, and allow you to watch the mice gobble them up as you lie there, dying slowly in a pool of your own blood. I must hand it to them, what it lacked in sophistication, it made up for in efficacy. I only bring it up now because that's almost as bad as I feel every time somebody breaks up with me. Even if, strictly speaking, they aren't breaking up with me because they were never going out with me, as Jorge kept on reminding me.

The good thing about being in agony is that it forces one to read. There is no better way to feel sorry for oneself than lying on one's back with a book in hand. I have spent the day reading *Consolations of Philosophy* by Alain de Botton. Granted, it's not the best choice: the author is yet another on my long list of Men Who Have Rejected Me. I once wrote him a fan letter, but he never responded, the bastard. And it's no good telling me that his publishers didn't give it to him. I don't buy that.

Anyway, I have decided to give Alain a second chance. He broke my heart once. Now he can bloody well fix it. I have to say that the chapter on Schopenhauer is cheering me up a bit. According to Botton (stupid name, anyway), Schopenhauer says that it's perfectly natural to feel suicidal when even the most fleeting of romances goes down the tubes. The reason is, having unconsciously selected the father of your offspring because his traits will complement yours to make the perfect baby, your body is gearing itself up for the job and once the machine is in gear, it doesn't backtrack easily.

I wonder what our baby would have looked like? Would it have had his dark, curly hair with my green eyes?

I'm going to slit my wrists. Damn Schopenhauer!

I'd better turn to another philosopher. Nietzsche is sure to do the trick. There is nothing that cheers me up more than reminding myself that my suffering is just another one of those tests that we *übermenscher* have to go through on a periodic basis to prove ourselves as the truly superior beings that we are.

I do realize that although it feels like it, I am not heartbroken in the strict sense of the word. Heartbreak is what you experience after a loss, while what I am suffering from is nothing other than a good old-fashioned blow to the ego. *But:* while a broken heart sounds more dramatic and less appealing than a blow to the ego, I would choose a broken heart any day. The first is mere amputation, while the second is death. A slow, agonizing death that gnaws away at you, like the mice from the London Dungeons.

Oh dear. I think I need to seek consolation elsewhere, since Alain's philosophers don't seem to be doing it for me. Let's see . . .

1. I have one less reason not to sleep with Javier.
2.

Well, I suppose one consolation is better than none.

May 15, 2000

I was sitting with Valeria and Monica at Almagro, when in walked Jorge with Pancho and Javier. I must have turned red then purple before going a not-very-attractive shade of green because both girls noticed and asked me what was wrong. I pointed out Jorge and they both made sympathetic noises to show they understood how hard it is to be bumping into exes at the *milonga*. Of course, I haven't told either of them the real reason that Jorge is my ex. The official story is that he is "scared to get involved because he is leaving for Europe in less than a month." I don't think they need to know that their friend is a slut.

Not that *I* think that I am a slut, but apparently others would beg to differ. Starting with Jorge and Pancho, who both decided that the best policy was to ignore me. The way they are behaving, you'd think they were two vestal virgins who had been raped by a depraved old satyr (me). It's not as if I had forced them into anything down by the river that night. It did take three in this particular case, and according to my recollection of things, they seemed to enjoy themselves as much as I did.

Anyway, I was busy fuming at Jorge and Pancho's hypocrisy when Javier signaled that he wanted to dance. At least one of the triplets was a man.

As I got up from my table and walked over to join him on the floor, I was taken over by the spirit of revenge. I wanted to taunt Jorge and I knew I could count on Javier as my taunting device.

And I was right. Javier, obviously annoyed at having missed out on the fun, was adamant that he should get a belated piece of the action. In other words, he was being an even naughtier fruit than usual. The obscenities he whispered in my ear as we danced were so obscene that I cannot bring myself to repeat them on an empty stomach. But in the heat of the moment, I didn't mind them at all. In fact, I was rather enjoying hearing in graphic detail what he planned to do to me later. It sounded very promising.

He was spewing forth quite happily when suddenly the flow of dirty talk stopped right in its tracks—in the middle of a particularly good bit. Damn! Talk about teasing, I thought as I opened my eyes. And there she was, standing in front of us: Romina.

"You didn't tell me she was back," I hissed, making no attempt to disguise my frustration.

"I forgot," he groaned. He sounded pretty frustrated too, which somewhat alleviated the burden of my own frustration. But still, I wanted to strangle him.

We finished the set in silence. Afterward, I went up to her and as warmly as possible said, "Welcome back!" even though this did not exactly reflect my feelings. Javier, who couldn't stand being with the two of us together, ran off to join the other triplets, while I condoled with her. Her father's funeral had been on Saturday and she looked as devastated as she felt.

You did the right thing, I thought later as I scrubbed myself with cold and soapy water. Of course, if Romina hadn't appeared in time, I might not have had the opportunity to feel so self-righteous—but I preferred not to go there. I am sick to death of doing the right thing is where I went instead.

May 20, 2000

I had just been subjected to a *setus horribilis* with someone I would rather not remember, both for his sake and mine. After that, I decided that I had been charitable enough for one evening. I was going to stay put until somebody decent asked me. No more of this "being nice" nonsense.

I have to be pickier, I thought. Not take so many risks.

That's when this man I had never seen before planted himself in front of me and extended his arm, assuming that I would get up and go off with him, just like that! It took all the courage in the world to do what any self-respecting *porteña* would do in the face of such nerve. I declined with a barely perceptible shake of the head before staring through him and into the distance.

He really ought to know better, I said to myself to justify my cruelty. He shouldn't expose himself to rejection like this. It's not my fault he doesn't respect the code.

"Suit yourself. That's the last time I ask *you* to dance," said the stranger under his breath.

I raised an eyebrow, as if to say, "Boo-hoo-hoo, I'm gonna cry."

But when I watched him glide across the floor seconds later with a girl who looked in absolute heaven, I almost did cry. I went up to Valeria, who was sitting at another table with Ezequiel—possibly the ugliest guy on earth, which is such a pity because he is an amazing dancer—and I asked her, "Who's *that?*" *That* was Diego: tango teacher on the weekends; moonlights as a doctor during the week.

Now that I got a better look at him, he was young (but not *too* young, for a change) and handsome and the right size and build. This was one of those occasions that called for some serious groveling. I put all pride aside.

"You are so wonderful! And I made a *big* mistake. Will you ever forgive me?" I pouted so much that I got a cramp in my lips. But no amount of pouting could persuade Diego, who was now taking his turn to stare through me and into the distance. He was letting me know that I had been blackballed. And if you think that elephants have long memories, you haven't met a scorned tango dancer.

May 29, 2000

They call him "el Gato" because he doesn't walk, he prowls. I will never forget the first time I saw him dance at La Catedral. It was a devastating vision of power and grace that made a cat look clumsy by comparison. The light he emanated was so bright that the space around him was plunged into darkness. From the moment I saw him, I prayed to God that he would ask me to dance. When He did not answer my prayers, I asked Valeria to intervene instead. This produced the miracle I had been waiting for.

El Gato may move like a cat, but he doesn't look like one. Indeed, he is decidedly un-feline in appearance. If he were green, el Gato would be the Incredible Hulk. Presumably, his massive bulk is left over from the days when he wrestled for a living. But el Gato is not green. He is every color of the rainbow. His body is covered with tattoos of all shapes and sizes. One on his left bicep is a heart, bearing the inscription "Mama." If this isn't the proof that he is a real *tanguero*, I don't know what is.

In spite of the fact that el Gato has recently been cast in one of the top shows, *Tango por Dos*, I have never considered him partner material. I may be hungry, but not hungry enough to spend eight hours a day with a multicolored version of the Hulk who is in love with his mother. Nope. But don't get me wrong: I love to dance with him and do so every opportunity I get at the *milonga*. Last night, for instance.

I was enjoying the feel of his velvety-smooth paws on my back when suddenly I noticed that the velvety-smooth paws were being more active than usual. At first I thought he was indulging in some harmless flirtation, until I realized that he was not caressing me, but signaling to someone behind my back. I was horrified. This was *totally* unacceptable. I couldn't see who he was signaling to, since I do not have eyes in the back of my head, but I could feel his hands gesturing madly as he led me into a series of back *ochos*.

"Sorry, *querida*, I've got to go and take care of some business," he said, using his gruff, smoke-and-whiskey-filled vocal cords, thereby jilting me halfway through a tango and leaving me stranded in the middle of the salon. This was the worst thing that could have happened to me. I'm not exaggerating.

With my self-esteem shattered into a thousand teeny-tiny pieces, I staggered back to my table. I noticed that his tumbler was still there. That was odd. He normally goes running back to it as soon as he has let go of me.

Unlike my friend, I never drink when I dance. It's terrible for my balance. But last night, I made an exception to the rule. My nerves called for a stiff one. I decided to finish the bastard's scotch. That would teach him. As I sat brooding, I replayed the one and a half tangos in my mind and combed them for faults, the way a mother chimp combs her offspring for fleas. I had a field day. I was able to find fault with my posture, footwork, axis, weight distribution—with everything about my dancing, in fact. I was surprised he hadn't dumped me sooner, in retrospect. All I wanted was to flee the site of my demise. I had finished his scotch, anyway.

I was getting ready to leave when Monica came up to me:

"Have you heard?" she asked me.

"No," I said morosely.

"The cops are raiding the place for drugs. They aren't letting any-body in or out," she said.

"Oh. Have they found anything?" I asked as I took off my shoes. I wasn't registering what she was saying. Alcohol has the effect of slow-ing me down, in addition to throwing me off balance.

"Of course not. They never do," she said, raising an insinuating eyebrow. I looked around the room for el Gato. No sign of him. Ding-dong! Suddenly, I remembered the rumors that he is the biggest dealer on the scene. I hate to say it, but I find these rumors plausible.

He must be "paying the rent" in some back room somewhere. Phew! The thought made me go warm and fuzzy all over. Was it the whiskey or was it the revelation that I had not been jilted because of my bad danc-ing? I put my shoes back on in a flash and danced the night away with Ezequiel, Mario, Pablo, Pupi, Fabrizio, Ernesto, Guillermo, and many, many more.

June 18, 2000

When my mother told me that she was coming for a visit, I was worried. I'll rephrase that: I dreaded it. She has not always been my number one supporter when it comes to the tango. I knew I would have to put on my shiny armor to steel myself against the onslaught of her fear (that I will remain a spinster) combined with my own (that I will remain a spin-ster). But lo and behold, instead of the enemy, I have met with an ally. I got a whiff that something had changed last Sunday at La Glorieta.

Diego was there. I was wrong about him: he isn't an elephant after all. Or if he is, he's an amnesiac one. After having stood me in the cor-ner with the dunce's hat on for almost a month, he has seen fit to forgive me. I think he took pity on the girl who displayed such genuine re-morse by looking at him with the saddest puppy eyes in the world. Fi-nally, he was satisfied that the point had been well made and even better taken.

Now he came over to me at the railings and without a word extended his arm in exactly the same gesture as he had the first time around, thus wiping the slate clean and erasing my misdeed from both our memories.

Wow! He was perfect! And I was perfect by association! I hated it when the music stopped because that meant I would have to let go of him. But he also hated it when the music stopped because that meant he would have to let go of me. So we made a silent pact and pretended the music hadn't stopped. We stood there, hugging each other (it wasn't an embrace—it was a hug), our colliding chests exerting the force of a pressure cooker about to explode. Our hearts were synchronized. I breathed with his every breath. My eyes were closed, as were his. I presume they were. They better have been! I was touching his soul and he was touching mine and we waited for a few seconds of eternity until they put the next track on.

With all this going on, you can imagine that I wasn't paying much attention to my mother or her video camera. Diego and I finally had to let go of each other—there comes a point when you simply can't take the pressure anymore, where you *will* explode (I can't say that I've ever witnessed this, but that doesn't mean I wanted to risk it).

When the *milonga* ended, I had to drag my mother away. At home, she showed me what she had shot. And that's when I knew that not only is she on my side, but that she *feels* the tango. She did a better job of filming the dance than many professional cameramen. I was amazed by how every time something "happened" between me and Diego, something visible—I don't mean the touching his soul bit—she was on top of it. It is so difficult to capture the spontaneity of tango. Even the dancers don't know what's going to happen next, so how could the person watching them? And yet, as if it were dancing with us, the camera followed us around the bandstand, capturing the freedom of our spirit and the density of our feeling. Out of the blue, it zoomed in on my legs just in time to catch a *boleo* or an embellishment that expressed the moment. Then as the piece reached its emotional climax, the camera knew to look for our faces, because where else do you find the tango at this critical moment? From that clip, I realized that my mother gets it. She has seen the magic of tango with her own eyes. Now *that* is what I call a miracle!

June 23, 2000

Last night, I took my mother to Canning. I was a bit worried about introducing her to el Gato, but he insisted, saying that he had a way with mothers and that I was not to worry.

"Señora, your daughter is *divina*," he said as soon as the formal introductions were over. My mother beamed. A compliment to her daughter = a compliment to her.

". . . I'm in love!" My mother did not flinch. She was still beaming. If she was at all horrified, she did a good job of hiding it. I laughed, just to make sure she got the joke.

". . . Will you do me the honor of giving me her hand in marriage?" he ended with a flourish. I was laughing so hard now, I almost choked. I looked over at my mother. Not only was she still beaming, I swear I saw a hint of gratitude on her face. That's when I understood that a proposal, even from a permanently drunk and stoned multicolored version of the Hulk, is better than no proposal at all.

"Your fiancé is quite charming!" she said once he had gone off to dance with somebody else.

"Didn't I tell you I'd find a husband?" I said before we both exploded into fits of (nervous?) laughter.

While it is a huge weight off my shoulders that my mother is less concerned about marrying me off these days, I have taken over her job in the worrying department. Especially when I think that this mock proposal is the only one I have ever received. I even managed to go to Cuba without anybody asking me to marry him. Before I went, everybody had warned me to watch out for *all* the guys who were so desperate to get out of the country, they'd do anything, including marry you. But they needn't have bothered. I didn't get a single proposal—not for marriage, at any rate. Why is it that the only proposals I ever get are of the indecent type? Even in Cuba?

July 1, 2000

The first time I saw him, I thought: Who does he think he is? Rudolph bloody Valentino? The stranger had one of those pencil-thin mustaches that literally screamed, "I belong to a slimeball!"

But by the time he issued an invitation to dance by way of the *cabezeo,* raising his eyebrow at an impossible angle and sucking in his cheeks to emphasize his cheekbones, I knew who he was all right. I couldn't very well turn him down. It *was* Pablo de las Pampas.

I decided, under the circumstances, that the best policy would be to play ostrich: I buried my head in its owner's neck so I wouldn't have to look at the mustache for longer than necessary. Oh . . . wait a minute . . . that felt surprisingly good. How could it feel so good with someone who had such a dreadful mustache? To avoid thinking about it too much, I buried my head in his neck even farther.

Although I find Pablo de las Pampas ridiculous—he isn't a person at all, he's a caricature—I play along anyway. If he's going to use me to look good, then I might as well return the compliment. After all, mustache or no mustache, he performs regularly in shows here and abroad. And he's looking for a partner. I know because he has placed an ad on the notice board of the dance studio where I go to practice. The ad specifies that his partner must have ballet training in addition to tango. Good, I qualify. I read on. She must be between the ages of eighteen and twenty-five. Ouch.

Long gone are the days when I was "twenty-one." I wasn't able to keep up the sham forever. I got caught up in my own web of lies. I'd told so many people different versions of the non-truth that I couldn't remember to whom I had said what. For some, I was twenty-one, for others, twenty-five and for others, I was ageless. I came to dread the question so much, every time I heard it, I went crimson in anticipation of the lie to come. I have always hated lying. Not because I am virtuous, but because of my terror, left over from childhood, that the person to whom I am lying can read my thoughts and will catch me red-

handed. I must have read one too many fairy tales and to this day at-
tribute magic powers to people—or perhaps I think of myself as super-
naturally transparent. I have come to the conclusion that the price for
lying about my age is not worth it. The truth is the only policy, no matter how awful.

What is the truth? It's that if I am not on the shelf yet, I am inches
away from it. Who in their right mind wants to dance with a wrinkled
old prune who has a saggy bottom? Granted, this is not a fair description
of myself. Yet. But the clock is ticking faster and faster every day and
soon it will be. The question is, *how* soon? How much time do I have before I become one of those grotesque old women whose flabby thighs
protrude from the slit skirt that fits too tightly over her swollen belly?
And will I know to give up before then? Will God have mercy on me
and send me a partner before it is too late?

July 6, 2000

At Niño Bien last night, el Gato gave me the signal. So far, so good.
Since he could not stand the idea of being separated from his whiskey
for even the short time it took to cover the distance from his table to
mine, he brought it along for the ride. Here too, there was nothing unusual. But normally, he leaves it on my table for recovery as soon as he's
finished dancing with me. Last night, however, he was reluctant to put it
down at all. I could see that he intended to dance with me, glass in hand.
I don't often kick up a fuss, but this is where I put my foot down. There
are limits to what *even I* will put up with!

It was too late by the time I realized I should have boycotted him entirely. El Gato was in a worse state than usual and completely oblivious
to the fact that the floor was packed, and that in order to avoid knocking
into people, the best policy was to dance small. On the contrary, he
seemed to enjoy playing bumper cars—and casting his partner (me) in
the role of the car. To be fair, it is often impossible to avoid the bruised
knees, kicked shins, stubbed toes, etc., that go with dancing tango so-

cially. I am not saying that el Gato is the only bad driver in Buenos Aires (when drunk driving). There are many, and I should know. But the bad drivers I have had the misfortune of being driven by at least *try* to be careful. Or have the good excuse of being blind as two bats (no names). And when they have been unable to avoid a crash, they look apologetic, grovel for forgiveness, and show some concern for the aforementioned stubbed toe or grazed ankle. Not el Gato. Not last night. There was no wiping the look of glee off his face when he had bashed into another couple successfully—using me as the instrument of punishment. He seemed to get an enormous kick out of invading OPS (Other People's Space). Which meant that I got an enormous kick out of it too—literally.

I am not saying that this is the first time in my life I have danced with an inconsiderate bastard. After all, tango is a macho man's dance and the line between macho man and inconsiderate bastard is a fine one. I often have to interpose myself between two alpha males competing over the same piece of floor. I have witnessed a number of fistfights and I've even seen the bullet hole that one *milonguero* I know left in the wall of a salon when another *milonguero* allegedly called his mother something not very nice. I don't know why my trigger-happy friend was so proud of himself, since he is obviously a lousy shot. He didn't hit a single innocent bystander, let alone his target.

The question is, what does a girl do when she is caught in the middle of a cockfight? My code of ethics dictates that "Thou shalt not be a backseat driver, no matter how reckless and/or incompetent the guy at the wheel." It is unfeminine and, anyway, it never does any good. The man will pretend to listen to you only to become a repeat offender seconds later, pushing and shoving his way through the traffic, not in the least bothered about the wreckage to the body of the car (= you). The only resort in these cases is to grin and bear it and swear never to dance with him again.

So that's what I did. I kept to my policy stoically, promising myself that this would be the last time and other encouragements of that nature.

"They've asked me to do an exhibition at La Catedral. I want you to do it with me. They've also asked Alejandro and Claudia and Eduardo and Gabriela," he said. I gulped. That *was* an impressive lineup.

"Has the cat got your tongue? Say something, *mujer!*" he slurred.

"I can't. I'm too happy for words," I said. "Of course I'll dance with you, my *gatito!*" I cried, as *we* stumbled—I was helping him to stumble—back to my table to recover his drink.

July 16, 2000

El Gato told me to meet him at La Esquina de Troilo to warm up before the exhibition. He had some "business" there he needed to discuss with the owner. At the appointed hour, I showed up outside the club, which is on a deserted street in a rundown part of town—not to say a no-man's-land. There was no sign of life inside the place or anywhere in the vicinity. I was going to have to wait for him outside. It was freezing and there was even some snow left on the ground from the other day's snowstorm.

I was wearing my sheepskin jacket and a woolly hat, but underneath, all I had on was a skirt that barely covered my bottom (el Gato had said, "Wear something sexy") and my fishnet stockings. To keep my limbs from freezing up—it's difficult to dance with frostbite—and to dispel the fear of being alone in the middle of nowhere, I started to dance—more like jiggle up and down. I was in full sway when I sensed I was not alone. A car rolled up to me and then stopped. It was a police car.

A young policeman got out. "Your papers," he said, deadpan, looking at me as if I were some kind of . . . oh.

I knew I should have waited to put on my makeup, but what was the use in crying over spilled milk? The snag was, I didn't have any papers on me to prove that I wasn't a hooker. I have never bothered to make my status here official. The less I have to do with bureaucracy, the better. As far as the authorities are concerned, I'm a tourist. The thing is, tourists are supposed to carry their passports with them, always.

It was time to turn on the old charm.

"I'm terribly sorry," said the maiden in distress, "I've left my papers at home. In fact, it's a good thing you stopped. I have a problem. You see, I'm waiting for my tango partner because we're going to perform at La Catedral tonight and he said to wait for him here, but there must be some mistake because the place is shut down. I don't know what to do." I stopped just short of crying. I kept that trick up my sleeve, in case I needed it later.

"Did you say tango?" asked the cop. I noticed a softening of attitude.

"Yes. Tango," I replied.

"Did you hear that, Raúl? The *gringa* dances tango!" he said to his colleague in the car. He turned to me again:

"I don't know how to dance," he said with a doleful shake of the head.

"Well, it's never too late to learn," I said.

"I've always wanted to, but it's so difficult . . ."

"It's not all that difficult if you take it one step at a time," I encouraged him.

"You're right . . . Maybe you could teach me?!"

"One day, *mi amor* . . . But right now, I've got to get to La Catedral. It doesn't look like my partner is coming. Where am I going to find a taxi?" I asked myself out loud.

"Allow me," said the officer. He opened the back door of the police car and motioned for me to get inside. This made me very uneasy. Everybody knows that the cops here are worse than the criminals. I danced with one the other night who they say moonlights as a contract killer. Who knows if it's true or not, but it's a reflection of how people feel about them. It's been less than twenty years since the "Dirty War" ended—the military regime that waged a war of terror on so many of its citizens between 1976 and 1983—and people are not going to forget so soon the part the police played in it.

The wounds have far from healed and this is made all the more apparent by the billboard advertising campaign all over the city right now, the headline of which reads: "Call us if you are unsure of your real identity." This is a reference to the thirty thousand people who "disappeared" and whose babies were taken from them to be given to supporters of the junta. No matter how many times I hear about it, I cannot come to grips with it. It seems impossible that something like that could have happened here. But it did. And many of those who disappeared were last seen in the back of a black Falcon, the police car of the time.

The car in front of me now was not a black Falcon but a beat-up old Peugeot. I was paralyzed with fear anyway. I couldn't think of a way out, so I got in. In front, the two cops were talking in lowered tones. I couldn't hear what they were saying. I had no idea where they were taking me. I once learned in a self-defense course that it helps to talk to the aggressor. So I talked. About this, about that, and about the other, hoping to stall them from doing whatever it was they had planned. As I talked, I saw bits and pieces of myself in black plastic bags, floating down the river. Then I recognized where we were. We were in front of La Catedral. The car stopped and the policeman got out and opened the door for me. Door-to-door service. They wished me luck, were sorry they couldn't stay to watch, but unfortunately, they were on duty. I thanked them, and as they drove off into the cold night, I let out a deep breath.

I went inside, and sure enough, there he was. El Gato looked like he was going to skin me alive, so I beat him to it:

"Don't make my balls swell, Gato." (Argentine balls don't break, they swell.) "You said meet at Troilo. I froze my butt off waiting for you," I said, right off the bat.

"I said meet at Homero Manzi [a different famous composer]!" His voice was booming.

"No you didn't. You said Troilo," mine boomed back. (But you were too drunk to remember—this I kept to myself).

"Don't you give me none of your lip, woman!" he growled.

"I was almost *arrested* because of you!" I snarled, showing him some canine. That calmed him down.

I then proceeded to milk the police episode for all it was worth, adding the odd embellishment here and there: "And then, when he put the handcuffs on . . ." The cat went quiet as a mouse. Good.

"Okay, okay. It's over. You're here now," he mumbled. "What counts—"

He hadn't finished his sentence when they announced us. We were next. And that was the end of our warm-up.

"If you fuck up, I'll kill you," he informed me as we made our way to the floor.

It's amazing what wonders a threat of execution can work. I had no choice but to become a pillar of strength and to hold up the by now completely legless Gato to keep him from crashing down to the ground.

Compensate! was the adrenaline-coated order rushing through my body.

There was nothing for it but to go all out on the seduction front. I don't think I could have been any more seductive with my clothes off. In fact, any puritans in the audience would certainly have described the display as lewd. They would no doubt have objected to my right leg's tight grip around his hip. Neither would they have approved of my shin as it started its slow descent down his thigh after coming a little too close to his you know what. But instead of grunts of disapproval, my shin's behavior met with a whistle or two as well as shouts of *"Esa!"* (Attagirl!), from whence I deduced that the audience did not contain a single puritan.

Now my hand stroked the back of his head, gliding through his not exactly clean hair before it cradled his head like a baby, while my half-open lips approached his, which were marinated in scotch, and stayed there for a long enough time to take away the collective breath of the crowd that surrounded us. I could almost hear their desire stirring beneath the music. Then my arm slid back down to rest on his upper arm, my bloodred fingers digging into his tattooed biceps. But before it found its resting place, my arm flung itself up in the air, where it stretched, fingers spread, my whole body expanded. (Like in real life, where I automatically stretch when I am turned on, my body growing as big as possible—presumably so that there is more of it to enjoy the lovely sensations going on inside.) After this final spasm, my arm, now a spent force, floated languidly back to nestle tenderly in the embrace.

The action shifted to my legs, which took over where my arm had left off. With each and every *boleo* and *gancho*, I could sense the audience's temperature rise as it warmed up to the sight of my naked thighs, trapped inside the fishnets, going about their business. In summary, the term "dry intercourse" was never more appropriate, though I wasn't sure who I was having it with: el Gato or the audience? Finally, the tango ended and the crowd erupted into thunderous applause as well as cries of *"Otra!"* (Encore).

The seduction had worked: they were mine! I felt a rush of happiness. I had actually *enjoyed* it! For the first time, I had been fully present during a performance—I did not float away as I had that first time with Chino. There was nowhere in the world I would rather have been than dancing in front of these people and sharing the emotions that the tango stirred in me. This night would go down in the history books as the night I overcame my stage fright!

As it happens, Pablo de las Pampas was there. He came over to congratulate me. As he spoke, the mustache made me uneasy, so I looked at his earlobe. We chatted for a while. And then, he casually mentioned he was looking for a partner.

"Yes, I know. I saw your ad," I said, blushing. I knew what was coming.

"Are you working with anyone?" he asked me.

"Nobody permanent—but I'm looking," I said. Mustaches *can* be shaved off, I thought.

He paused as he mulled over The Question: "How old are you?" he finally asked me.

"Thirty-one," I said, throwing myself over the edge. To his credit, he did *try* to hide his disgust. But unlike mustaches, it is not possible to shave off the years.

He turned rather quickly to talk to Eduardo and Gabriela, who had performed right before us. I had nobody else to chat with, so I made a beeline for the ladies' room, where I stood in front of the mirror for a good five minutes, counting each and every wrinkle on my soon-to-be completely withered face.

July 18, 2000

Diego can be so arrogant. Of course, this only makes him more attractive. Especially when his arrogance is directed at me. The thing is, Diego is the exception to the rule that all dancers are stupid (he *is* a doctor, let's not forget). Which makes it difficult to entirely ignore what he says, even if what he says doesn't make one feel too good. Here is a sample conversation. We had it last night at Tasso:

"You've got talent. It's a shame it's going to waste," he said in his usual laconic way.

"Waste? You don't think I'm growing?" I asked defensively.

"Not as fast as you should. Look at Valeria. Now *there's* someone who's growing." That was just what I didn't want to hear. How did he know? As I said, he's smart.

"I'm obviously not as talented as she is," I replied, gulping down my rage. I don't know who I resented more at this particular moment, him or Valeria.

"Nonsense. You're just lazy," he said.

"That's not fair! You don't know how hard I work," I said. He had touched a huge nerve.

"You dance with the wrong people," he said. He meant el Gato, who was dancing with some fat broad with bad peroxided hair. "I heard about the exhibition. They said it was lousy," he added.

I have a sneaking suspicion I know who "they" is. And since "they" can't dance to save "their" lives, this doesn't affect me in the slightest.

Well, maybe it affects me a little.

Okay. I'm crushed. Happy?

The truth is that criticism always hurts, no matter how badly its source dances.

But I did not want Diego to see that his words had reached their target. He had come far too close for comfort.

"I *like* dancing with el Gato. He's got *balls*," I said because I couldn't come up with anything better than an indirect challenge to his manhood—perhaps I was trying to provoke him. And anyway, he didn't need to know that I'd had it up to here with el Gato and that as far as I was concerned, I had danced my last tango with him. Because I didn't know it myself yet.

My comeback certainly shut him up for a while. It's funny how easy it is to shut up an Argentine man. Much easier than to get a real cock to stop crowing at six in the morning. But it was too late. I could not get what he had said out of my head. In retrospect, the applause wasn't all *that* thunderous. It now sounded tepid—chilly even. Come to think of it, they only asked for one encore. And wasn't that the sound of jeering I heard mixed in with the clapping? Diego was right: I was awful, the audience hated me, and I am a talentless waste.

"If you practice with me, I'll show you the meaning of work," he said as smoke wafted out of his mouth in a spiral staircase.

I thought I must have misunderstood. I went over what he had said a few more times in my head. It sounded very much like he was asking me to practice with him. I didn't know what to make of it: was it a backhanded compliment or a backhanded insult? Talk of twists in the plot!

That's when it occurred to me that I hadn't even considered him as a candidate. The reason, I now realized, was that deep down I thought he was too good for me. (And I too old for him: if nobody else wanted a soon-to-be shriveled-up old prune, why would he?) But I couldn't allow him to suspect this. I must play it completely cool and not let on that this came as a godsend to a desperate tango dancer at the end of her tether. It was imperative I act as if the offer were the most natural thing in the world, as if handsome young doctors asked me to be their tango partners every day. As a result, I went mute—worried that if I did say something, I would break the spell and the offer would be taken away from me.

"Is that a yes or a no?" he asked me.

"Let me think about it," I said. I was playing it cool, remember? After all, the arrogant prick deserved to be taught a lesson. He could wait till tomorrow, I thought.

He looked down and didn't say anything as he crushed his cigarette stub out in the ashtray. He lifted his eyes and scanned the room in search of someone to dance with, as if I had vanished into thin air, like the last breath of smoke from his mouth. Then I noticed he made eye contact with one of the best/prettiest new dancers on the scene and was dangerously close to giving her the *cabezeo*. I panicked.

"It's a yes!" I said. In fact, I think I may have shouted it out at the top of my lungs as I simultaneously threw myself at his neck and didn't let go of him all night long. So much for cool, calm, and collected . . .

July 27, 2000

Diego and I were practicing at my place. We have been working on a piece by Pugliese called "La Mariposa" (The Butterfly). People ask me: how do you separate the personal from the professional? The answer is: I don't. Even if you want to, you can't avoid the laws of physics: two bodies that rub against each other for four hours, three times a week cause friction; friction causes sparks; and sparks cause a fire. And by definition, tango is about containing the fire. You need a fire, because without it, there is nothing to contain. But if you let the fire get out of hand by giving in to your desire, that too spells the end of tango. In other words, tango is about *playing with fire* but *not getting burned*. Easier said than done.

As I was saying, on the surface it looked as if Diego and I were practicing. But in reality, we were doing everything but. The fire was getting out of hand. I could feel my cheek (among other things) burning against his and we were both shaking badly. As we danced, I fought an internal battle. I told myself it was a bad idea for the reason above. On the other hand, he is *really* attractive and sexy—especially when he's being difficult . . . Added to which, I knew that if I didn't sleep with him, sooner or later, he would leave me for someone who would, since the only reason men dance with you is because they are looking for a convenient source of sex.

So one thing led to another and, well . . . the fire got out of hand.

There is no point in crying over spilled milk. What is done is done. But it must not happen again. It's going to ruin everything. How many times do I need to learn my lesson? Tango and sex don't mix. I must think of myself as a nun, who instead of being married to God is married to the tango.

I have no idea, though, how I am going to keep Diego if I don't have sex with him again. He seemed rather eager to start all over again today and he didn't like it very much when I referred to yesterday as an "accident."

You are damned if you do and damned if you don't, as I have said time and time again.

August 5, 2000

Sometimes it seems like everybody and his dog wants to go to bed with me. And then there is Ezequiel, who doesn't even qualify as a dog because dogs are better looking. He has tried every trick in the book, and I have kept on telling him that he is wasting his time—though I haven't told him why exactly. I know it's best to be cruel to be kind—and that applies to human dogs as well as to pet ones—but I have never been able to bring myself to tell him the truth: that while I love dogs, I don't normally go out with them.

That was before I realized that dog spelled backward = god.

To be honest, Ezequiel's looks have never mattered to me on the floor: I dance with my eyes shut anyway. We have always had a special connection—but recently his dancing has skyrocketed. A few months ago, he quit his job in "construction" (he was a bricklayer) to devote himself full-time to tango and the results have been phenomenal. Having reached the farthest galaxies in the known universe, he is now preparing to go where no man has been before. Each time I dance with him, it's better than the last. I tell myself it can't possibly get any better, but it does. His thirst for the discovery of new figures and sequences is unquenchable, making him a pioneer in the true sense. It is a privilege to be invited along for the ride to these uncharted territories. However, no matter how breathtaking the trip, I have always managed to avoid the temptation of dilly-dallying with the pilot. Of course, the fact that the pilot is so extremely ugly meant that there was not much temptation to be avoided.

Until last night. I don't know what came over me, but the more we danced, the less I felt like dancing with anyone else. In fact, I started to feel that I *couldn't* dance with anyone else. This made Diego angry, even though he tried not to show it. He danced with all the prettiest girls in the room to make me jealous. But it didn't work: I was too fulfilled by Ezequiel to look elsewhere, let alone worry about who Diego was dancing with.

The chemistry was visible. So much so, that a number of people commented on our special brand of magic. Normally, I tire of a partner after more than a couple of sets. I am usually so promiscuous on the dance floor, it makes Don Juan look slow on the uptake. But the pleasure of dancing with Ezequiel was so exquisite, it hurt. To have danced with anyone else after him would have been like having a scoop of plain vanilla after having had a triple-chocolate-fudge sundae dripping with hot caramel sauce and sprinkles on top. I thought my heart would burst.

Finally Diego left in a huff, without saying good night to me. I knew I'd have to deal with it the next day, during our practice session. But tomorrow was another day. In the meantime, I climbed higher and higher up the ladder of bliss with Ezequiel.

"This is love," I said, unable to contain myself. I meant it. But it wasn't said with any intent. I just needed to share this feeling with him, call it bliss or ecstasy or whatever you want to call it. If I didn't get it off my chest, I was liable to explode. But he didn't see it in that light. He saw it in another light. One that had just turned green.

When the set ended, we went to sit down for a rest. He took hold of my hand with his, which was rough, weather beaten, and corroded by cement mixed with hard labor, and started to play with my fingers. He brought my hand to his lips and blew on it lightly before inserting the tip of the index finger into his mouth. He started to tickle it gently with his tongue.

"Imagine this is your nipple," he said, looking deep into my eyes.

I did as I was told and was surprised to find that I could imagine it with no difficulty at all. How could this be? This was *Ezequiel!* What on earth was happening to me? Then he asked me to imagine other things, which I had equally little difficulty in imagining. I started to feel a current flow through my body. It grew steadily until soon I had become a fire hazard and my loins a particularly dangerous minefield. This was disconcerting, to put it mildly.

Until my index finger had been introduced to it only minutes ago, I had always looked at that mouth with what can only be described as repulsion. How could anyone want to kiss such a mouth? The lips were too full, the teeth uneven. They jutted forth in the most anarchic fashion—each tooth going whichever way it pleased. And in many places, where you would have expected to find a tooth, there was none at all. Just a gaping hole. In fact, his whole body elicited feelings that ranged from mild horror to not-so-mild pity. I'm convinced that he suffered from malnutrition as a child. He is now a scrawny young man who looks like a scrawny old man with a hunched back from all the bricks he has carried. It is a body one would rather not think about. How do you explain that I was now shaking with desire for . . . this? Had I been beamed into *A Midsummer Night's Dream?* Had Puck slipped a potion into my drink that was making me mad with lust for the donkey-headed Ezequiel?

The next set had started and we were back on the floor. We were approaching the front section of the salon, where brocade curtains divide the dance area from the entrance. Suddenly, I found myself spinning like a dervish inside the curtains. Ezequiel had wrapped us up inside them. We were in our own world now: I melted into his mouth, which had become the extension of mine.

When we eventually disentwined from the curtain, I didn't care who saw us. I knew this would get back to Diego. So be it. We collected our belongings and left to go to my place. Once there, I didn't have time for the usual "Do I? Don't I?" debate since he was already inside me. He had come home. In every sense.

"It's as if you've been here all along, waiting for me!" he whispered. He was awestruck by the perfection of our fit. But not nearly as awestruck as I.

Until last night, I never really believed that two people could be "made for each other" or in the "other half" theory. Until last night, I never understood "Cinderella" and the true significance of the glass slipper. To think that I have been reading porn since I was five and I wasn't even able to appreciate it.

August 15, 2000

I don't have time to go to any of my dance classes anymore. I'm too busy cooking for Ezequiel. The day before yesterday, I made him a chicken casserole. Yesterday, it was lasagna. Today, I'm going to surprise him with pork chops. Looking after him is a full-time job. We get up at around two and I make him breakfast. Then he leaves to go practice with Valeria. That sort of annoys me, but I haven't told him yet that I want him to be my partner. Slowly does it. I won't spring the news on him until he's ready.

Off he trots to practice with Valeria and off I trot to the supermarket. I go almost every day, the reason being that cooking for Ezequiel means also cooking for Valeria, who gets hungry, poor thing, after all that practicing they do together. And since there's always plenty of food at "our" place . . . I really like Valeria, but I do wish she would give me and Ezequiel some space. She gets to dance with him all day long. You'd think she'd let me have a piece of him when she's not.

Once I've traipsed back from the supermarket with four unliftable shopping bags, I am able to squeeze in a couple of hours of practice with Diego. He has been acting out lately. In fact, he's turning into a real pain. I can't say I blame him or that it comes as much of a surprise. What he doesn't realize is that I'm going to dump him as soon as Ezequiel sees the error of his ways and gives Valeria the shove.

I did, however, briefly enjoy the sweet taste of revenge the other day. Ezequiel showed up at my place early, while I was still practicing with Diego. I was wearing a cropped top and very tight Lycra pants and we were in the middle of the most passionate bit of the choreography when he walked in. You should have seen his face. It serves him right. Usually, though, he comes back after I've sent Diego home. The dinner is already on the table when the vultures (note plural) arrive.

I'm convinced that there must be a correlation between love and cooking. As I fall deeper and deeper in love, I cook greater and greater quantities. Ezequiel is so skinny, he desperately needs fattening up. I do wish Valeria would eat less and leave more for him. The good news is that so far, the disease (love) has not extended itself to other chores. But I fear it's only a matter of time before I start to darn his socks. I won't have reached the terminal stage, though, until I iron them.

Anyway, when I'm done feeding them (note plural again) and have done the dishes, it's time to go to the *milonga*. For every minute of bliss I spend in his arms, I must pay the price of hours of torture as he dances with other women. I had hoped I might have evolved since Frank. But no. I don't know which is worse: watching him dance with Valeria, or watching him pick up the foreign ladies in order to seduce them into taking lessons with him. That is how he scrapes together a living, now that he is no longer "in the construction industry." As I watch him from the arms of other partners, the suffering grows until it reaches an unbearable climax. I swear he can read my heart because that's when he takes me back into his arms, saving me from my torment. That's when I am reminded that it's all worth it. Every second, every minute, every hour of torture. I wouldn't exchange it for the world.

August 27, 2000

On Tuesday, I found a love bite on Ezequiel's neck—one that I hadn't left there. He did nothing to hide it. It was almost as if he were flaunting it. I don't know why he takes such pleasure in hurting me. But I don't allow him to see that he has succeeded. I do everything in my power to hide it. I refuse to give him the satisfaction of knowing how jealous I really am. I am a lousy actress onstage, but in moments like these, I deserve to win an Oscar. I am supremely talented when it comes to putting on a dazzling white smile when I feel like death inside.

In this instance, I admit I was caught off guard by the purple-red stain on his neck, the size of a birthmark. I tripped up on what I was saying (I can't remember what it was), losing my train of thought for a second. He asked me what was wrong. He was hoping, no doubt, that I would confront him about it. Instead I told him that I was very tired, that was all. Would he mind terribly if I stayed in tonight? I promised that I would be back on form tomorrow. I made sure to say my lines as tenderly as possible.

"Good night, my love," I said, wondering what marks I would find on his body tomorrow. I kissed him good-bye, avoiding that particular spot.

As soon as he was out of the door, I crawled over to my bed. I didn't have the strength to get undressed. I lay there in the dark, but I didn't go to sleep. I was trying to make the pain go away. I tried all the meditation exercises in the book, but none of them worked. My mind kept going back to pick obsessively at the wound. I kept trying to steer it away from self-destructive thoughts. I tried giving it carrots, but that didn't work. I tried the stick, but that didn't work either. I tried talking to myself and then I tried to empty my mind. I tried breathing deeply. I tried repeating a mantra. I tried saying the words, "This too shall pass." I tried changing positions, lying on my stomach, putting my legs up against the wall, facing south instead of north. I tried it all, but nothing worked. It was like quantum physics of the soul: impossible to successfully locate the suffering particle. As soon as you locate it, it is no longer where you thought it was. The suffering particle is nowhere and everywhere at the same time. Before you know it, it has seeped into every corner of your being. You are defenseless as it flows through your veins, penetrates your heart, your lungs, your stomach, your arms, your legs, your head. It spreads like cancer—the fastest-spreading cancer known to man.

But here is the good news. Unlike cancer, it takes very little to go into remission. You don't need chemo or radiation treatment. All you need is a small miracle. It doesn't happen very often, but when it does, recovery is instant. The tide of pain turns and you find yourself with the soles of your feet splashing in shallow puddles, where you had been drowning in deep waters only moments before.

My mind had latched on to the love bite like a dog to a bone and wouldn't let go. The more I shook it, trying to take the bone away from it, the more it growled and locked its jaw around it. Finally, I gave up. It could keep its stupid love bite. Which is precisely when the miracle happened. That's when I understood that by showing the love bite to me, Ezequiel was in fact inflicting the same sweet torture on me as the sweet torture he had felt when receiving it. The love bite on his neck was *mine* now. And it was as much a token of his love as it was of mine. He hurt me *because* he loved me and I hurt because I loved him. The love bite was there to remind me that with love comes pain, and as I embraced the pain, it disappeared, to leave in its place only love.

And with that, the dog dropped his bone, went to curl up by the fireplace, and promptly fell asleep.

September 7, 2000

Hector the Collector asked me to an event last night they were holding at Gricel for him. They were going to present him with a "Tango Lifetime Achievement Award." It turned out to be quite a big do. There were film cameras from Solo Tango (the cable station) as well as from a Japanese documentary-film company. And there to honor him were a number of big names, including José Vargas and La Rosarina. A lot of water (flat, not sparkling) has flowed under the bridge since we committed sacrilege. To think I once looked up to him as "God"! It makes me laugh. Especially when I see how he lets Graciela treat him. Now here's a couple where there is no doubt who's wearing the pants. She can get away with it, though: she *is* a living legend. I do wonder, though, if they are sleeping together. And whether he runs off to confession straight afterward? I bet she handcuffs him to the bed.

There were a number of other well-known dancers, both young ones and older *milongueros* too, all lined up to perform in honor of Hector. He invited Ezequiel and me to sit at his table.

"*Che*! Do you mind if I borrow your little China girl?" he asked Ezequiel, as if I weren't there. I was wearing the red Chinese dress that I'd bought on Canal Street before leaving New York.

"Go ahead! Be my guest!" replied Ezequiel, also as if I weren't there.

He led me to the floor. During a pause between two tangos he said: "The organizers have asked me to exhibit tonight. Are you up for it?"

"Absolutely!" I replied.

I used to worry that if ever it became public knowledge that I was dating someone at the *milonga*, none of the others would ask me to dance. But I'm finding this not to be the case. On the contrary, they flock to me even more than before (which was already a lot). My revised theory on Argentine males is that they don't *really* want to seduce you. They want to *look* as if they want to seduce you. Without running the risk of getting trapped if the seduction should prove successful. But I also have another conflicting theory. And that is that they figure if Ezequiel can get me, surely they can. After all, in their eyes he is the ugly lowlife that I once thought he was, when I was still blind. They can't understand what I am doing with him—a number of them have told me so to my face—and they are sure that it won't last. So they are already positioning themselves to be next in line. Now that I've succumbed once (that they know of), surely I'll fall again. Moral of the story: I have absolutely no idea what is going on in their warped little heads.

It was a nice exhibition, though no room for showing off. We danced exactly the way we would have in a salon. No frills, just the bare bones of tango. That is the way the older generation likes it. After the warm applause and a few cheers, we went back to our table.

"What did you think, *amor?*" I asked Ezequiel. Triumphant would be overstating it, but I was feeling happy with myself.

"It was okay. Except for your knees. You should keep them together more," he said as he got up to dance with La Rosarina. I was mortified. That is the worst thing you can say to a tango dancer. I sat, knees locked together under the table, until he forgave me. But for what, I wonder?

September 10, 2000

Practicing with Diego has turned into a daily tug-of-war. He keeps making me tug on something I would really rather not touch, thank you very much.

I haven't been completely honest. I have been keeping a deep, dark secret. It's so embarrassing, I couldn't bring myself to talk about it before. But I can't keep why I didn't want to go back to Diego "for seconds" a secret any longer. Of course there had to be something. Think about it: he is handsome, a doctor, *and* a fabulous dancer. What more could a girl (and her mother) want? No, I have been protecting him from the venom of my pen but the time has come when I must own up because otherwise, it's impossible to understand the full extent of my predicament.

It's his dick. There, I've said it. It's the most extraordinary thing! When he unzipped his fly and it was out in all its glory for the world to see, I was only able to keep a straight face by thinking very sad thoughts.

What is *that?* I've never seen one of *those* before. Don't tell me I'm going to have to get up close and personal with it. Do I really have to touch it? Please say I don't. Please make him put it back inside his briefs, where it belongs. But my wishes never do come true. And this one was no exception.

Had it been straight as an arrow—which it was—and stuck out at a ninety-degree angle from his belly button (i.e., in front of him), it would have had the immediate effect of Cupid's arrow on me and I would have been delighted to let it pierce me repeatedly on its way to my heart. But alas, Cupid's arrow it was not. The problem with it was that it was straight as an arrow but stuck out at a forty-five-degree angle to the right of his belly button—I wish I knew how to draw. I think that the technical term for this is "Abnormal Penile Curvature." How do I know? Spam. (I've registered with Yahoo! as a retired man, thinking I would get less spam that way. As it turns out, I don't. But I do get more interesting spam. You'd be amazed by the variety of sexual dysfunction that afflicts retired men and the gadgets designed to cope with said dysfunction. It goes without saying that the very idea of them having sex in the first place is yucky.) Anyway, it's one thing seeing the words "Abnormal Penile Curvature" on your screen and quite another coming face-to-face with it in the flesh. I wouldn't wish it on my worst enemy.

How on earth am I going to get through this without laughing? I wondered. It was no longer an option to say, "Sorry, I've changed my mind." That would have been rude. For once I wouldn't have minded a touch of impotence. But it was not my lucky day. So I closed my eyes and was polite.

It wouldn't be so bad if we could move on and forget it ever happened. But he won't let it rest. He keeps trying to coerce me into sexual favors (i.e., by placing my hand on his crooked dick in the middle of a tango), and I am fast running out of excuses for not obliging him.

I don't know how many times I have told him that it was "special" (I wasn't lying) but that it would not happen again. I have given him every excuse under the sun, but my excuses seem to go in one ear and out the other. I have even thrown him the old "I'll let you know if I change my mind" bone. (There I was lying.)

"I become really insecure when I'm with a guy. I turn into a dependent freak show. A black hole of need waiting to be filled. And you should see how possessive I get. You don't want that, believe me. It's for your own good. Just ask any of my boyfriends," was yesterday's brain-wave. Unfortunately, this approach backfired, just like the rest. If any-thing, it has fanned the flame of his passion. I am at my wits' end. He keeps insisting that I break up with Ezequiel.

"He can't give you what you need. I can," he said. And he was so sincere, it made me feel even worse. How could I tell him that he can't possibly give me the one thing I need since Ezequiel already has it.

September 16, 2000

Yesterday, Diego changed tactics. He switched off the physical and turned on the psychological pressure. He said that if I didn't feel like go-ing to bed with him, then he didn't feel like practicing with me. What did I tell you? And I'm not Einstein. I was about to send him to hell, then something held me back. I'm not sure what that something was. Fear? Cowardice? Pity for the Handicapped?

I prefer to think of it as: "Love of Tango."

And so for the "Love of Tango," I was polite for a second time.

But of this you can be sure: there will not be a third. Because no mat-ter how much I love tango, I don't love it *that* much.

September 19, 2000

Ezequiel has asked me to "lend" him some money. A hundred and fifty pesos. He needs to buy himself a suit. He has a gig with Valeria at a café and he has nothing to wear. I feel . . . uncomfortable about it. And not only because the money is for dancing with her. I want to help him as much as I can, of course I do! There is nothing I wouldn't do for him. And he knows it. But I can't help wondering about his motives. Do I look like a cash cow, or what? That's a rhetorical question. Of course I do.

But I'm not doing either of us any favors if I say yes. It's as true of life as it is of tango: a woman must put up some resistance for the man not to step on her toes. The question is, how much? When is it appropriate to resist and when is it not? I'm starting to tire of these no-win situations. If I say yes, I'm helping him but I'm setting a precedent. He's going to think he can rely on me whenever he is short of cash (which is always), and I don't want that. On the other hand, I can't imagine any good coming out of saying no. (I know what it looks like, but if I do decide to give him the money, it has nothing whatsoever to do with feeling guilty about what happened with Diego.)

Monica tells me not to. She's quite adamant about it. In fact, she wishes I would stop seeing "the creep" once and for all (her words, not mine). But that's because she doesn't know what it's like to have found your "half orange," as the Argentines say. Even if he doesn't look anything like you thought he would.

September 30, 2000

I went to Café Dandi to watch Ezequiel perform with Valeria. He looked so handsome in his new suit. He didn't say thank you (not that I expected him to), but I knew he was pleased. Diego came too. I only asked him because I needed a fourth to square the triangle. I knew that I would feel like shit if I sat alone watching Ezequiel and Valeria do their thing. I needed some moral support.

As the show started, the lights dimmed, prompting Diego to grab hold of my hand, which prompted me to shoo his away. In retaliation, he whispered rude comments about Ezequiel's style and did not stop with his insulting remarks until the end of the performance. It had been a terrible idea to ask him to come and I felt more demoralized than ever. I should have foreseen this. How can such a clever girl be such a nincompoop?

I thought Ezequiel and Valeria looked great together, although I didn't want to think so. The demons that I thought I had eradicated have come back with a vengeance. Watching them dance together is pure torment. I have tried to spare our friendship from my baser instincts, but I can't anymore. I have started to dislike Valeria. Intensely. There, I've said it. In fact, I HATE HER. I hate her perfect peachlike bottom. I hate her perfect long legs. I hate her perfect blond hair. I hate her perfect long neck (that is begging to be wrung by me). Most of all, I hate her perfect tango. I've never hated anyone so perfect in my life. It's gotten to the point that if I had any needles, I'd be practicing voodoo, sticking them into dolls with her name on them, repeatedly. It's a good thing I don't sew. I feel so ashamed of these evil thoughts that I bend over backward to compensate for them. I have never been a better friend.

"Congratulations! You were *fantastic*!" I gushed. She knew.

"And what about *me*?" asked my love.

"You know that you are the best," I said, forgetting for a moment that I was sitting next to Diego. "I mean that you were terrific," I rectified quickly.

The two guys talked shop for a while, comparing notes on figures. Every now and then, Diego played footsie with me and I kicked him away. Ezequiel appeared to be completely oblivious to what was going on under the table. Or was it simply that he didn't care?

As the boys talked, I listened to Valeria complain about her backache. I've never *not* heard her complain about something hurting: if it's not her back, it's her head and if it's not her head, it's her foot. I listened to her with the patience of a saint. I'll rephrase that: with the patience of the guilty. My patience was rewarded, though. Ezequiel saw to that when we got home. And once again, my soul—my ugly soul—was at peace.

October 14, 2000

I didn't know it, but at 5:23 on Tuesday morning, Ezequiel withdrew from me for what would be the last time. My eye happened to slide over the alarm clock at that very moment, which is how I know what time it was. That was fifty-nine hours and twelve minutes ago. They have been the longest fifty-nine hours and twelve minutes of my life.

Everything seemed normal that morning. We had fallen asleep in each other's arms, as usual. And then we had gotten up at two, as usual. And I had made him breakfast, as usual. And he had left to go practice with Valeria, as usual.

But by nine o'clock that evening, he hadn't shown up at my place, as usual. I waited until ten o'clock when I finally caved. I called Valeria:

"*Che*, is Ezequiel around?" I asked casually.

"Sure—it's for you," she said. (Sounds of phones being accidentally dropped and then passed to people.) He was on, but he didn't say hello.

"When are you coming over? The filet is getting cold," I said.

"I'm not," he said.

"What?! Why not? Didn't you say you would, this morning?" I asked him. A creeping sensation was invading the pit of my stomach. A mix of dread and nausea.

"That was this morning," he said. I knew what he was talking about, of course I did.

"What are you talking about?" I asked.

"Diego told me," he said.

"Told you what?" I said because I couldn't think of what else to say.

"You're a whore," he said. His words burned my cheek more than a slap.

"Do you think we could have this conversation calmly, like grown-ups?" I said, feeling far from calm myself.

"No, I don't," he said. And then he hung up on me.

I sat by the phone, staring at it. As the minutes went by, I went from being sure he'd call back, to hoping he might call back, to knowing he wouldn't call back, and finally to being sure he wouldn't while praying that he would. I sat completely still, reflecting on how my world had just collapsed around me. I knew that if I got up from the chair, I would collapse too. I sat there for a long time.

Finally, I found the strength to move to the sofa, where I curled up like a junkie on a public bench. The only difference was that the track marks were on my heart. I was numb from the self-administered anesthetic that was circulating in my blood. I don't know exactly when it wore off, but it did.

The pain is so bad, I don't know if I can endure it. It has been fifty-nine hours and twenty-five minutes since I went into withdrawal. Since I knew that I will never be a whole orange again.

October 18, 2000

I practiced with Diego today, even if it kills me and even if I want to kill him. But I don't have any other option. I must dance with the enemy. I've been asked to give an exhibition at Viejo Correo and I don't have another partner. I said yes even though it's the last thing I want to do. We have a month to complete the Pugliese choreography. Work is a blessing, they say. I wonder if that's true when you are working with a prick. A crooked one, at that. To think that once upon a time, I found him attractive.

"So how are things with Ezequiel these days?" he asked.

"You know how they are," I replied.

"No, I don't," said the sadist.

"We broke up," I said. I was too depressed to have it out with him now.

"Does that mean we can have sex?" he asked.

"Maybe. But not today. It's too soon," I said.

I'll get to the truth (that I would rather die) another time.

Surprise, surprise, the practice session went much better than usual.

October 26, 2000

Last night, I saw Ezequiel at Niño Bien. I knew he'd be there. Going to the *milonga* has become like putting my hand on a hot stove, knowing that it is going to give me a third-degree burn and that I'm going to get blisters, which will pop and then take forever to heal. But that doesn't stop me.

"Let me go to him," begged my heart.

"Me too!" said my body. These two are pals.

"Don't you dare move! Stay right where you are," said my mind. Why does it have to be so bloody strict?

"He's coming toward us now. He's going to ask us to dance!" they cried out in unison. They were very excited.

"You're not going to let him walk all over you," said my mind.

"But we *want* to be his carpet!" they cried.

"It's not going to happen." And my mind meant what it said.

"So, how are you?" asked Ezequiel.

"Fine. How are you?" I asked him, my voice sounding unnaturally cheerful.

"Fine," he said. His did not.

"Good," I said. My voice was now bordering on hysteria.

"Good," he said. His was not.

Unable to find the words, we stopped looking for them and danced instead. But it was not I who was dancing with him. It was an empty shell. My mind had performed a magic trick. It had put both my heart and my body into a hat and made them vanish, whisking them away to a safe place where Ezequiel could not touch them. When the dance was over, my mind brought them back out of the hat.

"We hate you," they said in unison.

"You're welcome," said my mind.

November 4, 2000

I have had my answering machine switched off for over a week now. It's to avoid the horrible sight of the blinking red light, which makes the absence of *his* voice on it even more painful. I know that if I listen to any more messages from my mother, from the health insurance company, from an ex-lover who used to make me dread listening to my messages as much as *he* does, but whose messages now leave me completely indifferent, in other words, from anyone who is *not him*, I am sure I will slit my wrists. So to avoid the irreparable, I avoid my answering machine.

I thought this was clever. I thought that if I didn't turn on my answering machine, it would prove that I was not expecting him to call, and since I was not expecting him to call, he was bound to call, since the only things that ever happen are those you don't expect. But it hasn't worked.

To be fair, he did call once, before I switched off the machine, and left a message asking me to call him back. But I didn't because Monica made me swear not to. She said that if he wanted to speak to me so much, then he would call back. Apparently, he doesn't want to speak to me so much.

Why do I think he would call? I ask myself as I toss and turn at night. It's my last resort, that's why. I fantasize that he will overcome the barriers between us and use the phone as his sword. That he will thrash through the jungle of our unsaid feelings and storm the castle by declaring in no uncertain terms and over the telephone that he still loves me and that it was a mistake to break up. My brain knows that this is delusional. But my brain is not my strongest organ. I have another that is full of blood and it is bleeding and it won't stop.

November 6, 2000

Doesn't Diego know that you don't knock somebody when she's down?

I finally told him in no uncertain terms that while I felt very serious about our dance relationship, I did not see a romantic future for us. Result: he is punishing me by practicing with someone else on the side. In retrospect, I would have preferred he dump me completely. But he's smart, as I've said before. He knows that it's more humiliating to force me to compete with Another Woman.

The other woman's name is Cecilia. Or am *I* the other woman? Whoever is the other woman, I feel like a piece of shit. One that has been trodden on several times. And stamped on for good measure. I might have been able to put up with it if he didn't keep shoving her down my throat. It's really hard for me to ignore the fact that he is being "unfaithful" to me when he keeps talking about her, and comparing me to her. Unfavorably.

"Cecilia's steps are longer than yours," he says (long = good).

"Cecilia never rushes to the cross like that," he says (to rush = bad).

"Give me more resistance, the way Cecilia does," he says (Cecilia = good).

"Cecilia is learning fast," he says (I = bad).

I don't know where people get the idea that tango is "sublimated warfare." If you ask me, there is nothing sublimated about it.

We have two weeks to go before the exhibition. The veiled and not-so-veiled threats are becoming more frequent and less bearable. I try to disguise how much they hurt me. I smile meekly and try to fix whatever it is he doesn't like about my dancing. I bite my lip and think Zen. I tell myself not to take his criticism to heart. After all, this is his way of getting back at me. I also try to be understanding of his performance anxiety. But I am finding it difficult. We had gotten 90 percent of the way through the choreography when he decided he no longer wanted to dance to Pugliese, but to Di Sarli. So we started everything again from scratch. But three sessions into Di Sarli and he decided that he didn't want to dance to him either. Now he wants to do a piece by Pedro Laurenz. I am trying to be patient. Unfortunately, patience is not a virtue I possess in great quantities.

November 17, 2000

My lip was going to bleed if I bit on it any harder, and you know how difficult it is to stop a bleeding lip. There was no avoiding it: we had to have "The Talk." There is nothing I dread more than having "The Talk." In my experience, having "The Talk" = getting "The Sack." As a result, one usually postpones having "The Talk" for as long as possible. And when one cannot postpone it any longer, it is too late. In this case, I should have postponed it a few more days. Until after the exhibition. I knew that now was not the time to rock the boat. But I don't always do what I know.

After Niño Bien, I gave him the old "it's either her or me" speech. (Will I ever learn? I didn't think so.) His answer, predictably, was: "I can't decide." I knew a happy ending was no longer in the cards. I just needed to hang in there until after the exhibition. That was the plan. This is what happened.

On Monday, he came around to practice. He was being even more of a jerk than usual, picking on me at every opportunity: "Loosen your grip on my arm, will you?" Then two minutes later: "I can't feel your grip, woman. Firmer!" I was going mad. Finally, I did go mad. I knew that it was irreparable the moment it came out of my mouth: "Don't worry, dear, just five more days and you'll never have to practice with me again."

He froze. Then very quietly he said: "In that case, I'm not sure I want to do the exhibition."

How professional, I thought. "Look," I said, "you've got to tell me now: do you or don't you? If you don't, it's okay. I'll find someone who does." (Take that!)

"I don't, then," he said.

Shit. Fuck. And every other four-letter word I know in English, Spanish, French, and Greek.

Fives minutes later, he was walking out of my apartment and I was doing nothing to stop him.

November 21, 2000

It happened the night of the day that Diego walked out of my apartment. Without any notice, I started to throw up. I didn't make it to the toilet on time. (And when I say "toilet," I mean "toilet." That night, it was definitely not a "loo," a "lavatory," or a "WC." And the room it was located in was neither "rest room," "powder room," nor "ladies' room.") After being caught out the first time around, I knew not to take my head out of the bowl. It was a good thing I didn't, because I puked another five times. But I was not done. No, sirree! I then proceeded to empty my already empty bowels, while simultaneously sweating I don't know how many bucketloads of cold sweat. They say that the body is made up of 70 percent water. I think I evacuated at least 75 percent of my body that night: all the liquid it contained and then some. That was before my head froze, crashed, and then shut down, like a computer. Finally, it exploded.

Luckily, I had managed to crawl back into bed before it happened. Now I was paralyzed. From head to toe. I couldn't get to the phone for help. I couldn't blink. I thought I would die without being able to tell anyone about it. Funnily enough, I was not sad. By now, I saw death as a release. As I lay in bed like a vegetable, I waited for it to come. For three days and three nights. Every now and then, the phone would ring. And the doorbell went a couple of times. But I didn't have the strength to cry out. I just lay there. Waiting. But it did not come.

Instead, the spell was lifted as if by the wave of a magic wand, early this morning. Suddenly, I could move again. Now, I'm almost back to normal, though feeling a bit on the dehydrated side. The exhibition is tomorrow and I don't have a partner.

P.S. The good news is that I have lost at least ten pounds. (Though you'd have thought that 75 percent of my body would weigh more than that.)

P.P.S. Do you think it's possible that somebody was sticking needles into a doll with *my* name on it?

November 21 (technically 22), 2000

It's four in the morning and I'm back from Tasso, where I went in search of a partner for tomorrow's performance. Inspiration struck at one o'clock: el Gato, I thought. I know, I know . . . I swore never to dance with him again, but dire straits call for . . . el Gato.

I got out of my pajamas and took my first shower in three days. I'd forgotten how nice it was not to smell of vomit. Next, I did my best to cover up the gauntness with lots of makeup and a bright blue dress. Black was out since I wanted to avoid looking like the ghost of a widow if possible. I checked in the mirror before leaving: I looked the picture of health, convincing me that I had made a complete recovery. Until I made my way toward the elevator and my shaky legs told me otherwise. Had walking always been this difficult? It's only when you've stopped using them for a while that you realize how hard your legs work to take you places. And I hadn't even changed into my heels yet. I got inside the elevator and pressed Lobby. The sudden drop made me wish I hadn't. It's a good thing I didn't have anything in my stomach to throw up. "Mind over matter," I repeated to myself as I walked out of the building, smiled weakly at Salvatore, who offered to wave me down a cab— so I couldn't have looked *that* healthy. But I simply had to get to Tasso. I had some important business to attend to.

"My Gatito, how I've missed you!" I purred as I batted the lashes on which I had put far more mascara than usual to cover up the last days' damage.

"Where have you been all this time?" he asked me.

"I've been sick. In fact, I've never been so sick," I said, pouting. I had put on my most "luscious red-number-five" lipstick, which I normally reserve for shows.

"You look okay to me," he said. Perhaps I shouldn't have worn quite so much makeup. I wasn't getting the sympathy I counted on.

"Listen, darling, I have some great news. I would have told you before, but I was so sick [there was no harm in stressing the point]. You know Natalia Carbajal? Well, she's asked me to dance at Viejo Correo. And I immediately thought of you. In fact, I even told her: 'I will *only* dance if el Gato dances with me." And she said: "You could get el Gato? Really?!" He chuckled. "My Gatito will dance, won't he?" I hoped I didn't sound too desperate.

"When?" he asked.

Now we were getting to the tricky part: "Tomorrow. At four?" I hoped I didn't sound too tentative.

"Tomorrow? At four in the afternoon?!" As if to say, "You must be joking."

"I know it's last minute, darling." I was at a loss to find an argument.

Until inspiration struck a second time.

"The press will be there," I said. I prayed that the press would be there.

"The press, you said?" The fish was taking the bait!

"Absolutely. And even Solo Tango," I said, getting carried away with myself.

"I'll be there," he said.

"*Barbaro!* Fantastic!" I cried. I hoped I didn't sound too relieved.

My mission now accomplished, all I wanted was to go home and lie down. I'd forgotten how dizzy it made one being vertical.

November 22, 2000

I was lucky: the press was there. Let me rephrase that. I was *un*lucky: the press was there. It was there to record the lowest point of my career for all posterity. (I hope very much it was the lowest point.)

My stomach was tied in a million knots. I hadn't recovered from the Diego debacle, the ensuing nervous breakdown, and the need to run around looking for a partner at two in the morning the night before an exhibition. When my stomach is in knots, it turns into a gas chamber. You try dancing tango while trying not to fart at the same time. It can't be done.

Monica had promised that she would help me with my hair. She showed up at 3:55. In every film I've ever seen about show business, everything is always in chaos and everybody panics until the last minute, but by some miracle, things turn out all right in the end.

Unfortunately, this was not a film.

"Forget about it, Monica, we don't have the time to do anything fancy. Just help me put it in a simple bun, will you?" I pleaded with her.

"Don't be silly. These things never start exactly on the dot," she said as she poured water all over my head. That's when I heard Natalia Carbajal announcing, "El Gato with La Griega," followed by loud applause.

"Christ!" I shouted (in English) as I ran out of the ladies' room and into the limelight. The water from my hair, which was half in a bun and half wild, was trickling down my forehead and into my eyes, making my mascara dribble down my cheeks.

As I said earlier, luckily, or unluckily, the press was there to take lots of pictures. And as for the million knots in my stomach, they are still there and I doubt they will ever come undone.

December 10, 2000

It's been a year to the day since Fernando de la Rúa was elected president. I remember the cheering as if it were yesterday. Today, the cheering has died down and given way to quite a different sound.

It's the same every Wednesday afternoon. Loud, very loud, the rhythmic drums of protest and the shouting voices of *"bronca"* that fill my street. The demonstrations start like clockwork, at one P.M.—the only thing that ever starts on time in this country—and turn my apartment into an amplifying box of the country's discontent.

They say that these are anti-unemployment rallies. Funny how when Menem was still in power (and unemployment had already peaked at 18 percent) my Wednesdays were no more noisy than any other day of the week. Do you think it might have something to do with the fact that the trade unions that organize these protests are aligned with the Peronist Party (Menem's party)? It's a rhetorical question: these demonstrations started as soon as the new president was elected to power, so that it became apparent right from the start that he was not going to be allowed to govern.

Beyond what this act of sabotage is doing to Argentina, I am concerned about what it is doing to me. It's driving me crazy. How am I supposed to relax with all that screaming and shouting going on out there? And if I'm not relaxed, how am I supposed to withstand the torture, otherwise known as my stretching routine? I had hoped that the demonstrations would let up after a while. But it's looking unlikely that they will. And I'm going to have to go elsewhere on Wednesdays to inflict pain on myself in peace and quiet.

December 15, 2000

Valeria and Ezequiel have left. They've gone to try their luck in Amsterdam. It was Diego who told me at Niño Bien last night. I refrained from killing the bearer of bad news. But not from smacking him. Really hard. That certainly wiped the grin off his face. Better still, he couldn't hit me back in front of so many people. My hand is still stinging. God, it feels good!

Of course, it would have felt better if Valeria had been around for me to slap too. Actually, it's a good thing she left the country before I got a chance to wring her neck, in addition to slapping her. Because I've heard that Argentine prisons are not the most comfortable. To think I once considered her my best friend. Just goes to show that tango and friendship don't mix any better than tango and love.

I suppose it's a good thing she is out of my life. With her gone, so is my envy. At least, I hope so. Because if my relationship with Valeria has taught me anything, it's that black magic is more harmful to one's own health than it is to the health of the person one is trying to harm.

December 31, 2000

So to make a long story short:

1. El Chino: OUT
   I wish there was a way of finding out where they sent him. I've never been to see anyone in jail before. Maybe they'd let us practice together during visiting hours?
2. Pancho: OUT
   I wonder if I didn't misjudge him. That night down by the river, he wasn't nearly the *flan* I had him pegged as—if I guessed correctly whose hands were whose. But it's too late now: he's taken.
3. Jorge: OUT
   He is in Bologna, from what I've heard. Apparently, he is

teaching with a partner he met over there. I hope he is no longer a practicing Taoist—for his sake as well as hers.

4. Javier: OUT

Though strictly speaking, he was never IN. I do hope, however, that Romina never found out how close I came to having sex with her boyfriend while her father lay dying in a hospital in Cordoba.

5. El Gato: OUT

But at the end of the day, this ex-wrestler, drug-dealer, perpetually drunk and stoned Incredible Hulk lookalike was more reliable than all my other partners put together.

6. Diego: OUT

I do feel bad about the slap, though. It's not his fault he has a crooked dick.

7. Ezequiel: OUT

I know it's "for the best," as everybody keeps on saying. But I don't want what's for the best. I want my half orange back. I'll even iron his socks, if that's what it takes.

8. Pablo de las Pampas: OUT

I was going to eliminate him because of his awful mustache, but he beat me to it for being too old.

9. My Ideal Partner: OUT

Or he will be if he doesn't appear in 2001. Either he shows up in the next twelve months or I'm going back to advertising. That's my New Year's resolution.

Colgada

1. Tango move in which the follower is thrown off
her axis, so that she is left hanging in the air and
on to the leader for dear life.

2. A girl who has been left hanging, i.e., "stood up"—
for instance, by her tango partner.

3. A slow-coach; someone who forgets things
all the time. More often used in the masculine:
colgado.

January 16, 2001

After two weeks of eating dog food from a can—that's what it felt like—Ariel, my composer friend, came to the rescue.

"Make a video! How many times do I have to tell you?" he shouted. (He always shouts—even when he's not angry.) "You need a portfolio! Show it around! Get yourself some gigs lined up! Forget about Prince Charming! He's not coming! Nobody's going to sweep you off your feet! Haven't you learned anything by now?! It's up to you! You have to make it happen! Do I have to remind you what lazy bastards those tango dancers are?!" (No.) "You've got to bring them the work on a silver platter! You've got to *pay* them! Forget about romance! Be professional about it, for Christ sake! Stop moping! Get your ass to work!"

It was just the kick up the aforementioned ass I needed. Anyway, it was time I got up: the bedsores were starting to become a problem.

The first thing I did was write up a shortlist of possible partners. To make my dream team, the candidate had to be (1) a top dancer, (2) neither too young nor too old, (3) as attractive as possible, (4) not in prison, and (5) still talking to me.

The last criterion severely curtailed my initially long list, turning it into a shortlist in the literal sense. I was down to three names: Claudio, at the top (in spite of being a borderline case since I didn't know where we stood on number five), Julio "Blind as a Bat" Vargas as second choice, and Pablo, the Man from the Pampas himself, as a last resort and only if I was really, really desperate. (And only if he agreed to shave off the mustache.)

Time to make those phone calls.

The telephone had turned into Godzilla. How do telemarketing people do it? I suppose they don't have much choice since cold-calling *is* part of their job description. But there must be some mistake here: When I signed up to dance the tango, there was no mention whatsoever of cold-calling in the contract. It was in the small print? Damn! I didn't see it. At the mere thought of picking up the phone, I felt a huge lump of grizzly fat get stuck in my throat. The idea that I am offering guys money to dance with me is a hard one to swallow. It certainly does take the romance out of it. In spite of what Ariel says, it wasn't supposed to happen this way. I was supposed to be swept off my feet by a Knight of Tango on his White Horse who, if anything, should have been the one paying for the pleasure of dancing with *me*. Or at a stretch, who didn't mind terribly dancing with me for free. Finally, after almost choking on it, I swallowed the lump of fat and dialed Claudio's number.

It was ringing. He picked up. Oh shit.

"*Tanto tiempo!* It's been such a long time!" I cried, trying to sound as chipper as possible. But he could smell the fear, all right. We hadn't spoken since that unfortunate incident, when I hadn't heard the doorbell ring because I had been in the shower. I hoped he had forgiven, if not forgotten. I stalled as I tried to ascertain whether he liked me or hated me, by chatting about this, that, and the other. I couldn't tell. Finally, it was time to take the plunge. I asked him in a shaky voice whether he was available for a project. I wanted to produce a video (nervous cough) and it would involve dancing with me (loud rattling cough ending in clearing of throat) and he would be paid (near death resulting from choking) the sum of $500. Now that I had gotten the painful bit out of the way, the rest was a piece of cake. I was about to get into the logistics: it would involve thirty hours of—but before I could finish my pitch, Claudio jumped in:

"Look, love, I'm sorry, but we're swamped at the moment. Maria and I are off to Japan in a month and we have a really heavy rehearsal schedule. And what with the classes and—when are you going to invite me over for some *mate?*" he said. It was a no. Bastard.

"You see, it wasn't *so* terrible," I lied to myself. I decided to get all the pain out of the way in one fell swoop. I was on a rejection roll, so I might as well continue. I also knew that if I sat idle, I would reach for a bottle of pills and empty it down my throat. So I called number two on my hit list: Julio Vargas. Now there's a name nobody would ever have foreseen anywhere near it. All I can say is *thank God* I kept my big mouth shut that night we went to Almagro with his brother, José. Because Julio, though still blind as two bats, has become simply outstanding. Thanks to his looks, he has made the most remarkable progress in record time, since it is as true for boys as it is for girls that the better-looking ones dance more than the less attractive ones and therefore progress more quickly. (See Darwin and his theory of evolution.) Julio has become so good that it is *he* who ignores *me* now at the *milonga.* (Surely, *that* is not progress.) I dialed his number and he picked up. I started the spiel again. I was on automatic pilot, racing through my lines to get his "I'm sorry, I'm busy" bit out of the way as quickly as possible.

"Yes! I'll do it. When do you want to meet to go over the details?" he said before I fell off my chair.

January 25, 2001

Every day, Julio and I meet at La Glorieta to practice. We arrive with my boom box, place it in the middle of the bandstand, and put on *"Desde el Alma"* by Pugliese. Pugliese again . . . He has a *magical* effect: stray dogs, homeless people, tai chiers, and skateboarders all run away immediately and leave us with the whole place to ourselves.

It has been unbelievably hot and sticky these last few days, reminding me of the heat wave that very first time I came here on holiday to see Heleni and Jacques. When I think back to those early days, I feel a slight pain in the left side of my chest. It is like remembering the first blush of love when you have been married for twenty years. It hurts to remember what your dreams and aspirations once were—before you found out that you would have to *pay* people to dance with you . . .

The irony is that even though I'm the one paying him, Julio acts like he's the boss. And for some reason, I let him get away with it. He's gotten quite a reputation for being "difficult"—which is a euphemism. He is more volatile than a diva and flies off the handle at the smallest provocation. Often, none is needed. I swallow the recriminations—since it's always my fault, it goes without saying—with the same revulsion as one swallows a vile-tasting medicine that the doctor insists will make you better. I tell myself not to take his tantrums personally, since I know that deep down, when he blows his top, it's because, really, he's angry with himself. In spite of the emotional cost of working with a tyrant, I prefer it a million times to working with any of the lazy bastards I've had to put up with so far. But even though I tell myself not to take the little "episodes" personally, I can't help it.

"For Christ's sake, control your hips!" he lashes out when he has kicked me in the shin because he can't see where it is located.

"You're not trying!" he shouts when I'm giving it my all.

"Who's boss here, you or me?!" The answer is pretty obvious. But now is not the time to set him straight.

"We *both* are," I say to humor him.

Why do I put up with it? Why all this treading on eggshells? Because when it's good, it's *very, very, very* good. And I was going easy on the *"verys"* to save ink. Normally men tire quickly. They don't have the stamina. But he's different. I often feel exhausted (not to say extremely sweaty) at the end of our practice sessions. My cravings have been sated and for once I don't go home humming "I can't get no satisfaction," by the Rolling Stones. Which is why I put up with the diva, no matter how *very, very, very* temperamental he is—and I was going easy on the *"verys."*

So when he announced to me today that he had just dumped his partner, my heart started to pound with such eagerness that I was in danger of going into cardiac arrest.

"What happened?" I asked with fake concern in my voice.

"There are things I can do with you that I can't with her." If ever I felt triumphant, now was the time. I held my breath. Any minute now, he was going to "propose."

"That's why I've decided to dance with Veronica." My heart stopped.

"That makes sense, Julio. It makes complete sense . . . ," was all I could find to say.

What else *could* I say? She *is* his girlfriend, after all.

January 30, 2001

It's a damn good thing I'm paying him. Because if he weren't in dire need of the little green bills, Julio would be impossible to work with. It's the only reason I have any power at all in the relationship. I think I'm going to pay all my partners from now on. Things got particularly tense when Veronica, his model girlfriend (as in "fashion," not as in "well-behaved") put him in the doghouse over some misdemeanor he'd allegedly committed. He wouldn't tell me what it was, but I take it that it must have been naughty since she was refusing to return his calls.

On Day 1, he was all swagger and smiles. On Day 2, he was still swagger but no smiles. On Day 3, he was a complete wreck. And as a result, I was in grave danger of becoming a bruised wreck, given that he always takes everything out on me. If they didn't patch things up quickly, I could wave bye-bye to the video. We had a week to go and were in the middle of choreographing *"La Pavadita,"* the most demanding piece of the three. We were supposed to be doing lifts, but it's impossible to practice lifts with someone who can't lift you because he is falling apart. He dropped me three times yesterday and then blamed me for it. I'm lucky I didn't twist an ankle or break a leg. I'd had enough. The time had come to take action.

"*Che*, Vero, I'm calling about Julio," I said.

"What about him?" she asked. Why was she being curt with *me?*

"He's very upset, you know," I said.

"*He's* upset!" she snorted. This was an indirect invitation to probe, which I ignored. Frankly, if there is one thing I dislike more than my own domestic disputes (in the days when I used to have a boyfriend to dispute with—it's so long ago that I can barely remember, but that's another story) it is other people's domestic disputes. I find them depressing. And anyway, I didn't have the time to hear her side of the story—I had a video to save.

"Vero, I know how . . . difficult Julio can be at times. Trust me. But I'm sure he's really, really sorry. Why don't you give him the chance to make it up to you? I can tell that he'd do anything to get you back," I said without (a) the slightest idea if this was true or (b) what exactly it was he had done. But it was immaterial. The point was for him to stop collapsing under me every time he tried to lift me. I know I always go on about being fat, but 105 pounds isn't all *that* heavy, is it?

"Let him stew," she said, and she meant it. Here is a woman who knows how to treat men, I thought. I must ask her to give me private lessons.

"I agree with you, in theory. But in practice, I have to shoot the video next week," I said.

"What do you want *me* to do about it?" Oh dear. She was playing hardball.

"Please find it in your heart to forgive him. I'm sure he's paid the price already. I am begging you." If we had been in the same room, I would not have hesitated to get down on my knees and kiss her feet.

"Is he *very* sorry?" she asked me, fishing. This was more encouraging.

"*Very, very* sorry," I said most earnestly. I could hear her grinning on the other end of the line.

"Okay, I'll give the bastard a call," she sighed.

"Oh, thank you, thank you, Vero!" I cried, trying not to draw any conclusions from the term of endearment she had just used for her boyfriend. All I felt was relief that (a) the video was saved, and (b) I was not living in the daily hell otherwise known as a relationship.

Day 4. I am happy to report that the swagger is gone and the smile is back. The broadest smile you ever saw. Phew.

February 12, 2001

I have just come out of the editing room. The video is ready and it's exactly what I dreamed it would be. No, it's not. It's *better*! I never imagined that reality could live up to, or even *surpass*, expectations. I keep playing it over and over. I can't take my eyes off the screen. In disbelief I watch that woman dancing with the handsome young man. Did they use a distorting lens without telling me—one that makes me look thin? I can't believe that *she* is *me*! To what, I wonder, do I owe the miraculous transformation from ugly duckling into swan? Have the hours of daily torture otherwise known as my stretching routine finally paid off? It certainly looks like it! I do look longer. In fact, it reminds me of those funny mirrors they have at funfairs that play with you as if you were a piece of bubble gum. And I am now in front of the one that pulls you out of somebody's mouth and stretches you into a long piece of string.

I analyzed the images of myself on the screen from every possible angle in order to assess whether the change I noted was real, or whether it was the make up and lighting people who had done a fantastic job. Or had I always looked like this but not realized it? Perhaps I had never been such an ugly duckling after all? It was difficult to tell.

But more than my physical appearance, I liked the air of confidence that this woman—she was definitely not a girl—exuded, her stage presence, or *angel*, as they say in Spanish.

"You look great," said Julio, who was watching the final cut with me. That was the biggest compliment I will ever get from him.

"So do you, Julio," I said.

God it was frustrating. The video confirmed what I have known all along. We look great *together*. A real match. But if he can't SEE it, there is nothing I can do about it. Apart from putting on a smile and handing him a copy of the video so that perhaps one day he might see the light.

Okay. I have the video. Now what?

February 14, 2001

Whether you're a beautiful swan or an ugly duckling makes absolutely no difference when nobody loves you.

It's the X year in a row that I have been punished with empty mailboxes—both real and cyber. As for chocolates and roses and heart-shaped boxes, let's not go there. I'd rather keep it at X because if I try to remember when exactly the last time was I received a Valentine's card from someone other than my grandmother, I might do something stupid—or clever, depending on how you look at it. I'm sure that nine out of ten scientists would agree that suicide is the correct course of action under the circumstances since I would only be accelerating my journey down the same evolutionary path as the one I am already headed in: extinction. The chances that I will ever reproduce have become slim to the point of anorexia, judging by the contents of my mailbox. In Darwinian terms, I am an endangered species, a dying breed, a weak link in the chain. I'm sure that if I lived in the animal kingdom, I would have been sacrificed by now for the greater good of the flock. No doubt, the other swans would have pecked me to death for being nothing but a liability, a waste of precious food and oxygen. Unless mistaking me for an ugly duckling, a hunter shot me first.

February 19, 2001

No matter how tired and depressed I am after a very long week, La Glorieta invariably works its magic on me. Though there has been the odd exception to the rule when, because of an important soccer match or because of some freak constellation of the stars, nobody worth dancing with shows up. But as I said, that is the exception. Usually, if I make the effort to drag myself there, I am rewarded. With the wave of a magic wand, the heels that I reserve for La Glorieta, which are no longer shoes but the remains of my most comfortable sling-back stilettos, once black suede but now white with dust, turn into glass slippers. My gray track pants and thick woolly sweaters turn into the most sparkling gown at the ball and the wreck that I am turns into a fairy-tale princess. I know that everything will be all right with the world if I pluck up the courage to hop onto the 64 bus, my very own pumpkin carriage, and take the forty-five-minute bus ride there.

I was starting to wonder whether last Sunday might not be one of the rare exceptions. I sat on the bandstand railing and surveyed the crowd. I couldn't see anything decent at all. I asked the girl sitting next to me if there was a big match going on today. She didn't know.

That's when I spotted Gustavo and heaved a sigh of relief. This was more like it! Something to get the adrenaline going: a conquest!

I remember being awestruck the first time I saw Gustavo do an exhibition, when I was still a beginner, back in New York. He had the dark, pointy features of a character out of the Bible and the jet black hair, which he wore gelled back and up in a ponytail. The drama of his looks was heightened by their contrast with those of his partner. You've never seen a more Swedish-looking Swede. He was night and she was day and together they made a big impression on me. Not to mention their dancing, which had all the ingredients I love: drama, humor, musicality, passion, irreverence—you name it, it had it. It was an exhibition I will always remember, fusing the unfuseable as it did.

Afterward, when the *milonga* had resumed and the floor had been invaded once more by a hundred or so couples, I remember watching him from afar, feeling humbled as he glided across the room with one more experienced follower after another. And I remember promising myself that one day I would dance with him. And here we were—I don't know how many years later. My opportunity had come at last.

I asked the girl who was still sitting on the railing next to me about him. All she knew was that he was fresh off the boat from Madrid, having split up with the partner he had been working with over there. Music to my ears.

But before he could be mine, I had to get him to dance with me—once would be enough. The question was, how? He was never going to know whether I was any good if I dangled on the railing forever. I had to show off the wares, so to speak. I was in the process of trying to solve the conundrum, desperately looking around for my least bad option (the showing was unusually dismal, as I mentioned), when lo and behold, I noticed from the corner of my eye that he was approaching. And then he stretched out his arm to help me off my perch! I was so shocked by the synchronicity—for once my wishes had not landed on deaf ears—that I almost broke a heel, my landing was so rough. I laughed nervously, to cover up that I felt like a klutz, while I prayed that I wouldn't mess up my one and only chance to impress him.

And then IT happened. The moment I have been waiting for since I moved to Buenos Aires. It was like electric shock treatment, in the pleasant sense of electric shock treatment. I was instantly revived and all tiredness was gone. Dancing with him was such a jolt to the system that I now had enough energy to climb not one but two Himalayas. And the more we danced, the more excited I got. Each tango confirmed it: I had found Him, the One I have been looking for! Together we would conquer the world! I had not a doubt in my mind, and La Glorieta had kept its promise once more.

"I saw the video. Nice work!" he said between two tangos. "Flattered" is an understatement. My ego was about to explode with pride. *That* was why he had asked me to dance.

"Thank you. Did Julio show it to you? I didn't know you two were buddies," I said.

"He showed it to the teaching staff at La Rosarina's, the other day," he said. Julio, at least, was not shy about it. I haven't shown it to anyone yet—other than friends. I'm dreading the question: "Is that your partner?" And having to answer, "Well, no, as a matter of fact, it's not. I don't have one. I was hoping you might lend me one." It's too humiliating. It's worse than going to a dating agency. I can hear them say: "Sorry, love, but we don't have any openings for single female tango dancers. We're looking for couples." Nope. I can't do it.

Then I was in Gustavo's arms, which made me forget for a second that I was the leper of tango.

"So what are your plans?" he asked me during a break.

"Do you mean in the immediate future or generally speaking?" I asked, tiptoeing around the question, not daring to interpret it in the way I hoped he meant it. I didn't want to let the idea through the door that my dream (you know, that stubborn one of me finding a partner, yeah, that one) might be on the verge of coming true for fear of the disappointment that would follow as inevitably as the moon does the sun.

"Generally speaking," he said. Gustavo meant business!

"Well, I was kind of looking for somebody to hmm . . . work with," I said, unable to look him in the face.

"How about you and I give it a shot?" he asked me.

"Oh. My. God!" I cried. "YES!"

"But I must warn you," he said.

(Oh no. What is it this time? Wife? Three kids?)

"I expect total commitment from my partners," he said.

If I had felt high when dancing with him, now I felt like a hydrogen balloon that had escaped into outer space and there was no bringing me back down to earth. Not now, not ever. Was I dreaming or had he just said the C word?

February 25, 2001

I entered Salon Canning and froze. What was *she* doing here? Valeria! Wasn't she supposed to be in Amsterdam? With *my* boyfriend? Speaking of which, where was the bastard? I scanned the room for Ezequiel but couldn't spot him. I didn't know whether to be afraid that he was here or afraid that he wasn't. My heart was beating so wildly I was convinced that Emiliano, with whom I was dancing the set, would think I had developed a sudden and overwhelming crush on him.

The only way to find out Ezequiel's whereabouts was from the horse's mouth. So I went up to the horse and gave her a big, phony hug. I asked her when she'd gotten back and how long she was in town for. That's when she told me that Ezequiel had stayed behind but that she wasn't going back. I was stunned, though I had been praying for this day all along. There hasn't been a single moment when in some dark recess of my mind I haven't fantasized about the day he would dump her, the way he dumped me. (Bastard!) Sometimes, I could see it so vividly that I would forget it was a figment of my imagination. Once I even caught myself in the act of rubbing my hands together as I gloated over their breakup. And now it was no longer just a figment of my imagination. My avenging angel had done his (or her?) job.

But before I could fully adjust to the reality that my dream had come true, before I could savor the sweet taste of revenge, Valeria served me a big, fat helping of the truth. And the truth, sadly, tasted less sweet than revenge. Apparently, he has met a girl. She's Dutch. But that's not the punch line. The punch line is that he has *married* her! My stomach will remember that punch line forever. I stood there, facing her, feeling winded and dazed. It was as if she had hit me on the head with a heavy iron skillet. I desperately wanted to faint, but I didn't think it would look right. I couldn't believe it: this moment that I had looked forward to for so long was being sabotaged. And now, instead of triumph, all I felt was pity. I don't know who I felt more sorry for: her or me. How could I be angry with her now? I couldn't hate her anymore. Bummer.

Hearing the news also made me realize something else. All this time, I have secretly fantasized—so secretly, in fact, that not even I was aware of it—that Ezequiel would come back to me one day when I least expected it. Instead I found out that he is married to someone else when I least expected it. And once again, reality has refused to play ball with my fantasies . . .

March 3, 2001

We are choreographing a piece called *"Corazón de Oro"* by Canaro.
We've got a couple of gigs lined up, and as soon as *we* have at least three
choreographies under *our* belt, *we*'ll be ready to go. *Our* ultimate goal is
to go over to the States and Europe sometime next year to give workshops. You'd think all these *we*s and *our*s would make me happy. It's
what I have been dreaming of, isn't it? So why, far from feeling elated,
do I feel queasy every time a *we* or an *our* comes out of Gustavo's
mouth?

Why is it that when I FINALLY land a guy who is willing to commit, he is so TERRIBLY flawed that his commitment feels like a hole in
the head? I hate to complain. But it's his organizational skills: he doesn't
have any. I think I have landed the World's Most Disorganized Person. I
mean it, literally. I've never met anyone more dysfunctional. It's mind-
boggling the amount of time we waste trying to locate the cassettes that
he has either lost or overdubbed by mistake. He owns a CD player, but
for a reason I have yet to fathom, he refuses to play CDs. And that's not
where the test to my patience ends.

It is only the beginning. Sometimes I show up at the studio that he
owns to be told that we can't use the salon because he has rented it out.
At others, I ring the doorbell once, twice, three times. Finally I hear a
groggy voice on the intercom: I've woken him up from a siesta. Which
means that we are now going to be forced to spend an hour in the
kitchen drinking *mate* to wake him up. I'm starting to think that *I* must
be the cuckoo one! There must be something wrong with *me* for being
so organized. I must learn to be less organized, I tell myself as I sip the
mate that he has handed to me. This is a test of my patience, I tell myself
as I listen to the deafening sound of my mental watch go tick, tick, tick,
marking the time that we are *not* dancing the tango.

Every tick is agony, and soon I am in the throws of a full-scale panic
attack. But I'm careful to hide the palpitations from him. On the outside
it looks as if I could happily go on drinking *mate* all afternoon. And

sometimes we do. And I come dangerously close to failing the test. At other times, God takes pity on me. The *yerba* loses its flavor, signaling the end of a *mate* drinking session, or he's found the cassette, or he's found us another room to practice in, or he's hung up after a half-hour phone call . . . anyway, FINALLY we are dancing and the agonizing test comes to an end. My (im)patience is rewarded and he takes me once more to that place where, if there are any watches ticking, I can't hear them.

March 13, 2001

As hard as I am trying to keep my relationship with Gustavo professional, he is trying harder not to. It's only normal, I guess. This *is* tango, and by definition T-A-N-G-O spells T-R-O-U-B-L-E.

I've said this before and I'll say it again: friction causes sparks and sparks can cause a fire, if you're not careful. I admit that it does take two pyromaniacs to start one. The thing is not to let the fire get out of hand. That's why you should always place a grid in front of it. Unfortunately, Gustavo keeps removing the grid to stoke the fire. He certainly likes to stoke it a lot. When he is done stoking, I make sure to place the grid back in its place, hoping to postpone for another day the transformation of the house into a heap of ashes. But no sooner have I put it back where it belongs than he removes it again, and back and forth it goes a hundred times during each practice session. This can get pretty tiring.

Gustavo, bless his soul, doesn't come on to me directly. His seduction is very subtle. Like when he "accidentally" takes off his T-shirt while attempting to remove his sweater, so that I may get a glimpse of his six-pack, which is nice, I must say. Or like when we dance. I can tell when a guy is dancing with me to dance versus a guy who is dancing with me to get it on with me. And Gustavo is not dancing with me to dance.

So why am I being such a stick in the mud? Why don't I just get it over with? After all, he's my age, attractive, smart, with a roof over his head, *and* an incredible dancer. What more could I want from life? I can't deny that there are times when the dancing is so good that I forget to put the grid back in its place immediately. But there is something holding me back from making a bonfire with him. I can't quite put my finger on it . . . something that tells me to wait until I get to know him better.

The question is, how do I buy the time I need? By pretending I don't understand his insinuations: "Stand here next to me, in front of the mirror . . . we make the perfect couple, don't you think?" By pretending I don't see the way he looks at me furtively, out of the corner of his eye. By pretending that I don't feel his not-completely-professional hands. By pretending I don't know that a covert war is being waged between us. I'm acting like a coward, I know. But the bottom line is that I'm afraid to lose him. I'm fast running out of candidates, and this could very well be my last shot. I don't want to waste it.

March 22, 2001

Five minutes after I gave my credit card details over the phone for the nonrefundable ticket to New York, Gustavo called me to inform me that we have been booked to do a gig at a restaurant. He had forgotten that I was leaving. Typical.

I didn't kick up a fuss. I didn't nag him or groan, "Oh, Gustavo . . ." I didn't dare. When you're down to your last candidate, you become a lot more accommodating. Trust me.

"If you think this is worth it, I'll change my ticket," I said. But as I said it, I was thinking: Please say it isn't, please say it isn't! It's not as if I have lots of money to be throwing out the window. But if I had to, I would. But I really hoped I wouldn't have to.

He must have heard what I was thinking because he assured me that it was no biggie. He'd speak to the organizers about postponing the gig until after I got back. I heaved a sigh of relief.

Gustavo may not have the best memory in the world, but he is going out of his way to make this partnership work. Nobody has ever done that before. You should be grateful. *That* is what counts. The rest is unimportant, I told myself, ecstatic that I had a real partner at last.

The next time I went to practice with Gustavo, he was not alone. He was dancing with another girl, Florencia. She and I have shared a number of partners. I think her feelings for me must be as mixed as mine for her.

"Stay away from any guy I dance with . . . ," she'd warned me once. "It's a sure sign he's a dud." It's nice to know that I am not the only one who is cursed. But what was she doing here with Gustavo? I was dumbfounded. It looked like they were practicing! I was confused. Wasn't he supposed to be *my* partner? I stood and watched for half an hour. Half an hour on *my* practice time. When they were done, Florencia and I kissed and exchanged pleasantries even though I was not feeling very pleasant inside.

"You said you couldn't make the gig, so I asked her to dance with me instead," Gustavo offered as an explanation after she had left.

"Oh, I see," I said.

"Is there anything wrong?" he asked me.

"No, no, nothing at all," I said, my performance not up to its usual Oscar-winning standards. I looked as miserable as I felt.

Since then—about a week ago—Gustavo has made sure that Florencia and I cross paths a number of times, to show us who is the rooster and who the hens.

Yesterday was the last straw. I wasn't going to be chicken for a second longer. "Gustavo, I don't think this is going to work out," I said. "I'm sorry." I was, truly. After all, as I am only too acutely aware, there are far fewer men on the market than women. And I have danced with nearly all of them. Furthermore, I am easily replaceable, as he has spent the week demonstrating to me.

I did not foresee the positive result that my outburst would yield.

"I've been bad. I promise I'll change. It'll be different from now on. You'll see. Believe me." He looked so sincere. How could I not give him a second chance?

(Note to self: say no to men on a more regular basis.)

March 30, 2001

I'm in New York, where I've been catching up with friends and family. I even saw Frank, which was awkward but good for both of us, I think. He's not dancing with Isabel anymore, but with some other equally tall and stunning girl. Good for him. I did get a kick out of showing him my video, though. I could tell he was impressed. I don't think he expected me to get this good.

"You've put a lot of work into it," he said. I think it was meant to be a compliment. But one can never be too sure.

The biggest compliment, though, and the one that means the most to me came from my father, who is also here. When I showed it to him, he didn't say anything at first. He sat in his armchair in stunned silence, doing an imitation of the Buddha. I didn't want to ask him "What do you think?" because it was abundantly clear to me that he didn't think very much at all.

Over the years, I have become immune to his special brand of non-demonstrativeness. More precisely, I have learned to shut down my system before the pain shoots to my heart. But life has a funny way of giving you things once you stop caring whether you get them or not. I suppose that is the meaning of a gift, since the things you need, you go out and get for yourself. A gift, on the other hand, is not something you need, but if it is offered, you accept it with joy.

"I'm so proud of you!" were the words that finally came out of the Buddha's mouth. I never thought I would hear him say this. It was a gift far greater than any material one he has ever given me.

"So it wasn't a complete waste of money, then?" I asked, fishing for more compliments. The only problem with them is that the more you get, the more you want.

"No, it wasn't a complete waste of money," he conceded. "It was a better investment than I thought," he said.

"That's made my trip, Daddy!" I said as I gave him a huge hug.

April 12, 2001

I was barely off the plane from New York when Gustavo told me about
an audition for *Forever Tango*. I know we're not ready for what is probably the biggest and most competitive show in the world. We haven't
been together long enough and we don't yet have a finished choreography under our belt. But it's too good an opportunity to pass up.

"Absolutely! Let's do it!" I said excitedly.

First, I need audition practice. And second, it's important to show
your peers that you're in the ring. So we're practicing madly, putting the
finishing touches to *"Corazón de Oro."* Since my talk with him before the
trip, Gustavo has been making a concerted effort to be more professional
and waste less time. He's being surprisingly good.

God, I've gained weight, though, with all those fudge brownies in
New York, and I don't know how the hell I'm going to fit into my dress.
I'm thinking sequins.

P.S.—I forgot to mention that the gig he was supposed to do with
Florencia never happened. Good—but I wonder why not?

April 20, 2001

I arrived at the audition early to avoid the crowds and to secure us a decent place in line. Which was a good thing because it soon turned into a
python, weaving its way up two flights of stairs, into a dance studio, and
out of it again before making its way toward the closed doors of the audition room. By the time Gustavo arrived, half of Buenos Aires was
there to try its luck. Everyone was stretching and air-kissing, stretching
and air-kissing, stretching . . . It's such a fake environment. Everyone is
sick to their stomachs with fear and willing to annihilate each other for
the chance to dance with the biggest tango show in the world, and yet
they go around pretending that this is a cocktail party and aren't we all
having a fabulous time?

Gustavo tried to disguise the fact that he was nervous. But he was
green—not cool-as-a-cucumber green, more like a shade of I'm-going-

to-puke green. It felt like our turn would never come. This was worse than being stuck in a traffic jam. To kill time, I asked Monica, still my official coiffeuse (I have forgiven her for the fiasco at Viejo Correo), to do my hair. We set up shop in the middle of the staircase. She combed, gelled, tugged, and pulled at my hair as dancers squeezed past us on their way up (the Hopefuls) and on their way back down (the Dejected). I was finally ready, every hair sprayed into place a hundred times, lips blood crimson, and lashes thick with tear-proof mascara.

That's when Gustavo chose to tell me, "I've rented out the studio to a couple. I thought we would have finished by now. There's no one else to let them in. I have to go. But don't worry. I'll be back by the time you get to the front of the line. Ciao!" And he was gone. I hadn't even had the time to blink. I couldn't have anyway, the mascara was so thick. I was now blankly staring at where he had been standing only moments ago. Then a voice announced: "We will be recessing for lunch. Will all remaining dancers please come to the front desk to pick up a number for this afternoon's session?" Was this the voice of an angel?

I went back home and called Gustavo to tell him about our stroke of luck. I did not bring up the little detail of his desertion. This was not the time. I'd wait until after the audition was over. For now, I needed to remain focused. I told him that we had been called back for four o'clock. We agreed to meet on the staircase.

I arrived at four, lipstick, hairspray, and mascara freshly reapplied, and waited. And waited. Of course, I had known from the start. I asked myself from when exactly? Had it been from the moment of his disappearance or had it been before? From this morning, when I saw the look of terror on his face, or before then even? From the moment he had told me about the audition and I had sensed his ambivalence about the whole thing? No, I had known from way before then, from the first time I went to his place to practice and we spent half an hour trying to find one of his homemade cassettes. That's when I should have run out of the place screaming, I realized in retrospect. No use in crying over spilled milk now. And to continue with another proverb, I had made my bed and was going to have to lie in it.

I decided to play this grotesque comedy of errors out till the bitter end. It's not that I held out any hope, for in this case, it had died a quick and painless death. But I wanted the satisfaction of seeing how the story ended. So I waited patiently in line, which mysteriously seemed to be growing at the head. I tried to hide my humiliation at having been stood up by my partner by making light of it with my friends in the line—both the real and the fake ones. Among them was Florencia. She was not at all surprised that Gustavo had pulled a disappearing act on me.

"Did you hear about my gig with him?" she asked me.

"Only that it didn't happen," I said.

"It turns out that he got the dates mixed up. There was this huge fight with the owners when we got there. Finally, they said they'd *try* to fit us in. I wasn't going to take this unprofessional shit. So I left. But listen to this: he danced anyway! With some girl he picked up on the spot! Can you imagine?" she asked me. Unfortunately, I could.

We laughed at our shared misfortune as we inched closer to the audition room, which had become our Holy Grail.

I was within a yard or so of it when again, the voice of the same angel as before made another announcement: "We only have time for three more auditions tonight. Those who have not auditioned may come back on Monday. The last three numbers to dance tonight are. . . ." Mine was one of them. I had a split second to make a decision. I decided: "Fuck him! I'll audition alone on Monday." I tossed my number to Florencia, who was desperate to get the audition over and done with. So for the second time in one day, I left the building, muttering: "I *will* be back!"

April 21, 2001

Gustavo had called while I was still waiting in line and had left a message on my machine. He sounded sheepish. I finally got around to calling him back today.

"I fell asleep," was his alibi. And then came the best bit: "What's my punishment going to be?"

That's when I understood what type of guy he is. He belongs to that category of little boys who get their kicks from being spanked. Being naughty is the only way they know to get a woman's attention. You do have to feel sorry for these perverts. But I don't have what it takes to prop him on my lap and take out the cane. I won't do it. Even if it does mean losing him.

I was unable to react to something so pathetic, so instead I informed him of my decision to audition alone.

"Won't you give me another chance?" he asked.

I started to giggle nervously before exploding into a fit of uncontrollable laughter.

"I take that as a no," he said.

April 23, 2001

I finally stepped inside the audition room. I couldn't believe the moment had come. The Holy Grail was mine! But I shouldn't have been so thrilled. I was met by a stone-faced jury, reminding me of the one I'd faced at that ballet exam when I was five. The day I had the flu and a 104-degree temperature. The day I couldn't remember any of the steps, my head throbbing so badly as I tried unsuccessfully to spy on my neighbor's footwork. The day I failed. The day I can't forget. And here I was again, as unprepared as I was then, back for more punishment.

"Why do I keep doing this to myself?" I wondered out loud.

"Are you presenting yourself alone?" one of the jury members asked me, adding salt to the wound.

"Yes. Alone." I don't think there has ever been a stiffer upper lip in the history of stiff upper lips.

The assistant they gave me to dance with was useless. He did nothing to make me look good. All I could do to control the damage was to look passionate. After I had looked passionate for three minutes, the jury said a most dispassionate thank you and I thanked them equally dispassionately upon leaving the room. Of course, I had known from the start that this was not going to be my passport to Broadway. But rejection hurts, even when you're expecting it.

"Why do I keep doing this to myself?" I asked myself once more.

There was nobody else around, so I had to answer.

"Because there is virtue in showing up, that's why," I said.

"Good answer," I said.

"Thank you!" I said.

As I made my way back down the stairs and onto the street, who should I bump into but Gustavo, who was entering the building at that moment. And by his side was a girl I've seen at the *milonga* but whose name I do not know. Given what she was wearing, it was apparent that she wasn't out on a casual stroll with him. He was going to audition with her! Suddenly the idea of spanking him didn't seem so revolting.

When he saw me, he pretended to be embarrassed. But it was obviously fake, since he had gone out of his way to create the situation with the express intention of provoking me. In retaliation, I made sure to look as unflustered as possible, and with a smile that I normally reserve for family weddings and births, I said: "Break a leg!" I meant it literally.

April 27, 2001

Today I received a bouquet of a dozen red roses with the words "Forgive me." I would have returned them to sender if it weren't such a drag. Instead, I gave them to the wife of my building's super. She loved them.

May 1, 2001

Normally, he is on my mind the second I wake up. It's a nervous twitch of the brain. An automatic reflex I can't control, like a weak bladder. I'm awake = Ezequiel. But this morning was different.

As usual, the first thing I did when I got out of bed was to feel my way into the kitchen with my eyes still shut tight, fumble around for a filter in the cupboard, scoop three tablespoons of coffee, getting half of it in the filter and the other half on the counter, fill the coffeemaker with water (with great difficulty), and switch it on. What was not usual about this morning was that Ezequiel hadn't crossed my mind in all the time it had taken me to execute this task. I had a pee: nothing. I checked my e-mail as I drank my three cups of coffee: still nothing. I did my morning stretch: nada. I had some breakfast: nope. I took a shower: not even in the shower. It was only as I left my apartment and put the key in the keyhole to go to ballet that he finally popped into my mind: Ezequiel. Just the name—not the face.

Only then did it occur to me that I had been up for almost two hours and this was the first time I had thought of him all morning (afternoon, technically). And instead of being accompanied by the usual heaviness in the chest and nausea, today the thought of him had the same effect on me as hearing the results of a soccer match—i.e., none at all: it left me completely indifferent.

I never thought this day would come: I had resigned myself to a life sentence. But I have been let out early on parole! The sun is shining and the birds are singing (literally) and I am skipping along the sidewalks of Buenos Aires (literally). I can see the sky at last. I had forgotten how beautiful it was. I don't care if people call me *"loca"* (crazy). I'll skip as much as I want—and if I feel like it, I'll even throw in a hop or two!

I can't believe how *quickly* I got over him! I know they say that to get over a breakup, it usually takes about half the time you actually went out with the bastard. But that calculation has never applied to me. It normally takes me *at least* ten times the time. So imagine how thrilled I am that, in this instance, the ratio of time spent together/time crying over him is: 1½ months/*only* 7 months—which brings us to a ratio of *less than 5*! Isn't that great?!

May 4, 2001

"I have a suggestion," said Florencia over the telephone.

"I'm listening," I said.

"If we can't join them, let's beat them!" she said.

"Come again?" I said. What on earth was she talking about?

"I've been selected to dance at the festival next month at the Teatro San Martin," she said.

"That's great, Flo! Congratulations! That's a huge achievement!" I said. It really is.

And then, when I least expected it, she said: "Do you want to do it with me?"

Since I didn't respond immediately—I was too stunned—she continued:

"Look, you and I are in the same boat. And it's sinking fast. There simply aren't enough guys. Good ones, I mean," she said. (Tell me something I don't know.) "So what are we going to do about it? Not dance? Just because there are no guys to dance with?" She had a point.

It's not as if I hadn't thought of it myself. I regularly fantasize about dancing with a girl. Especially when guys don't show up at auditions when they were the ones who asked you to go in the first place. But there is a leap between fantasy and reality. And I wasn't sure if I was prepared to make it. It was too risky. How would male tango dancers react once they found out about it? I've seen men on more than one occasion separate two women dancing together at a *milonga*. They take it as an affront. "We'll have none of that in here," I've heard them say. So wouldn't dancing with Florencia kill any remaining chance of my ever finding a partner?

Who am I kidding? I said to myself. There aren't any remaining chances left to kill. Florencia is right. I have nothing lose. I might as well dance with someone—even if he's a she—rather than sit on my ass waiting for a miracle to happen.

"Sure, Flo! I'd love to!" I said.

"*Barbaro!* I'm so happy, *negra*! Let's show those bastards!" she cried.

"Fuck Gustavo!" I cried.

"That's the spirit, girl!" she cried. "Fuck 'em!"

Since then, we've been training intensively. The festival's in three weeks and it's going really well. What a nice change not to have to stroke a guy's ego all the time! What a relief to feel free to give and take constructive criticism, without worrying about the repercussions! What a novelty not to have to mince words, step on eggshells, or beat around bushes! How relaxing not to have to explain everything all the time and to understand what the other means with few or no words at all! How mature we are that we can bring any disagreements to the table for open discussion! How fun to take turns leading and following! It's so nice not to be a second-class citizen for once.

Actually, the experience is confirming my theory that lesbians have it easier. Think about it. The biggest joke God ever played on humanity was when he created men and women, who, as we all know after having read the book, come from different planets, and forced them to live on the same one, trapped in the inferno of desiring precisely that which makes them miserable: the opposite sex. That is what I call a sick sense of humor. What a relief it is to take a vacation from hell. Frankly, I don't ever want to go back there again.

May 12, 2001

We don't have a finished choreography yet, but we have two more weeks to go, which is plenty of time, so I'm not worried. However, some cracks are starting to show as the deadline approaches. I guess that's normal. You can't avoid a certain amount of tension. Florencia does not seem as ecstatic as she was at first with my dancing. Or with me. I'm afraid that familiarity doth breed contempt—on both sides. She keeps sighing loudly every time I do something "wrong." She hasn't pointed the finger at me directly, but she has hinted on a couple of occasions that it's my fault that the various sequences of front and back *sacadas* (displacements) are not going as smoothly as they ought. She has told me—she can be quite bossy at times—to step in closer to her and not lean on her right arm so much. Then yesterday, it was my turn to get short with her when yet another one of her *ganchos*—

they're always late—got me in the shin. I think the trouble is with her *enrosques* (the leader's winding motion that gives momentum to the *giro*), but she wouldn't listen to me when I tried to help her fix it, so I gave up trying and sulked instead. I don't normally complain about injury, but for some reason, yesterday I decided to milk it for all it was worth.

But this is still far, far better than practicing with a man.

May 23, 2001

Panic stations! We have ditched the music and scrapped the choreography—the one we were working on wasn't working. We are starting all over again to another piece and the performance is the day after tomorrow. Long gone are the days of peace and harmony. When we are not openly hostile, we take turns sulking. There are plenty of opportunities to be hostile or to sulk. For example, when one of us forgets a sequence or the other anticipates, thus messing up the timing. Or when one accidentally lets go of the grip during a jump and the other has a terrible landing. Fingers are pointed, egos undermined, attacks more vicious than between two alley cats. This feels strangely familiar. Where have I experienced this before? Oh, yes, now I remember: dancing with a man.

What, if anything, have I learned from all this? That the problem is not with the *opposite sex* and, therefore, it is not a solution to turn gay. The problem is with *other people*. Jean-Paul Sartre said it. *"L'enfer, c'est l'autre"*: other people = hell. I think he was talking about tango. In fact, I'm sure he was. Try as you might to escape it, tango is war. If you thought you could dance it with a friend, you were wrong, since, invariably, tango turns friends into enemies.

Moral of the story: one might as well dance with one's existing enemies rather than make new ones. At least one expects the opposite sex to act like swine, while it feels like betrayal by one's own sex. And whereas one loves to hate men, it's not nearly as much fun hating women.

But the real issue lies elsewhere: as convenient as it might have been, the sad truth is that one has no desire to sleep with the enemy when the enemy is a woman. And if one has no desire to sleep with the enemy . . . it's not tango, is it?

June 14, 2001

Last night, I went to see the legendary Alberto Castillo sing at Torquato Tasso: the old man is a lesson on how to enjoy life instead of being a pathetic crybaby all the time. At the grand old age of ninety-five, he is still going strong. I suspect it's got something to do with the fact that he is *pickled* in alcohol. Indeed, he is a puritan's nightmare: he has drunk more whiskey, done more drugs, slept with more women, gambled away more money, and smoked like more factory chimneys than anyone—and he is still here!

On my way in, Osvaldo, the doorman/homeless guy who once delivered me into the hands of the clever con artist/taxi driver gave me a peck on the cheek.

"Where have you been hiding? I missed you!" he said.

"I missed you too, *mi amor!*" I said, not wanting to talk about the depressing reason for my absence these past couple of weeks. (What's the point in going out anymore when there is no incentive in the shape of either male *or* female partners?)

"*Che!* I've been keeping something for you," he said.

He reached into his pocket and out came a ring. A purple plastic one: the kind that you fish out of a bowl in a convenience store.

"I found it on the street and I thought of you" he said, handing it to me.

I was so touched, I couldn't say anything. How did he know that purple was my favorite color?

"Every time I take a look inside and you are dancing with someone, I see an angel!" he said. The man is either a liar or needs glasses.

"If there's an angel, Osvi, it's you!" I cried, feeling much better all of a sudden. Whether he was a liar or needed glasses, it positively warmed my heart to hear him say so.

I put the ring on and it fit perfectly. I haven't taken it off yet, either. I will wear it every time I feel low to remind myself that I am not alone in the world. Actually, I am starting to suspect that I really *do* have a guardian angel who appears in various guises to pick me up every time I fall.

Last week, for example. I was waiting for a bus at the stop.

"Don't worry, you'll be fine, dear," said the stranger next to me, from out of the blue.

I didn't hear him at first, so engrossed was I in thought: Why did you say yes to Florencia? Idiot! You knew from the start that it was a bad idea. Of course you did! It's too late now, though. It was your last shot and you blew it. You only have yourself to blame . . .

It's not that the stranger was a mind reader. It was that I had been mumbling to myself while shaking my head and pointing at people who were not there.

"Sorry? Did you say something?" I asked, trying to sound like a normal human being—i.e., one who doesn't talk to herself in the middle of busy streets.

"I said to stop worrying, everything is going to be all right!"

The guy obviously had no idea what he was talking about. Nothing was ever going to be all right again. But nevertheless, I thought it was sweet of him. One of those Buenos Aires moments . . .

July 17, 2001

Why is it that the best things always happen at the worst times? When you are in the middle of making moussaka for twelve guests even though you don't know how to make moussaka but you feel you should know how since you are Greek—half of you, anyway. I am giving the dinner party in honor of Inés, Jacques's sister, to celebrate her engagement to a certain Juan Carlos, whom I am going to meet for the first time. All I know about him so far is that he owns an *estancia*—a farm, basically—and that they met at a polo match in Windsor. And now she's moving here. I'm so excited for her. And for me too. It'll be nice to have family here again—my cousin's husband's sister definitely counts as family!

Luckily, the preparation for the dinner party had started the day before, since the béchamel was giving me an exceptionally hard time. I had already poured my first dribbly attempt down the drain. It was my wrist: in anticipation of the disaster, it had started to shake uncontrollably, so that the entire contents of the milk carton spilled into the bowl of the flour-and-butter mixture, thus fulfilling the prophecy. All my hopes went down the drain along with the white sauce. But I picked myself up, and undaunted (okay, a bit daunted), I started from scratch. I congratulated myself for my foresight at the supermarket—I had bought double of everything, just in case. I was now at the crucial stage of separating the egg yolkes from the whites. I held my breath, as this required super-human concentration. It's a tricky business. I was almost home free and dry . . . when the phone rang, disturbing me from my deep meditation. Too late: the damage was done. The transparent mucus was floating happily inside the bowl. What good did my foresight at the supermarket do now? The telephone was ringing but I was too depressed to answer it.

I'll scream—I mean *screen* it, I thought. Then I heard a voice I never expected to hear on my answering machine. It was the Man from the Pampas himself: Pablo! And his silly mustache!

I was going to have to make this a quickie before the neighbors called the fire department.

"What a surprise!" (Call waiting. Shit.) "Can you hold on just a minute, Pablo? There's someone on the other line," I said.

"Darling!" came the voice from London.

"Mummy, thank God you called—but could you hang on a sec? I'm on the other line." I pressed the flash key.

"Sorry about that, Pablito. What's up?" I said.

"Are you available for a gig? It's small, but it'll be worth it," he said.

"When?" I asked. (Has he gone amnesiac and forgotten how old I am? Or is he desperate?)

"Tonight," he said. (He's desperate.)

"Umm . . . all right, then. What time and where?" I sighed. (You don't deserve me.)

I had half an hour to change and get over there, thank you very much!

"Sorry about that, Mummy. It's the béchamel—" The smelly black smoke was now streaming into the living room. "I'm going to have to call you back!" I yelled before hanging up on her.

I raced to the stove to rescue the eggplants—the onions were beyond salvation; they had died and gone to heaven in a blazing funeral pyre—and then I ran into the bathroom to rummage through the cabinet, dropping half the contents onto the bathroom floor, breaking a few little bottles that I didn't even know were in there and finally retrieving the red nail polish I was looking for. Then I ran back into the kitchen to stir the ground meat and tomato sauce, applying the polish between stirs. I ran to the bedroom to get my fishnet stockings. Again this required a lot of rummaging, since as I have mentioned before, even fishnets can get holes in them and do, frequently—footsie and bumper cars being but two of the games that invariably result in holes in one's stockings.

I checked the clock. Five minutes to go. Just enough time to call my mother. I dialed her number, holding the receiver between my right cheek and shoulder as I rolled up a stocking and adjusted it to the garter:

"Mummy, as I was saying, the béchamel, it's gone wrong. First it was runny. Now it's got bubbles. How do I fix it?"

As it turned out, there was no fixing it. Once the air gets in, it's game over. I would have to start all over again tomorrow. I congratulated myself once more on the foresight I had shown by starting the process a day early. Insecure in the kitchen, me? Now, I was in too much of a rush to mourn the loss. I had to decide what to wear. The only cure for the blues is red, I thought. Red skirt (with white polka dots), red lipstick, red-and-black two-tone heels, and a black top that shows off my shoulders and just the right amount of cleavage. I had already recovered from my post-culinary depression. Whores in the bedroom are a dime a dozen, I thought, but to be a whore in the kitchen, now *there's* an achievement!

"Where's the fire?" was the first thing Pablo asked me when I arrived.

"What do you mean?" I said.

"Something smells like it's burning," he said. That something was my hair.

"Oh that! . . . It's nothing, it's just the moussaka," I said.

"The moussa-what?" he said.

"I'll tell you some other time," I said.

Small indeed was the way to describe the event. There were ten people in all and I wanted to kill Pablo for having interrupted me in mid-cuisine for *this*. (Just as I was starting to have fun.) Especially when he regaled us with his folk dancing for about an hour. I sat there admiring him and simultaneously wanting to shoot him.

He must have had a reason for asking me here, so I'll sit pretty until I find out what it is, I thought.

I found out soon enough. The time had come for us to do our thing. And boy, was he in the mood to show off! I wish I could say the same thing about me. The parquet was a dancer's nightmare. The floor had turned into a sheet of ice, but instead of skates, I was wearing heels, and I was dancing with someone who was completely oblivious to my predicament. "Pablo de las Pampas" (he had turned into his stage persona all right) was in the mood to spin like a top and I was not left with much choice but to spin along with him. He was not deterred by my terrified expression. He executed about twenty *giros* per second. Since the *giro* is a figure in which the man becomes a revolving center, while the woman draws circles around him, you don't need to have majored in trigonometry to understand that this means she needs to move faster than he to keep up. The concentration, not to say leverage, required to stay on the merry-go-round-gone-mad was tremendous. When it was over and I hadn't fallen on my face once, I graced the audience with a smile that said "easy-peasy-japaneasy."

Pablo seemed pleased enough with my performance. I think I passed the test, if that's what it was. But I had more pressing business to attend to. And so, as soon as was decent, I made my escape and ran back to my eggplants.

But it was too late. And whoever invented home catering is a genius.

July 21, 2001

When Pablo called me this morning to ask if I was available for a gig, my first question was "When?," since I assumed that if he was stooping so low as to call *me*, it must be because he was desperate once more. But lo and behold he said:

"It's not for a couple of weeks. It's not a one-time thing. It's a regular deal."

I couldn't believe it! A top professional dancer was asking me to be his partner! That night *had been* a test and I had passed it with flying colors! Wasn't *I* the brilliant tango dancer? The eggplants had not died in vain, after all.

I was still patting myself on the back when he informed me that the gig was not in a theater. Nor was it in one of the *casas de tango* to which they bus the tourists on organized tours—places like El Viejo Almacen or Michelangelo.

"Where, then?" I asked, confused.

"Calle Florida," he said, referring to my least favorite pedestrian street in downtown Buenos Aires. The sounds of cheering died a sudden death. Surely he wasn't being serious? Surely he wasn't asking me to be a beggar?

But when I said, "Sorry?" and he repeated his proposal, I realized that he was being serious and that I was indeed being asked to be, if not exactly a streetwalker, then a street dancer.

I don't know if it is a good "career move"—in fact, I am pretty sure it is not. But then again, I have nothing to lose. Where nothing = no partner and no prospect of one in either the near or the distant future. So I said yes.

"Now don't go taking this as anything serious. It's *sin compromiso:* no commitment. Got that? I'm only asking you because my steady part-ner doesn't want to do it. I need the cash, though. My ex is suing me for child support. But that's not really any of your business," said Pablo.

Charming! I thought.

"No problem, Pablo! *Sin compromiso!*" I said, while I thought: How presumptuous of you to think that I should want to commit to you and your silly little mustache! Don't make me laugh!

But today, I don't feel like laughing. In fact, it pisses me off. When it comes to commitment phobia, I have my double standard to maintain. It's okay if it comes from me, but it's not okay if comes from them! Es-pecially not when the object of their phobia is me. I'm tired of hearing *"sin compromiso"* this and *"sin compromiso"* that. It seems it's all they are capable of saying. Why the fuck does "I don't want a relationship/com-mitment/anything serious" *always* have to be *the very first* thing they say to one? Why can't they *wait* to take their vanilla-ice-cream-covered tongues out of one's throat before they say it? (Or is it me?)

Of course, I see where they are coming from. The idea of commit-ment is even less appealing in Spanish than it is in English. Who wants to commit when you've got the word "compromise" built into the word right from the get go? But still, it's annoying. I hate it that they keep bringing up the stupid C word only to say that it's something they don't want. Frankly, I would prefer it if they didn't bring it up at all. It makes me feel like I have some contagious disease. And the question is how on earth am I going to dance the tango with someone who behaves as if I had the plague? But it's too late to backtrack now: I've said yes. And unlike a certain sex of a certain nation, commitment is not something I talk about but something I do.

August 6, 2001

I met Pablo and the other cast members in front of the Galerías Pacífico. He showed me to the "dressing room," otherwise known as the public restrooms of the shopping mall, where I locked myself in a cubicle and got changed. I had decided against any of my "good" gowns, since they would get ruined in a jiffy, and went for the simple and elegant knee-length dress that I'd worn for my first exhibition with Chino. It has very fine, almost invisible straps in the back, so despite its understatedness, it is quite sexy, if I say so myself. I had trouble deciding on which heels, given that all my shoes have suede soles—suicide on the cobblestones I'm supposed to dance on. I had to rush out to a shoe repairman this morning and have him stick some rubber on the bottom of my black-and-white two-tones.

Finally, I emerged from the cubicle in my costume. In the meantime, a long line had formed of patrons waiting to use the lavatory. I don't know if they were more surprised by my metamorphosis or annoyed by the fact that I had taken so long in effecting it.

Now, I put on my makeup and costume jewelry in full view of the fascinated audience. When I was done, having received the thumbs-up of the attendant and a couple of women in the line, I left the dressing room and walked through the shopping mall, my heels clicking loudly against the marble floors. I pretended not to notice the turned heads (of the male shoppers, in particular).

"Is that what you're going to wear?" were Felicia's first words to me. Felicia is my boss.

"Well . . . y-y-es," I stammered. "Is there anything wrong with it?"

"Don't you have anything sexy? Show us a bit of leg, woman!" she said with a wink. That's when I noticed that her dress barely covered her crotch.

"I'll see what I can come up with tomorrow," I said.

"Attagirl!" she exclaimed.

The *milonga* was already blaring from the loudspeaker. This was a signal to the living statue to step down from his pedestal, wipe off the green paint—remember the Statue of Liberty?—and evacuate the premises. We were claiming the turf. But there was competition from another quarter. The music from the Tower Records opposite the gallery was louder than ours. Felicia sent Ruben, the veteran cast member, to deal with it.

"Tell them to turn it down. How are we supposed to work with that racket, for fuck's sake?" I will spare you the intricacies of the "law" when it comes to matters pertaining to street vending because I doubt there are any.

With Ruben's mission accomplished, Felicia was ready to start her stretching routine. She was so flexible, it was depressing. She did have an advantage over me. There was literally nothing dress-wise to get in the way of her lifting her leg to impossible heights, or to interfere with her bending knees and lunging thighs.

"It's part of the show," she whispered to me. "If this doesn't stop them in their tracks, I don't know what does."

I followed suit. I am proud to say that I only tore two muscles in the process. I pulled my leg up behind me and contorted myself the best I could. I wished I had Miguel Angel to help. She was right: it certainly stopped people in their tracks. Onlookers gawked at us with their mouths wide open. I'm not sure it was in admiration, though. Five minutes later, we were officially "warmed up." (Thank God, because it's absolutely freezing! I'm going to catch pneumonia. Or TB. Like Mimi in La Bohème. Especially now that I have been told to dance with hardly any clothes on. She says I'll get used to it, though.)

Felicia told me to copy her. She grabbed one of the hats resting on a chair and threw me another. The hats that would later be passed around for the "contributions." She was dancing an intricate sequence that involved juggling with the fedoras, taking them off, flipping them this way and that, throwing them in the air and catching them again. Needless to say, I don't know how to juggle. Suddenly, I found myself in Chicago. I was doing my best to follow, but my best was not good enough. I was back in one of those dance aerobics classes—the one where the rest of the class has been working on the sequence for a month and you join late and the teacher says, "You'll get the hang of it! Just have fun with it!" And as you try to catch up with the others, you catch a glimpse of your out-of-synch-with-the-rest-of-the-class self in the mirror. And you are sure that every pair of eyes is watching you and laughing. And you're not having any fun with it at all.

After we had strutted our stuff for longer than I thought was necessary, Felicia said that it was time to start the show. There was a big enough crowd that Ruben and Pablo had corralled while I had been trying not to drop the hat.

"Come in closer, folks, the show is about to start!" cried Mauricio, the emcee. "No, you can't stand there! You're blocking the entrance to that store. This way, this way! In a circle, please. That's right. Move in together, closer. Nice and tight. Squeeze in. Good! Ladies and gentlemen: The most popular tango show on earth, enjoyed by more than a million people in over a year and a half. Let's hear a nice round of applause for the *Pacífico Tango Show!*"

August 8, 2001

The show opens with Ruben and Mauricio dancing together, and it certainly draws them in. For some reason, people who know nothing about tango love the idea that "Tango is a dance that was originally danced between men." Little do they know that that's nonsense! Sure, men *practiced* together—they still do today. But the reason they did this was because they wanted to *dance* with women. Men dance for one reason: to get women into bed—or at the very least, to *pretend* to want to get women into bed. And the better the dancer, the more likely the success. Let's not forget that tango was born in the good old days when there were far fewer women than men in Argentina, meaning that competition among men was stiff. Apparently, they were not allowed into certain establishments unless they danced at a certain level. And apparently, I was born in the wrong century.

After the opening number, it was my turn to present the centerpiece of the show, with Pablo. Unfortunately for me, it is Darienzo's version of *"La Cumparsita,"* which has got to be the longest and fastest recorded in the history of tango. And I have to dance it *eight* times in total—since we do the show *eight* times a day—and every time, I am sure I will not make it to the end. To think I'm going to have to start again tomorrow. And the day after that, and the day after that. I've been gobbling ibuprofen like candy for the pain. And also as a preventive measure against pneumonia. I don't think it's working, though. My cough seems to be getting worse.

On the bright side, I can look forward to losing lots of weight, if Felicia's emaciated figure is anything to go by. It is more likely, though, that I will be checked into an insane asylum first. I can't get the music out of my head. And it happens to be the only piece in the massive tango repertoire that I despise.

Just when I thought my body would not take another *giro* (Pablo's alpha and omega), I was granted a respite. I was gasping for air when Felicia signaled for us to pose for the cameras. The poor fools snapping away did not realize that no sooner had they snapped me with my thigh wrapped around Pablo's hip than a hat would be shoved under their noses and they would be required to put something in it. No coins, thank you. It's ironic that the world's most unphotogenic person has to pose not once but three or four times a set.

Between two sets, I noticed Felicia talking to what looked like two tourists, one of whom had a video camera around his neck. She called me over and asked me to translate. They explained to me in English— "Is that a Canadian accent?" "Yes it is"—that they were shooting a documentary on tango and wanted to film the show. I interpreted for Felicia.

"Tell him that he's not getting a piece of my ass for under one hundred dollars," she answered with terrifying aplomb. This was not the first time she had been in the position of negotiating the price of her ass, by the sound of it.

"She says that she would be delighted for you to shoot the show, providing, of course, you are willing to pay the standard fee of one hundred dollars."

"They say they are afraid they cannot pay a fee because that would compromise the integrity of the documentary," I told Felicia.

"Tell them to fuck off, then."

"Sorry, guys. She says that unfortunately, she is unable to help you with your project." I was sorry to be the bearer of bad news. They seemed to take it stoically enough, though. I realized why later, when I spotted them—or rather, their zoom lens, sticking out from behind a potted tree fifty yards down the street. Hopefully they got more than the green leaves they were using as camouflage.

After the *"Cumparsita"*—thank God, it's not just the good things that come to an end—the show ends with a *milonga*. Felicia and I take turns dancing with the old man, Ruben. There is one big benefit to my being the one to perform it instead of her: I don't have to pass the hat around. The hat gets passed around once during the *"Cumparsita"* and then a second time during the closing act. The first time Felicia pushed me toward the crowd with hat in hand, I thought the day I had prepared for all my life had come. It was official: I was now a beggar. But with each go-round of the hat, I learn that life in the gutter ain't so bad. Begging can be fun!

Another thing that isn't as bad as I thought it would be is losing the audience. Granted, it's not the best feeling in the world. I could tell you exactly how many people I have lost because I have kept count of each defection—but I won't. My eyes can't help being drawn like magnets to the ones who leave before the end of my piece. I can even spot them when I'm in the middle of the hundredth *giro* at 100 miles per second. But you come to accept it as a fact of life: like sheep, the audience will stray. I used to be devastated on behalf of street performers. I couldn't stand it when people pretended to suddenly turn deaf, dumb, and blind when one of them entered a subway car. But the thing I used to hate most was when a subway performer would do his thing and then try to get the audience to applaud by applauding himself, hoping this would precipitate an avalanche of applause, but instead you were left with the sound of one pair of clapping hands (his) ringing loudly in your ears.

But you get used to anything.

August 9, 2001

This morning, I received a form from my alma mater. They want me to fill it out in order to compile a *Who's Who* of their alumni. Officially, the purpose of the exercise is to help us "old boys" keep in touch. Unofficially, it is to keep us all in healthy competition (by comparing ourselves neurotically) with each other. I am convinced, though, that there is a secret raison d'être for the form. It was designed with the sole and specific purpose of humiliating me.

Until this morning, I was able to remain in happy denial of the fact that it's been almost ten years since I graduated. However, after having read the questions on the form, it is no longer possible to go around ignoring the depressing truth. For in this most inquisitive of questionnaires, I am being asked to give my history—employment and personal—since I left Cambridge.

They want me to list all the companies I have worked for—well, here at least, I have one respectable item to put in the box. You can't get any more blue chip than Young & Rubicam. Let's see, what else? Past positions, leading to current stellar job, for example, CEO of Prestigious Bank or Head of Physics Department at Some University or Other or Big Name Reporter at Big Name Paper. Better leave that for later.

Let's see, what else? They want me to list all the awards that the Queen has bestowed on me lately at Buckingham Palace, the various knighthoods and OBEs for outstanding contributions to the arts and sciences, the world economy, and world peace, not to mention my pocket. They want to know, have I won the Nobel Prize recently or the Booker Prize or any prize at all, for that matter? How many bridge or chess tournaments have I won in the last ten years? How about badminton or squash? Well, do you have anything to show for yourself? Any achievements at all? Come on, rack your brains, girl! At least tell us you've been married then, even twice divorced is better than none, and the number of husbands, children, nannies, dogs, houses, gardens, gardeners, clubs—both town and country, but not the Rotary. Which do you own: Mercedes or Jag? Number of carats on your finger? Anything, give us anything to reassure us that you have been neither a complete waste of the college's time nor of the taxpayers' money. Anything at all.

After three hours of staring blankly at them, I finally solved the problem of how to fill in the blanks on the form. In each one, I wrote the letters **NA** in bold print so that they would take up lots of space. And under "Current Employment," I wrote "Dancing tango on Florida Street, Buenos Aires."

If nothing else, my entry is bound to provide entertainment for the "old boys." And I don't care if they *do* die of laughter.

August 13, 2001

Every day we meet at our new dressing rooms, a shopping gallery on Florida five blocks away from the Galerías Pacífico. Every day, I show up at 11:00 as I have been told and every day I wait for the others, including Felicia, to show up at 11:55. The panic begins since *we* are now running late. Felicia and I run up to the bathrooms to get changed. I take this opportunity to bond. It's important to bond, you see. I make sure not to reveal any details that indicate that I do not, in fact, live off the $15 a day she fishes out of the hat to pay me. If only she knew that $15 barely covers the cost of resoling my shoes and a new pair of fishnets every day. I have fabricated the story (I know . . . , I said no more lying . . .) that I teach English to subsidize the "living" that I make on Florida. She now wants to take lessons with me. There is no way I can show her where I live because even though it is a rathole by most people's standards, it's probably nicer than where she lives. I don't know how I am going to get out of it.

When we've finished putting on our makeup and costume jewelry and zipping each other up, we go downstairs to collect the sound system, the jumbo-size battery, the microphone with its stand, the loudspeaker, the directors' chairs, the hats, the trolleys . . . and the men. It sounds straightforward, but it isn't. There is always a drama to ensure that the day starts off on the wrong foot. And it's always Mauricio's fault.

Mauricio, I have figured out, is Felicia's recently-exed husband and the father of her six, yes, S-I-X, kids.

And just in case you thought it was an amicable separation, it's not. Felicia hates Mauricio's cheating ass and we all get to hear about it. A lot.

When the battery hasn't recharged properly:

"He's fucking doing it on purpose." I don't point out to her that this makes no sense since it would be financial suicide for him to sabotage his own show.

When we can't find the hats:

"He's fucking hidden them!" It's starting to dawn on me that Mauricio is not the only one with the cocaine problem in the family. Then again, if I had six kids, I wouldn't be doing coke, I'd be doing heroin.

When the tape has been overdubbed and instead of the usual sound of the *milonga*, the loudspeakers blare nothing at all:

"I'm going to kill that son of a bitch!" she screams as she pushes all the buttons at once, frantically. I have no doubt about which son of a bitch she is referring to.

Though I might be forgiven for having my doubts. Because when Felicia is not at Mauricio's throat, she's at Ruben's.

"She can't boss *me* around!" the veteran of the streets grumbled to me the other day. (She can and she does.) "We used to have such laughs with Mauricio. Now there's a fine fellow. Why he ever got together with that crazy bitch, I don't know . . ."

August 15, 2001

Felicia lied: I haven't gotten used to the cold. But the good news is that I don't feel it when I'm dancing since Pablo keeps me in a permanent sweat. It's in between sets, however, that I am most cruelly exposed to the elements, my hot sweat instantly turning into icicles as soon as I sit still for a second. I freeze and defrost eight times a day on average. The fact that since Day 2, I have been (un)dressed, as ordered, doesn't help. Felicia wanted sexy and she's getting sexy. I have to say, it's amazing the difference a few inches make. My miniskirt now has quite a fan club: mainly unemployed, homeless bums who have nowhere else to sit all day, so they hang out on "our" bench. They are addicted to the soap opera that is guaranteed to provide entertainment in the form of bust ups and reconciliations on a daily basis. Speaking of which, Mauricio has left the show. But he hasn't gone very far—a couple of blocks down calle Florida, where he is doing the same show with a new couple that he's hired. It's the *Pacífico Tango Show* franchise! Hopefully this means we will all be spared eardrum surgery.

Our fans love this latest turn of events. I overhead one of them, who had missed an episode, asking the others for a synopsis of the previous day's installment. Another of them has made a sign, which he holds up during my performance: "La Griega Fan Club." Although I find it touching, I doubt Felicia shares my sentiment. In fact, I'm worried that she might get jealous. But what can I do to stop it? And frankly, I don't want it to. It's nice that somebody loves me for a change. Even if it is an unemployed bum on the street. At least *he* doesn't treat me like I have the plague.

Actually, I'm in real danger of becoming addicted to my fans. As addicted as my muscles are to the ibuprofen. Being worshiped from afar does make up for a nonexistent love life. But at the same time, I have never felt so lonely. It's weird. I swing from exhilaration when I am in the public eye to despair when I am not; when I am all alone in my apartment and there is nobody to share any of this with. What's it all for? I wonder. Until the next round of applause, when I stop wondering and start thinking: Who needs the love of a man when you have the adoration of your fans? Even if they are strangers who don't have anything better to do than sit on public benches all day. I wouldn't trade their applause for the world.

And then I get home and all I feel is empty. I never knew that emptiness could weigh this much.

September 15, 2001

I've become best chums with the beggars I pass every day on Florida on the way to our spot. There's the one-legged guy in the wheelchair who always asks: "How's business?" Hedging my bets (I don't want him to feel bad in case it is not good on his end), I answer, *"Màs o menos,"* the expression you'll hear more often than any other down here, meaning "fair" or "so-so." Nothing is ever "good" or "bad." It is always "so-so." I have also made friends with the gypsy urchins who routinely run amok during our show, driving Felicia to acts of violence. She has told me off already a number of times.

"Stop being such a fucking nice guy! Give them a finger and they'll tear off an arm! I don't want those animals near the show. They're bad for business. They drive the customers away! You got that?"

"Yes, Felicia, loud and clear." But I can't bear the thought that these children have never experienced a single act or word of kindness. Even though I know there is nothing I can do for them, I indulge in the occasional selfish act of giving them a candy or a sandwich to make me feel better.

And then there's my friend Pablo. Things have gotten tense lately. His new hobby is to criticize me while we dance. It seems he cannot wait until we are off "stage" to air his grievances. This has precipitated a deep crisis of confidence, which had me on the verge of quitting the other day. He has *got* to be a closet-case. I can't see any other explanation for his bitchiness toward me. And here's the proof. The other day he pointed out a pair of twin sisters on the street:

"Do you know what I'd do to those twins, given half a chance?" I didn't have the time to tell him that, frankly, I wasn't all that interested in finding out, before he was lavishing the details on me I hadn't asked for. The words, however, did not ring true. It sounded to me like he was trying way too hard to convince me of his manhood.

"How interesting . . . I've never heard *that* fantasy before . . . ," I said. (It was extremely run-of-the-mill.) Gay, I thought. Without a shadow of a doubt.

"Point your toes! Lift your torso! Stop wiggling your hips!" he peck-peck-pecks all day, as if I were corn and he a chicken. I try to console myself as best I can: what else can I expect from someone with a mustache like that?

The other day, I tried to defend my style by mentioning Gustavo Naveira, founding father of the new tango. Big mistake. But it was too late. Now Felicia has joined in the chorus line. They are ganging up on me and it's two against one. This has sent my confidence on a free-falling spiral. Luckily, not everybody agrees with them. Not my fan club. And not the people who regularly tell me how much they love me. The best endorsement this week came from a Brazilian woman and her daughter who came to watch the show two days in a row. During a break, she came up to me and said, "You have what they call an 'angel,' a gift. Cherish it, my dear." I wanted to cry. There is nothing I like more than receiving a compliment from a woman. Women don't have ulterior motives. Of course, it doesn't hurt to get a compliment from a man, either. For example, I was taking the subway the other day, on my way to a ballet class, when a guy came up to me and said, "Aren't you the one who dances on Florida?" I nodded. "I just wanted to tell you how much I like your work," he said before he disappeared into the crowded car. Pity he disappeared so quickly: he was really cute. And I glowed for a long time afterward.

October 7, 2001

Spring is here! A little earlier than usual, this year. You'd have thought this was a good thing after all my grumbling about the cold, but try and dance for five hours under a sunny, blue sky and you'll soon discover what a miserable thing it is! Give me back the frost! And those lovely gray skies! Why is it always too late by the time one realizes one was happy?

Luckily, I have managed to locate a shady sanctuary at the entrance of the C&A department store, where I seek refuge between sets, but before my body has had the time to let off some of the heat trapped inside the synthetic fabric of my dress, it's time to go back to the galleys. I'll get heatstroke if this goes on much longer.

On Saturday, Felicia took the day off, with no explanation. She must have had a rough landing from the night before, if you know what I mean. Consequently, somebody had to take the reins. And guess who that somebody was? There was nobody else, frankly, since I don't know who is more useless, Pablo or Ruben. It's a close call. Rather than wasting twenty minutes before each set rounding up a crowd that doesn't want to be rounded up, I did it *my* way, which involves less time and effort. I exposed my philosophy to the guys thus: "As soon as they see the pair of you dance, they'll come like moths to the light. Forget about trying to corral them before the show. It's too time consuming. Do you want to get the eight sets done as quickly as possible, or don't you?" They did. "Well, then." I hate to say it. Not only did we have bigger crowds than usual, but we did our eight sets in four hours, a record in the history of the *Pacífico Tango Show*! We were like schoolkids who have been let out early because a teacher is sick.

I may have been president for the day. But there was no doubt who was treasurer. Ruben was so anxious to count the dough, he couldn't wait to go back to the gallery where Felicia normally counts it. We had collected around $200. Not bad! I felt like Donald Trump. Ruben pulled me aside.

"Take thirty pesos. I promise, *she'll* never know," he whispered. I was taken aback. I hadn't expected my ethical standards to be tested in this way. Not here, not now.

Inside me, a voice went: "Listen to him. *She'll* never know. You *are* being exploited, after all. It's only right you take it. For once, you'll get your fair share. Especially since Pablo makes twenty pesos. Does he make more than you because he's a man? Or because he's 'famous'? Or is it because he's better than you?" The voice was egging me on. It was unnatural *not* to take the money. Isn't it a golden rule that when the cat's away, his employees steal all the silverware? But I could not bring myself to do it.

"I'm fine with my fifteen. Really I am. But thank you for offering," I said.

Ruben shook his head. He was deeply disappointed in me. After all, I made him look bad. Now I regret it, of course.

October 13, 2001

As it was Felicia's birthday today, I took a dozen *empanadas* with me to work. I hoped the gift might act as a peace offering, an olive branch so to speak—okay, as a bribe. Under normal circumstances, I hate sucking up, really I do, but I couldn't stand her picking on me anymore. I had to find a way to make her stop (before it ended in a bloodbath) and this was all I could come up with. And if I was lucky, I'd kill two birds with a dozen *empanadas* and get Pablo to warm up to me a bit as well. I've never known a colder fish!

I tried to make these ground beef, ham and cheese, and chicken-filled marvels once, but now was not the time to play it dangerously. There was far too much at stake. These *empanadas* had to be PERFECT since they were going to buy me not one, but two people's affections. So they were going to have to be from Gourmet, which in my opinion makes the best *empanadas* on the market. And we're talking about an enormous market. They're absolutely everywhere. I even saw some of them dancing in the street the other day. Humans dressed up as *empanadas*. What people are forced to do to earn a living . . .

I don't know what possessed me to try to make *empanadas* myself that first and last time. I thought there would be nothing to it, I guess. They looked so simple, so unassuming, sitting in their snug little rows in the display cases of every café, pizzeria, and *empanadería* in town. But I was clueless. Making *empanadas* is an art, and since that thwarted attempt, I have not been able to go by a display case without stopping to contemplate the plump little masterpieces. I am awed by the mystery of their making. How do THEIR *empanadas* come out looking so healthy? So chubby? So crisp? So golden? So completely and utterly different looking from mine? It's a metaphysical question—a mystery that shall remain forever impenetrable.

Anyway, I'm glad to report that the *empanadas* did the trick. There's no telling, of course, how long their benign effects will last. But for today at least, I was off-limits for Felicia. In fact, she was so touched that I had remembered her birthday, and so charming as a result, that I felt guilty about my deviousness. I wished she would go back to being her normal bitchy self instead of giving me the thumbs-up or winking at me every time I did something she approved of, like a really high kick or a really low lunge that stopped short of the splits, because I still can't do the splits no matter how many hours a day I stretch. In fact, I'm going to give up stretching and stick to *empanadas* from now on. They seem to be a lot better for my technique, judging by Felicia's reaction. I'd have to stretch for YEARS before I got the same results.

As for Pablo, the *empanadas* also worked miracles. I couldn't believe it, but today, he actually SMILED at me! I almost fainted.

October 15, 2001

Since Inés moved to Buenos Aires, I have been spending a lot more time in the murky world of Argentine "high society." It's not that I used to avoid it exactly, it's that I didn't have time for it: I was far too busy "networking" at the *milonga*. Now, though, after an exhausting day of flaunting my wares on Florida, the last thing I want to do is go to a *milonga*. And anyway, I don't need to anymore since I am working and I have a partner—even though he's not really mine. He's gone back to being his normal self—I didn't think that the effects of the *empanadas* would last forever.

As I was saying, these days, I'm much more inclined to accept nontango invitations. And to be honest, it does make a pleasant change to hang out with people who, in Mummy's words, know how to hold their knives and forks. And there is nothing more soothing, after a long day of being battered by the sidewalk, than to be offered a flute of champagne and a canapé on a silver platter by a white-gloved hand. But it's a secret. I don't want anybody from Tango to know. Especially not Felicia.

Last week, for instance, Inés and Juan Carlos had a dinner party for sixty on their roof terrace. As usual, I was introduced as the eccentric tango dancer. And as usual, after the initial embarrassed silence— nobody quite knows what to say at first—there was no stopping the tidal wave of questions. They all belonged to the class of Argentine who wouldn't be caught dead dancing the tango—it is far too proletarian— which is why they relied on me to give them a vicarious frisson. I'd been to the dark side and back and they wanted a full report. And as usual, I obliged them. The only reason I can get away with it is because I am a foreigner. In me, it is charming—but only because I am not their daughter, sister, or wife. They especially loved the bit about my $15-a-day salary—no doubt, their staff makes more than that. That always gets big belly laughs.

And yet as much as I enjoy the sound of it, their laughter saddens me because it is the wall that separates me from them. I often feel like a schizophrenic—I belong in neither world. Neither here nor on the street. Condemned to being a *bicho raro* ("a weird bug," an object of curiosity) in both. But at other times, the glass looks half full when I tell myself that I am lucky to have two homes instead of one.

October 17, 2001

I didn't recognize him at first, but something in the glint of his eye made me suspect that it was not entirely attributable to the masterful technique that Pablo and I were currently displaying in the form of a sequence of overturned back *ochos*. And then I placed him: it was the boy from the subway! And for the second time, I noticed how cute he was. What was he doing here? Did he work nearby? That's when I saw that he was carrying a pouch and that leaning against his left hip was a bike.

Only in Argentina do they make errand boys that look this good, I said to myself, feeling as disappointed as I did wistful.

When we finished the set, he came over to say hi and to make more flattering comments about my "work." He stood very close to me, and all the while he spoke, he drilled into me with his eyes that made me think of a Persian prince. He looked even better in close quarters. I don't normally find unibrows attractive, but in his case, there was something sexy about it. It heightened the intensity of his gaze. Sadly, he didn't only look better in close quarters. He also looked younger. My guess is that he's been out of puberty for at least a year—possibly two. I know, I know . . . But I swear I don't do it on purpose. I'm not a female version of Maurice Chevalier, in spite of what some people might think, and I don't go around singing "Thank heaven for little boys." (Apart from in the shower.)

But what is a lonely girl to do, Your Honor? Is it her fault if she's a little-boy magnet? Should she turn down an opportunity to become "acquainted" with a guy just because he happens to have been born in the wrong decade? Wouldn't that be harsh of her? Especially considering the fact that there are no prospects for *um . . . romance* on either the near or distant horizons? Furthermore, hasn't one been taught that it is always more gracious to accept the offering, even if the scratchy angora sweater, say, under the Christmas tree was not exactly what one was hoping for? And if you do turn down the offering on the grounds that "it won't lead anywhere" only to be hit by a car the next day? Then what? Wouldn't that be a waste? Therefore, doesn't it make much better sense to give the little boy one's e-mail address when he asks for it? I knew you'd agree with me, Your Honor!

And there it was, this morning: a message from him—so he can't be *all* that young, if he can write. The message opened with *"Princesa"* (a good start, I thought) and continued just as promisingly with references to my talent (that always goes down well), and to eyes that set souls on fire, and more along those hackneyed but effective lines.

And this afternoon, when he asked me out for a drink, after going to all the trouble of coming to see the show again, what was I to do? I owed it to him, didn't I? And if not to him, then to myself. It has been such a long time since I have seen any action—I can't even remember when the last time was. Oh. Yes. I just remembered. I wish I hadn't. Now I've got to forget all over again.

October 21, 2001

I made sure to tell subway boy to meet at the café opposite my apartment. Always a step ahead of the game, that's me!

The waiter came to take our order of two *cortaditos* and two pancakes, dripping with *dulce de leche*—caramelized milk, to put it more prosaically, although there is nothing prosaic about *dulce de leche*. I once considered becoming anorexic, but when I realized that meant no more *dulce de leche*, I quickly changed my mind. What I don't understand is how everybody is so skinny, since every spoonful contains about two million calories and they put it on everything when they don't spoon it straight out of the pot. Personally, I don't bother with a spoon.

As I listened to him tell me how beautiful I was, I debated whether or not to order a second *dulce de leche* pancake. It took all the willpower I have and then some not to. And while I fought with my *dulce de leche* demon, I asked myself if subway boy had commissioned Cyrano de Bergerac to write his e-mail. In spite of the fact that his looks kept getting better with each viewing—those penetrating eyes!—I'm afraid that his conversation had taken a turn for the worse. Though I can't say that the opening *verso* (the standard Argentine blah-blah about how fabulous one is) had been all that inspired or original, it was better than the talk of soccer with which he was now regaling me. If there is anything even more boring than cars, it is soccer. Don't ask me how I got from A to B, but I found myself daydreaming about Frank, and then, one thought leading to another, I asked subway boy if he wanted to come up to my place. Maybe I didn't ask him. Maybe I told him.

He looked a little taken aback. He hadn't planned on it being this easy. Then again, he didn't know that it was time for a little spring cleaning—spring *is* here! As I have mentioned before, Argentine men don't expect to score as easily with women as they do in soccer. But somehow he managed to overcome his panic and refrained from bolting out of the café, as most Argentine "machos" would have done under the circumstances. This might have something to do with the fact that I had gotten a firm hold of him and was now forcefully dragging him across the road.

Once we were in my apartment, his shyness escalated, and it was contagious. I didn't know if I still knew how to do it. I told myself it was like riding a bicycle, but I wasn't sure I still knew how to ride a bike, either. To dispel the awkwardness, I showed him my music and asked him to pick out a CD. He was amazed by all the tango CDs I own. While he went through the collection, I went into the bedroom, changed out of my clothes, and put on a slinky nightgown. I hoped it might put both of us in the mood. I, for one, needed all the help I could get since the conversation at the café had not been exactly titillating. When I emerged, Ernesto (if I am only mentioning his name now it's not because he was nothing but a sex object it's because . . . okay, you win). Anyway, Ernesto had put on Adriana Varela, the most popular female tango singer today. He had finished playing deejay, but he wasn't taking a step closer to me. He seemed to have become rooted to the spot and showed no sign of budging anytime, now or ever. Forcing me to go and uproot him myself before leading him to the sofa. When I offered him something to drink, he said he didn't want anything, so we sat in silence, listening to the music.

I was starting to feel a bit silly in my nightie when finally he leaned over and kissed me! It had been worth the wait: the kiss was as smooth and as sweet as the *dulce de leche* that had filled our pancakes. Even though I spend my days in the arms of a man—if one can call Pablo that—I had forgotten how nice it felt. As a result, my body was not long in waking up. And was that his waking up too? I thought so. And then I don't know what got hold of him, but from slow coach, he turned into express carriage. He seemed to be in a terrible hurry to remove all his clothes at once. But the racing demon had not dressed for the occasion. He was wearing the kind of shirt that has a million buttons made for teeny-tiny little fingers. There were buttons everywhere. The most annoying of all were the ones at the wrists. In the end, he gave up fumbling with them and tore the shirt off his back, sending buttons flying all over the place. Now he was frantically trying to get out of his pants, but his belt buckle got stuck in a loop. After much pushing and pulling, he was finally able to extricate it. Thank goodness, his jeans were not button-downs! He unzipped the fly and down they went, displaying a pair of boxer shorts bearing his soccer team's insignia. There was a snag, how-ever: he had forgotten to take his shoes off, so his jeans had nowhere to go beyond his ankles. As he stood there, looking helpless, I went to the rescue, bending down, undoing the laces of his sneakers and pulling them off his feet as he hopped up and down on one foot and then the other. Finally he was shoeless and the jeans and boxer shorts could come off. They did. He was now standing stark naked in front of me.

Oh no.

How was I going to do the spring cleaning with *that*? You need a much longer broom than *that* to reach the cobwebs. Those who say that size doesn't matter obviously have no idea what they are talking about. There's a reason it's called sexual ful-FILL-ment. And I wasn't going to get anywhere near it by the look of things.

You can't find decent help these days, I thought, sighing. Frustration has never been more of an understatement than it was at this particular moment.

I'm afraid to say that this time around, my manners were not up to par. I was far too demoralized to be my usual polite self. All I could do, by way of a consolation prize, was extend a bit of charity in the form of a blow job. Though if anybody needed consoling, it wasn't him. He seemed happy enough with his end of the bargain, which only served to make me feel more wretched. And so I blew away, only just managing to choke back my tears at the thought that after he was gone, I was going to have to remove the cobwebs myself. As bloody usual.

In retrospect, I wished Ernesto *had* bolted out of the café, since it would have saved me a lot of time and aggro, and his shirt six buttons.

October 30, 2001

I got into the cab and prayed that I would be allowed to enjoy a chat-free ride for once. I was feeling exhausted. It was psychosomatic. It always is. But knowing this didn't make it go away. All I wanted was to be left alone to wallow in my misery, assisted only by the symphonic sound of Aníbal Troilo's orchestra, even though La 2×4 FM, the local tango radio station that my driver was tuned in to, was currently losing the battle with the crackling interference. It would have been nice, as I said, but it wasn't to be.

"Are you married?" asked Néstor—that was my driver's name, according to the license hanging from the back of his seat. This is among the top three FAQs along with "Where are you from?" and "How old are you?"

"But *you do* have a boyfriend?" he said, assuming this was a rhetorical question after I had responded to the prior inquiry with the negative.

"*How on earth is it POSSIBLE?! SINGLE?!* A pretty girl like you?!" he cried, aghast, when I found myself in the unfortunate position of having to contradict him once more. His tone reminded me of the one people adopt upon hearing about a heinous crime.

How indeed? I have lost count of the number of times I have heard this refrain. Why do people automatically assume that if you are single, there has to be something wrong with *you*? Why don't they stop to think that perhaps the reason you are single is because there is something wrong with *them*?

"Take a look in the fucking mirror!" I feel like shouting, but I am so enraged that I can't even speak, let alone shout.

I'm tired of explaining to everyone that I'm not single to spite them. "I'd be more than happy to cooperate," I say. "Just introduce me to someone who is (a) attractive, (b) smart, and (c) nice, and I'm there!" I say. But apparently, this is too much to ask for. Apparently, I'm supposed to be satisfied with one of the following:

nice & attractive but not smart
attractive & smart but not nice

smart & nice but not attractive

smart & nice & attractive & has a teeny-tiny dick

No! I would prefer to bear my cross of solitude forever rather than settle for one of these permutations. Yes, it gets lonely—in spite of the riveting conversations one conducts with oneself at bus stops. But hey, it's lonely at the top! Of course, I can't come out and give it to them straight because they will stone me for being an arrogant bitch. So instead, I shrug and look humble and go along with the unspoken assumption that there must be something wrong with me, as I shrug some more and look terribly apologetic for not having a boyfriend.

I was putting on my shrugging act for Néstor, who had adjusted his rearview mirror so he could get a better look. I had resolved to avoid small talk at all costs, being as I was on the verge of a physical (nervous) breakdown. However, I couldn't avoid marking the time with my head as I listened to *"Uno,"* the tango that was now playing on the radio. And unfortunately, Néstor, who spent more time looking at me than at the traffic—we almost crashed into the car in front of us a couple of times—caught it.

"Te gusta el tango?" (Do you like the tango?) he asked. Another FAQ.

If I had been less tired, I would have told him that this was the understatement of the century. I would have said: *"Amo el tango!"* (I *love* the tango!) I would probably even have thrown in: "I live and breathe for it!" I almost certainly would have gone on to explain how it has changed my life before telling him about dancing it *a la gorra*—i.e., passing the hat around—on Florida. At any rate, that's the conversation I have with 99 percent of my drivers. But not today. I knew that if I mentioned that I am currently starring in the "most popular tango show on earth," he would never shut up. So in order to avoid unleashing the usual torrent of verbal diarrhea, all I said was, *"Sí."* Not a word more—which was really hard since normally, the people pleaser in me feels compelled to respond to every question fully. But I wasn't going to please anybody today. Nope.

But Néstor had a different agenda:

"I'm a musician. Not a cabdriver, really. I play the bass in a tango orchestra. I only started doing this shitty job last week. After twenty years, they let us go! We played at La Ventana. Have you heard of it? The *casa de tango*? That's where all the tourists go. Or they used to. Business has been slow. But still: they can't do that! Not after all these years. I'm suing," he said.

"I'm sorry to hear that," I couldn't refrain from saying. How could I stay mum? But I was adamant that he would not trick me into opening my mouth again.

"They say they had no choice. People aren't spending anymore. This country . . . it's going to pot! It's worse than Africa!" I've lost count of how many times I've heard this. I settled on groaning as the best halfway house between saying and not saying something. But still Néstor would not be deterred:

"What in God's name is a foreigner doing here in the *culo del mundo*? It doesn't make any sense! Everybody else is trying to leave!" Lately, this has hit the number one spot in the FAQ rankings. Of course, I feel compassion for everybody who is suffering because of the recession. But I wish they would stop asking me that! It doesn't make me feel at all welcome.

I refused to take the bait and pretended it was another of his rhetorical questions. There was no way I was going to fall into the trap of telling him that I have a very good reason for being here—even though I am doing it on the street.

Néstor did not seem to notice that I hadn't answered his question:

"Here's my card," he said, as he turned around to inspect me from closer up. "Call me and we'll go out sometime!" he said. And then I swear he licked his lips. I do not wish to be cruel, but Néstor was not exactly my type. Though I do see why he thought I might be his.

To put it mildly, I was not looking my best. Behind him there sat a female, anywhere between the ages of 31 and 101, the greasy state of whose hair highlighted the urgent need to make an appointment with the hairdresser to cover up her three-inch roots; and whose severely spotty face was as swollen as the rest of her water-retaining self, especially her thighs, which were about to explode out of her gray sweatpants. Under the circumstances, it was easy to see why Néstor thought he might be doing me a favor.

"*Suerte!*" (Good luck!) he said as I climbed out of his cab.

"*Igualmente!*" (You too!) I said with a cheeriness that, granted, was odd given my unmistakably non-cheery attitude during the ride. One may ask: why the sudden bout of cheer?

(1) I was ecstatic at the prospect of entering my EMPTY flat and of being left ALONE in it since that meant that I wouldn't have to TALK to anyone or hear any more of their STUPID QUESTIONS. (2) The desire to compensate for what I now considered to have been horribly unfair of me: namely the passive-aggressive silent treatment to which I had subjected Néstor and which I now felt he had not deserved, thereby causing me to feel tremendous guilt, which translated itself into the absurdly cheerful leave-taking.

That's why.

November 15, 2001

When strangers approach me to say that they have shed a tear, or that I have brought back memories, or that I have inspired them is when I feel it's all worth it. Also, I won't deny it's flattering to be recognized:

"*Hola*, Griega!" they say, assuming that because they know me, I know them.

In fact, this can lead to some rather embarrassing situations. The other day, I was walking along Avenida de Mayo when I heard somebody shouting out my name. I turned around and the stranger caught up with me. I had no idea who he was. He was in his forties and spoke to me with such familiarity that I thought I must know him. He wasn't giving me any clues apart from mentioning his job at Banco Rio. It didn't ring any bells, though. He looked too smart (in the well-dressed sense) to be a tango person. Had I met him at Inés and Juan Carlos's? I tried to keep the conversation fluid as I racked my brain trying to remember where on earth I knew him from. I was terrified that I might offend him. He was asking me a million questions about the show. So he knew about the gig on Florida, but that still didn't help me to place him. I certainly didn't know him from the *milonga* because I remember every face and every name of every man I have ever danced with. Who *was* this man? I spent fifteen long minutes worrying that I would let slip that I didn't have the foggiest idea who I was talking to. He said that he had been meaning to call me but that he had lost my number. Would I give it to him again? This was worse that I'd thought: how could I have forgotten somebody I had given my number to? I gave it to him, hoping that the usual rule would apply: he'd take it and never call, like the other 99.99 percent. Although knowing my luck, he'd be the .01 percent exception and he wouldn't even tell me his name when he called, he'd say: "It's me!," and I would still be none the wiser about who I was talking to. And anyway, he wasn't my type—he was too old and "a suit," but I felt so guilty about having forgotten who he was that I overcompensated by being super friendly. The fact that I call everybody *mi amor* is helpful in situations like these. Finally, I said it had been lovely to catch up but that I had to dash.

"Surely I'm too young to have Alzheimer's," I said to reassure myself. And it's not that I've done too many drugs, other than ibuprofen. It was only a couple of days later when I saw him in the audience that I realized that the reason I had not been able to place him was because I didn't know him from Adam. He was a random guy (stalker?) who had seen the show a number of times and thought this qualified as "knowing me."

For once in my life, I got lucky and he was no exception to the rule. My telephone number was a good enough trophy for him. He didn't want anything more from me. (It's come to the point where I give out my number fearlessly, because I know that they won't call.) To think I was on the verge of going to the hospital for an emergency brain scan, so convinced was I that I had a tumor. But one learns to take the bad with the good, and to accept these unnecessary health scares as the negative side effect of fame.

November 29, 2001

Today Felicia tried to do me out of my (un)fair share! I could see her coming from a mile away. After each set, she shook her head and mumbled incoherently as she assessed the meager contents of the hats. She didn't need to count the coins, there were so few. And as for bills, there were none.

"It's the end of the month," she said for my benefit.

(Speaking of which, Monica is coming over to my place tonight for gnocchi, the potato-based pasta that is the traditional meal on the twenty-ninth of each month. That's because everyone is broke by the twenty-ninth and they're cheap. And then the month's paycheck clears and everyone can start the whole riches-to-rags cycle all over again.)

Felicia stopped the show twice in midflow after the hat had done its first round and had come back almost empty. This made her furious and she took it out on the audience.

"Boludos!" she shouted at them. This is the most common form of address in Argentina. Roughly, it means "asshole." Interestingly enough, similar to its Greek equivalent, *malaka*, it can be used as an insult or a term of endearment, depending on the context. Right now, Felicia did not mean *boludo* in the endearing sense.

"If you think I'm going to work my ass off for *this*," she said as she made an O with her thumb and index finger—coincidentally, this also means "asshole"—"you can think again!" She stuck her finger through the O, for the benefit of any foreigners or deaf people in the audience. She was not in one of her better moods.

I knew that she was going to try to talk me into a pay cut and I was indignant. I was not going to let her trample all over me. Enough already! This worm was about to do a U-turn. I started to warm up, like in *Raging Bull*, before getting into the ring. I prepared my speech, in which catchphrases such as "a deal is a deal" and "fair is fair" figured prominently, thus working myself into a fury of my own.

Our shift ended and we hobbled back to the gallery with the heavy chairs, heavy sound system, heavy loudspeakers, heavy hearts—and tragically light hats. It was as we were changing out of our costumes that she started to say, "Today has been a bad day—" But I stopped her right there. She could save her breath.

"Feli, I don't give a damn how bad today was! My salary is fifteen pesos and I'm not taking a penny less."

To my amazement, she didn't try to fight back. Without a word, she fished out the five- and ten-cent coins from the hats. Fifteen pesos looks like a lot more when it's in five- and ten-cent coins. She was scowling, but she wasn't shouting for a change, teaching me a valuable lesson: it's easy to bully a bully. The hard part is plucking up the courage to do so. I was shaking for an hour afterward, there was so much adrenaline pumping through my veins. It's taken three cups of chamomile to soothe my nerves.

I predict that my newly sharpened assertiveness skills are going to come in handy when I go to buy the gnocchi at the grocery store around the corner. It is owned by a Chinese family—I think they really *are* Chinese, versus Korean/Japanese/vaguely Asian looking. The surly wife at the checkout counter is not going to like it when I pay for the gnocchi with my five- and ten-cent coins. Knowing her, she is going to kick up a fuss since she's almost as tough a cookie as Felicia. What she doesn't know is that she's about to face some formidable competition. But I'd better have a bit more chamomile first.

December 2, 2001

I can still hear the crowd cheering the day that President de la Rúa won the election. But now the sweet taste of victory has been replaced by a bitterness that I can taste in their mouths as if it were my own. I can't believe it's been two years already. It feels like yesterday.

Last week, the president made a televised speech in which he made a plea to the nation to come together to save Argentina from imminent bankruptcy. At the time, I did not realize how imminent imminent was.

I'll say this for him: he wasn't crying wolf! When he said "imminent," he meant imminent!

People say he's an alcoholic and that he was slurring when he made the speech. I didn't pick up on that, and I should know: I hear a lot of slurring at the *milonga*. If anything, I thought his speech was sobering. I got goose bumps as he begged the viewers to support the government's fiscal measures to counter the financial collapse of the country, "even though many of you may not like my style," he had said.

Well, now we know what these measures are. On Friday, the government announced the introduction of *el corralito*. It's got nothing to do with cattle and horses and everything to do with people's money. They can take out only $250 pesos in cash a week. The idea behind this measure is to put a stop to the recent increased flow of cash out of the Argentine banking system and into places like Switzerland and Uruguay. But it looks like the measure has backfired badly and has had a reverse effect from the one intended. People are lining up in the hundreds of thousands to try to get their money out of the system by any means in order to put it under their mattresses. And there is another snag: people can't pay their bills on a $250-a-week allowance. To find a way around the problem, they are opening multiple bank accounts. Their constitutional right to dispose of their money as they see fit has been taken away from them and they are fuming. But I doubt they'll do anything about it. What *can* they do?

The Argentines are big complainers, but when it comes down to it, they see it as their destiny to be fucked over by their leaders. They shake their heads, grumble, and pick fights in the lines. But that's where it ends. Many have brought fold-out chairs with them to pass the time more comfortably. Most sip on *mate* to ease the pain. And are those sandwiches they are eating? Apparently the banks are providing snacks to appease their customers—possibly the world's most expensive sandwiches?

December 10, 2001

Ruben called last night to say that he is leaving the show. He says he's had it up to his neck with Felicia bossing him around and he wanted to know whether I'd switch turf with him. He's going over to San Telmo. We would be "equal" partners, he made sure to stress, splitting the dough fifty-fifty. Tempting as it was, I had to turn him down. Pablo may be obnoxious, but his name looks good on my resumé: "Pablo de las Pampas" is big enough to neutralize the damage that dancing in the street might do to my reputation as a "serious" dancer.

The same, however, cannot be said for Ruben's name. It's not that he's a bad dancer. It's that he's the *wrong kind* of dancer. Although, truth be told, I prefer dancing with the wrong kind of dancer than with the right kind. Ruben doesn't hold me at arm's length as if I were some vile, creepy hag. He dances the tango the way it's supposed to be danced. Close. While he may not have the technique of a professional of Pablo's caliber, Ruben embodies the authentic spirit of tango. His style retains the *"mugre"*—the filth or muck—from whence the flower of tango originally sprang. *La mugre* was and will always be the life source of the tango.

Indeed, if the *Pacífico Tango Show* is serving any purpose—other than giving me premature varicose veins—it is to remind me that tango was the original "dirty dance." It's easy to forget when I dance with Pablo, who stresses technique over substance. By cleaning up one's act too much, one inevitably loses the erotic quality that makes the tango the tango. The way I see it, by stripping the tango of its *"mugre"* one throws the baby out with the bathwater. As a result, one ends up with a pristine but lackluster approximation of the dance. And by "one," it's obvious who I mean.

But. While I feel indebted to Ruben for reminding me of the importance of "keeping it dirty," I cannot accept his offer because it would amount to career suicide. I tried to let him down gently. But he took it in true *tanguero* fashion—i.e., not well. He accused me of being a snob, among other things. It's amazing how perceptive he can be.

I hope I haven't made a big mistake. Now that we are down to three, Pablo, Felicia, and I take turns dancing with each other. The upshot is that I am no longer the only target of their criticism. They have started to take aim and fire at each other too, which is refreshing for me but does not go down well with Pablo, who has threatened to leave the show several times already. I really hope he doesn't act on his threat. Because then who am I going to dance with? A cold fish is better than no fish at all.

"She's impossible. I can't dance with her. She won't let me lead. She's too bossy," he complains to me constantly. Of course, he's too chicken to complain to her directly. I sit and listen and feel smug.

As part of the new format, Felicia and I do a number together. She's not a bad leader, but she's not perfect, which means that sometimes I have to second-guess her, which means that sometimes I get it wrong, which means that sometimes she barks not very nice things in my ear. I have noticed, however, that our lesbo tango draws in the crowds even more than the man-2-man tango did. Hence my theory: two women dancing together captures:

a. the gay and lesbian crowd
b. men with lesbian fantasies—which is pretty much all men.

No matter how large the crowd of curious onlookers and human-rights supporters (I swear I spotted a rainbow flag the other day), it is not large enough for Felicia's taste, who has become terribly insecure since Mauricio left. So guess what she did? She asked him to come back and make a "guest appearance." As much as she hates his guts, she can't deny his charisma, which *does* draw in the crowds. I'm sure it made him feel good that she was forced to beg for help. When he appeared, the regulars on the bench buzzed with excitement, speculating about a reconciliation. But when Mauricio opened the set with me, you could feel the disappointment in the air as they realized that the speculation had been idle. He, on the other hand, seemed pleasantly surprised. I don't think he was expecting me to be any good, my being a foreigner and all. It always amuses me, the double take guys do when they dance with me for the first time. They simply cannot believe I am not a *porteña*. The fact that I dance like one without being one definitely gives me an edge.

"Boy, does this *mina* dance!" he exclaimed as he winked at one of the regulars on the bench. Girls in Argentina are neither birds nor chicks, they are "goldmines"—another reason I like it here.

Then he whispered in my ear, "Let's go out to a *milonga*, you and me, one night this week, okay?" He pinched my bottom to reinforce the invitation.

"Maybe, *mi amor*, we'll see," I said. (Is he out of his mind?! I might as well get the grinder out now, turn myself into hamburger meat, and save Felicia the trouble.)

December 18, 2001

The show was canceled today. Felicia couldn't get a bus ride into the downtown area. Everything is in chaos. Looters are ransacking super-markets all across the country! The government has declared a state of emergency. On the news, one of the looters they interviewed claimed "he was hungry." I hate to be cynical, but to me he looked like he needed to lose a good twenty or thirty pounds. The rumor is that Eduardo Duhalde (the current leader of the Peronist movement now that Carlos Menem is under house arrest) is behind this. Everybody in the service is nervous. They don't know what to expect. Or rather, they know all too well. They've been through more than their fair share of chaos in the past.

Since being forced to take the day off today, it has hit me how ad-dicted I have become to the *Pacífico Tango Show*. I'm worried that if I don't get my fix of cheers, applause, and adulation tomorrow, I'll go into withdrawal.

December 19, 2001

I was having dinner at le Biblo with Inés and Juan Carlos and a friend of theirs, Santiago. It was too late by the time I realized it was a setup. As I told Inés, when we went to "powder our noses," I thought he was very nice but . . . he doesn't dance the tango! Inés shook her head in distress at the lost cause who was soaping her hands beside her. I felt bad about rejecting her gift, so I told her not to give up and to keep on trying.

There's nothing wrong with the man, per se. He is extremely nice to look at. Indeed, if Robert Redford and Paul Newman had a child together—such a pity they don't—he would come out looking exactly like Santiago. And at thirty-five, he is the perfect age. On top of that, he's from a "good family," owns a large *estancia*—another way of saying he's rich—plays polo (don't they all?), and is everything my mother would love. I wish I *could* like him. But. He. Doesn't. Dance. The. Tango. It's not his fault. Nobody's perfect.

Anyway, all we talked about all evening was the brewing storm. But nobody predicted that the storm would break tonight! Why is it that nine times out of ten, one gets caught without an umbrella, even when one knows it's going to rain?

As Santiago drove me home after dinner, we got stuck—not in traffic, but in a sea of bodies. Protesters were banging on pots and pans outside the residence of Domingo Cavallo, the minister of finance, on Avenida Callao. There was nothing unusual about that. This has been going on for days, ever since the government decreed the *corralito*. A few detours later and we arrived at the back of my apartment building. We couldn't approach it from the Avenida de Mayo side because it was closed to traffic. Now we saw why. There were mini-bonfires lining the avenue, and flowing down it was a torrential stream of people. Santiago let me out of the car. I insisted that it was NOT necessary for him to accompany me to the door. I wanted to avoid any awkward situations. He complied unwillingly.

"Whatever you do, promise to stay indoors," he said.

"Yes, I promise," I said.

"You won't do anything foolish, will you?" he said.

"Of course not," I said.

I waved him off and ran upstairs to my apartment. I hadn't opened the door and already I was kicking off my heels. Once inside, I flung the Chanel bag (inherited from my grandmother) into a corner, put on a pair of sneakers and my jeans jacket, and ran back downstairs as quickly as I could. I left the building to join the throng that was marching down the avenue to Plaza de Mayo.

The protesters were ordinary, middle-class folk, ranging in age from one to ninety-one. It was like a mass picnic outing, except that it was a bit noisier because people were chanting slogans, clapping their hands, and singing songs of protest. But mostly they were banging on things. When they weren't banging on pots and pans, they were banging on lampposts, dustbins, anything they could get their hands on. It felt like carnival, as they beat out a *candombe*, the rhythm of the Rio de la Plata. Every now and then, there was a lull as the crowd went quiet. I will never forget the sound of that silence, the hushed sound of people's feet against the tarmac. Then the silence was broken as somebody led the crowd in a new refrain and the banging started up again. I did not feel entitled to bang on a pot or a pan. I tried to open an account once, but they wouldn't let me because I'm not an official resident. Ironically, it was the red tape that saved me. But even though I am not directly affected by the *corralito*, I am proud of Argentina today. By taking matters and kitchenware into their own hands, they have proved me wrong. And I have never been so glad to be wrong in my life.

The throng deposited me at Plaza de Mayo. It was already chock-ablock with demonstrators who had poured into this large but enclosed space in front of the presidential palace. People were chanting obscenities about Cavallo's mother. I couldn't help but feel sorry for him. It's not all his fault (I don't think), but try telling that to the people. Then I heard excited shouts of, "The son of a bitch is gone!" Immediately, people improvised a ditty on the subject. It was like the aftermath of an important soccer match. But instead of celebrating under the Obelisk, which is the meeting point for the supporters of the winning team, tonight's celebration was here in front of the Pink House. The people felt empowered and they were reveling in it. They had demanded Cavallo's withdrawal and now he was gone! I'm sure it surprised them as much as it did the government, which must have been counting on the usual complacency.

But it was too good to be true. Seconds after the news of Cavallo's resignation, the cheering stopped, giving way to the muffled sound of chaos. People were rushing toward me, away from the palace. I wondered what was going on. My eyes started to sting and then to water. I felt a burning sensation in my throat, which descended into my lungs almost immediately, making breathing very awkward. I was trying not to choke in between coughs.

"Tear gas?! On children and grandparents? Shame on them! Shame on the bastards!" went the voices of outrage.

I switched into automatic pilot and followed the herd out of the square. I tried to find the right balance between getting the hell out of there without actually running away: speed walking. The tide was reversing as the news spread about the tear gas.

The euphoria had turned into anger. On my way back up Avenue de Mayo, I noticed young men wearing black masks. Had they been there all along? Where had they suddenly appeared from? They had bits of street in their hands, stones and other missiles, and they were looking for targets. If I was lucky, I wouldn't get between them and their targets. I saw some people trying to contain the situation, shouting, "Don't run!," while others were looking to start fights. I saw a girl physically restrain her boyfriend from getting into one. He ended up hitting her instead. Tempers were flaring. It was getting ugly.

Now, I was back on Plaza Congreso, outside the Parliament building. There were people all over it. They had clambered up onto the steps, onto the statues of the lions, onto the lampposts all around it, onto the balconies and the roof, waving flags and making the same amount of noise they would at the River-Boca final (the two biggest soccer teams). I couldn't believe it when I bumped into Monica and Martin in the middle of it all! And guess what? They're engaged! I was so happy at the time that I begged them to make me a bridesmaid. But hopefully, they'll forget. Anyway, we hung out together for a couple of hours as if we were at some huge *milonga* or at the biggest engagement party in history. From here, the tear-gas episode seemed like a bar fight that would soon be forgotten. Finally, I left them to party on late into the night. As far as I was concerned, the festivities were over. I was exhausted from all the excitement. Though I thought it unlikely that I would get any sleep with the racket that was going on out there. It was three A.M. and the party was still going strong. I hoped it wouldn't end with artillery fireworks. I also hoped I could get my Florida-fix tomorrow.

December 20, 2001

As I left my apartment this morning to go back to work—yes!—I noticed that the windows of the café downstairs were shattered and that the streets looked a bit worse for wear. But they were replacing the glass and it looked like business as usual.

The crowds on Florida were a bit thin, but that was only to be expected. In fact, I was surprised that there was anybody there at all. I couldn't imagine that these were the same people who had been banging on pots and pans furiously the night before. It was as if none of it had happened. They were going about their normal business, buying and selling things, running errands, making their way to the office, to a café, or to the cinema. It was surreal. Could these really be the same people?

Felicia said she'd gone with Mauricio and their S-I-X kids. She said she had been terrified when she almost lost one of them in the crowd. Pablo went too, apparently. I was amazed when he said that he had taken a pan with him. I simply could not imagine him getting riled up enough to bang anything at all, let alone a pan. Just goes to show that you never really know anybody . . .

I stopped off at a café on the way home for a *cortado* and *medialunas*. On the television screen, I saw images of continuing clashes in front of the Pink House, between protestors and the police on horseback. I heard the people at the table at the far end of the café say Duhalde's name numerous times and loudly enough for me to hear it from where I was sitting. The (loud) rumor is that these *piqueteros*, or hard-line protestors, are his henchmen. While at a table next to mine, I overheard another word. A word that was being whispered: *"represión."* They were referring to the bad conduct of the authorities, both the government and the police. The military dictatorship and its thirty thousand victims are still far too close for comfort.

Back at my apartment, I was writing an e-mail when the familiar sounds of a demonstration started up again. Not a Wednesday has gone by in two years that I haven't been forced to endure these noisy rallies. But the sounds were different today—more threatening. Today they grated on my nerves. I tried to block out the growing unease and continued to write my e-mail.

I didn't know I had reached saturation point until Inés called to say she was concerned about my being in the epicenter of unrest and asked me to please come and stay with her and Juan Carlos. Until then, I hadn't thought of escape as an option. Now I did, and at once my heart started to race. I wanted out. I wanted out *now!* I started to pack frantically, making sure to take both passports and whatever cash I had laying around the house. Just in case. I also wanted to give my six doormen their Christmas presents—also just in case I never saw them again. As I was busy throwing things into bags, the phone rang again:

"They have called in the army. You must leave at once!" said Inés.

I didn't know what that meant, but I wasn't too keen to find out. I put the finishing touches to my packing—I admit I didn't fold everything as well as I should have—grabbed the doormen's gifts, and bolted out of the door. On my way out of the building, I threw the presents at the doorman on duty.

"Happy Christmas, Ramón! Could you make sure the others get their gifts? Thanks a lot!" He didn't have the time to reply. I was already out of the gate.

Outside, it was a war zone gone temporarily quiet. I hobbled under my duffle bag, stuffed with its arbitrary contents—how do you decide what to take with you and what to leave behind? I was not wearing the most sensible shoes. I couldn't bear to part with my platforms, but since they are heavy, I decided to wear them instead of carrying them. As a result, I kept tripping on upturned paving and the holes where the paving used to be. There wasn't a taxi in sight since the square was now closed to traffic. And around me were a number of men in black masks, looking at me menacingly. For once, I wasn't being paranoid (I don't think). Did I have the words "My Dad Is a Banker" painted on my forehead, or was I imagining it?

I must remember to check when I get to Inés's, I thought.

After walking about ten blocks (in the platform shoes with a very heavy bag), I found a taxi. I waved it down and said, "To Barrio Norte!" and hey presto, I was out of the desert and headed for the oasis.

I have been glued to the TV all afternoon. The violence taking place outside what used to be my doorstep is mind-boggling. Surely that's not where I used to live? I can't connect these visions of hell with my street. They say there are twenty dead. I have called the superintendent of my building to check up on him and his family. They are holed up inside their apartment. He sounded surprisingly cheery about the whole thing, which made me feel like a complete chicken. I also tried to get in touch with Felicia and Pablo to let them know that I might have trouble getting to work tomorrow, but I haven't been able to get through to either of them so far. I'll say this: being a refugee is not all it's hyped up to be. In fact, it's not something I would recommend to anyone.

December 21, 2001

News flash: President de la Rúa has just resigned. Scrammed, more like. He was airlifted out of the Pink House by helicopter a couple of hours ago. He was trying to flee to Punta del Este, in Uruguay, with his family, but they didn't make it. Apparently this is reminiscent of some dictator (I didn't catch which one) who also ran away in a helicopter. In the meantime, I am watching delinquents take advantage of the leadership vacuum. Overnight, Argentina has turned into a lawless state and they, those men in black masks, are making a mess on what used to be my doorstep.

I did finally get through to Felicia. She and the kids are fine. But she says that for the next few days it's going to be virtually impossible to get into the center from out in the sticks, where she lives—in not exactly a *villa miseria* (a slum) but not far off. So she's decided that our "Christmas break" should start a few days early this year. I thought she was pretty philosophical about the whole thing considering how badly she needs the money. I do hope this doesn't mean empty stockings for her S-I-X kids.

"Don't worry!" she said. "I'll see you in the new year!" It's amazing how nice she can be. It's a pity the country didn't collapse into anarchy a long time ago, since that apparently is what it takes.

December 22, 2001

Inés and Juan Carlos have taken The Refugee with them to La Esperanza for the holidays. Ironic though the name of the *estancia* may be—it means "Hope"—there are worse camps to be interned at.

It is truly an enchanted garden, miles away from everything, thanks to the fact that Juan Carlos owns the miles of land around it. Surely this is not the same country as the one that fell apart noisily outside my window the other day! The silence is almost unnerving: I had forgotten what it felt like not to hear the constant sound of clashing pots and pans. True, I have to put up with the bloody birds that wake me up with their chirping at six in the morning. It's a good thing that Juan Carlos has so many rifles handy. I'm seriously thinking of using one tomorrow morning at six.

I've been taking endless walks across fields and equally endless rides across vast stretches of farmland that go on and on and on into the infinite horizon and never stop. I have come to love these pampas. I didn't, at first. The first time I came out to the country, I equated their flatness with boringness. But now I find their very monotony fascinating—

mystical even. The best bit is looking up at the vast, vast sky. Everything shrinks when you do that. It puts things in their proper perspective.

When I came back from my ride this afternoon for a spot of tea, Inés told me that elections have been set for March 1. They have made someone president in the meantime, but I didn't catch his name.

It's time to get changed. We're expecting the family from the neighboring farm over for dinner. That's the thing about life in the country. All one does is eat and drink (heavily) to compensate for all that fresh air. But the best thing about life in the country is that I can eat all the garlic I want. Viento, which means "Wind," the horse I have been given to ride, doesn't mind my garlic breath at all. Or if he does, he can't complain about it.

December 24, 2001

When Inés said that the neighbors were coming over to dinner the other night, she failed to mention that the neighbors in question were Grace and Luis and their son . . . Santiago! They never give up, do they? But I played along, and even flirted with him to make everyone happy. It wasn't the most unpleasant evening I've ever spent. As I said, the guy is incredible, physically speaking. So it didn't require too much effort. Such a shame he doesn't dance the tango.

The next day, Santiago's parents asked us over to their *estancia* for the day. As we rolled up the driveway to the house, I saw a corral in a field on the left, and inside a gaucho breaking a horse. I thought I recognized the gaucho, but I wasn't sure. After I'd said a brief hello to Grace and Luis, I wandered over to the corral. I was right: the gaucho and Santiago were one and the same. We acknowledged each other silently and then I propped myself on top of the wooden enclosure and watched him go about his business.

The humid atmosphere diffused the light and created a halo around his golden head as he stood still in the middle of the corral. The horse kept far away from him, sticking as close to the edges as possible. But gradually, he was able to draw her in—it was a she—until he was looking deep in her eyes. I thought I overheard him whisper to her. As he did, he slowly slid the bit over her head until it was inside her mouth. She barely flinched. Had he hypnotized her? He was certainly on the way to hypnotizing me.

I don't know how much time passed—it had stopped as far as I was concerned—but Santiago waited with the patience of a seducer for the next step. Gradually, her diffidence gave way to what looked like half-hearted cooperation. Now she was walking, trotting, galloping, slowing down, changing direction, and stopping for no apparent reason. I hadn't heard the sound of any cracking whips. As I sat on the sidelines, watching Alexander tame Bucephalas, I wondered why anyone—human or animal—would give up her freedom to a master.

The time had come to saddle her. The unfamiliar object made her shy away at first, but as he teased her with it, putting it on and taking it off repeatedly, so that it brushed her flanks, stroking them with each contact, she finally allowed the saddle to sit in place. Again, I asked myself: why? But she seemed to become accustomed to its weight on her back and to the girdle around her belly as he continued to stroke her and to whisper sweet nothings in her ears.

She was ready to mount. As he straddled her, she flinched at the sudden movement and the extra weight on her back, kicking up a fuss with a cloud of dust that rose into the air. But he soothed her fears and she settled down. Now horse and rider were one. Osmosis. It was like watching them dance the tango. And Santiago's features relaxed.

The average tango lasts three minutes but I think this one lasted thirty seconds. She had timed the stunt perfectly. Nostrils flaring, mouth frothing, eyes incandescent, she raised herself up onto her hind legs and then towered there majestically with her tail up and ears back before she came crashing down again onto her front hooves, all the while letting out an ear-piercing whinny. Up and down, up and down went Santiago on what had become an equestrian seesaw. Apparently, she was practicing to be a bucking bronco. Finally, he didn't come down at all. Instead, he took off in flight, performing a quadruple toe loop in combination with a triple axel, on his way back down to the ground, where he landed with the thud of a very heavy sack of potatoes.

My back hurt, and as he lifted himself up from the ground, my ribs creaked. He looked even more beautiful now—as beautiful as a wounded soldier. It was obvious that he was in pain, hard as he tried to cover it up. He limped toward her, his eyes flashing with anger. I think he was angrier with himself than he was with her. After all, the art of seduction requires patience until the very end. He had made a fatal miscalculation, rushing the conquest and skipping a step on the final road to victory. But he was going to break her, whether she liked it or not.

And as I sat there on the side of the corral, I wondered why it was that she let him. Before wondering when it would be my turn.

Who cares if he doesn't do the tango? I thought, It's *only* a dance!

December 26, 2001

Christmas Eve was perfect. Apart from the intrusion on perfection halfway through dinner. Juan Carlos had a table for twelve placed near the eucalyptus grove, at the far end of the grounds. The lawn was aglow with tea candles that twinkled back at the stars and flickered among the flowers in their beds, while the fire of the *asado* blazed bright orange flames skyward into the night.

I'm afraid I'm going to break the magical spell to talk about the *asado* for a minute. I must, since it is the most venerated of all institutions—even holier than *mate* in terms of the place it occupies in the collective Argentine psyche. It's a . . . barbecue. But if ever an Argentine heard I called it that, he would take such offense at the comparison that I would never be invited to an *asado* again, and that would be a terrible shame. It is undeniable that Argentines have a knack when it comes to meat. I know more than one vegetarian who has relented. Partly because there's not much else on the menu, so if you want to survive, you'd better start eating meat. But as is so often the case, converts make the most fanatical of zealots. Having renounced their religion, many ex-vegetarians go to the other extreme and indulge their newfound carnivorous passion whenever they get the chance. Just writing about it, my mouth waters. All this to say that Hernán, the *asador*, was doing a splendid job with the mutton.

Okay, now we can go back to basking in the warmth of that night. The stars were out and doing their job brilliantly. The table looked exquisite, cloaked in crisp linen and set with fine crystal and antique silverware. The wine flowed freely, spirits rose steadily, and the volume rose accordingly. I don't know what it is about alcohol that makes people shout. Do you think it affects people's hearing, so they have to talk more loudly in order to hear each other? It was coming dangerously close to turning into a rowdy affair when all of a sudden the lights inside the house went out.

Conversations were left in mid-sentence, jokes dangled in the air with nowhere to go, and faces froze in mid-laughter. I looked up at the sky to admire the stars that shone more brightly in the pitch-black. It seemed that I was the only one in the mood for romance. I was hoping that Santiago might take this opportunity to play a little footsie or take my hand, or grope my thigh or something. Anything! But now that I've decided that I *am* interested in him, it's as if I don't exist. Typical.

Anyway, the power outage had put everybody on edge.

"It's Duhalde. He's sabotaging the electricity!" cried Luis.

"Do you think it might be a coup d'état?" asked Inés.

When about half an hour later, the lights went back on, there was a collective sigh of relief and we could go back to pretending that we were on another continent in another century. The wine flowed abundantly once more and the jokes, laughter, and chatter were resumed accordingly.

Christmas Day was perfect too. Before I decided to engage in battle with a stirrup and the stirrup won. I wish I could say it happened as I was galloping off into the pampas like an Amazon. Unfortunately, I hadn't even gotten on top of the horse yet. It happened in the saddle room as I was bringing the massive leather saddle with its weighty metallic stirrups down from its high perch—when *bang*! And now I am disfigured: I have a white gauze bandage covering the entire left side of my face. It wasn't my best side, anyway. But looking like an Egyptian mummy—or half an Egyptian mummy—is not going to help my chances with Santiago, I don't think.

The only positive I see is that when I get back to Buenos Aires and people ask what happened, I might be able to get away with: "I got into a skirmish with the cops at Plaza de Mayo!" which is far, far less silly than the truth.

December 28, 2002

I'm writing standing up. I'm worried that if I sit down, the blister will burst. In addition to the white gauze bandage on my left eye, I now have a symmetrical white gauze bandage on the right cheek of my bottom. It got there from trying too hard to please Grace.

"Brush the saddle!" she instructed when we went out for a ride together. I brushed and brushed until I could feel my pants burning my skin off. But I kept on brushing anyway. Why? Because Grace is the mother-in-law of my dreams and I wanted to impress her with my riding skills, thus telegraphing that I would make a perfect country wife. (Tango? What's that?) But I wasn't successful. If she was impressed, it was no doubt by the size of my bottom, as she put her veterinary training into practice and dressed the wound. I bet you she's never seen such a large one in her life! I don't mean the wound. (Wouldn't it be nice if the saddle had burned off some of the cellulite with the skin?)

The feeling is mutual: she has told me verbatim that she wants me as her daughter-in-law. So it's a match made in heaven, right? Wrong. Her son is being a complete spoilsport.

As she dabbed the raw flesh with iodine, she gave me a fishing lesson:

"Catch and release, catch and release—that's the way to get Santi," she said. "And whatever you do, don't sleep with him! Not yet. Not until he's ready."

I don't know what stung more: the lesson or the iodine. I have told her that I don't think he's interested in being caught. Unless it's by a horse. Santiago is more infatuated with his mare than he is with me, and once again, I must contend with the "Other Woman." Except that in this case, the "Other Woman" happens to be a horse. (Does that make *me* the "Other Horse" in her eyes?) Worse still, the horse is thirty years younger than me. I don't know what is more humiliating: competing with a human rival or with a rival of the horsey variety. What I do know is that once again, I am stuck in a love triangle and once again, I am the angle too many.

But Grace insists that it's too soon to give up. What she doesn't realize is that I am and always will be an F student when it comes to winning men's hearts. How can I tell her the truth? That in Santiago's eyes, as in the eyes of all men, I'm not wife material. I'm not even girlfriend material. They take one look at me and think: SEX! (sex and love being mutually exclusive when it comes to me.)

December 30, 2001

So I ignored Grace's advice. I knew for a fact that no amount of catching and releasing could win me Santiago's heart. Therefore, why hold out? If you can't beat 'em, you might as well go for a roll in the hay with 'em, is my philosophy. It must be said that in that respect, Grace's son has turned out to be most cooperative. Given the respective states of my face and bottom, it's amazing that he should want to have sex with me at all. I can't imagine that I look terribly appetizing in my begauzed state. But one thing we can't fault Santiago for is a lack of appetite. In his case "I don't want a relationship" means "Let's do it in the fields, in the stables, and anywhere else that animals are liable to leave droppings." In a nutshell, it's been well worth the straw stuck in my wound and the subsequent itchiness of infection. One certainly couldn't fault Santiago for not seizing the sexual day!

Of course, I know that I'll pay the price tomorrow, when I turn into a pathetic blob of self-pity. I always do, afterward. It's like drugs. You feel high at the time, and, well, I don't think it's necessary to spell out how you feel afterward. I know that when I get over the excitement generated by great sex—and by great sex, I mean sex with a penis that (a) is bigger than my thumb, (b) stays up for more than two seconds, and (c) is attached to the body of the son of Robert Redford and Paul Newman—as I was saying, all I'll be left with tomorrow—I know this from previous experience—is the knowledge that he finds a horse more lovable than me. All I will remember are the words "I don't want a relationship."

The only thing that will make me feel better is going back to work. I'll hear the sound of applause and instantly, I'll forget about my wounds. And when I dance—how I've missed the tango!—I'll be in such a state of bliss that I'll forget about the tragedy that I was not born a horse. And my fan club with their sweet little signs and their occasional stalker is bound to make me forget that I am the world's least lovable person. Only a few more days to go before I get back to life in the limelight, to being a "celebrity," to forgetting about Santiago. Since it's not going to be all that hard, I might as well go for one last roll in the hay. To bring in the New Year. Why not? Grace will never know.

P.S. It's a good thing I didn't catch the president's name, because Inés has just informed me that he's already been replaced by another one, whose name I didn't catch either.

December 31, 2001

My butt hurts! Which is one way of summarizing the year:

1. I had to *pay* a partner to make a video with me since nobody would dance with me for free.
2. I waited in line for hours on end only to be rejected like a used sock after having been stood up by the only partner who ever said the C word to me—and I didn't even spank him for it.
3. My attempts at being a lesbian failed miserably.
4. I killed many, many eggplants.
5. I now beg for a living in the gutter. My body has aged ten years due to the constant battering by the sidewalk and the

freezing and then boiling weather conditions, leading to TB and premature varicose veins.

6. And I am only marginally thinner than I was before.

7. I have a boss who makes Fagin in *Oliver Twist* look adorable.

8. My partner is colder than a cod. And less animated.

9. I am even less attractive to polo players than I am to tango dancers. And they haven't invented the operation to change humans into horses yet.

10. Finally, the country is in a worse state than my love life. A complete shambles is a nice way of putting it. People are lining up for days on end outside the Spanish embassy with their sleeping bags, desperate to get out, to start life afresh in a country where it's still possible to dream of a future.

No, no, no! You can't start the New Year off like this. You must make more of an effort to look at the glass as half full. Think positive! Even if it kills you:

1. I looked fabulous in the video, even if it's just me who says so (since I haven't had the guts to show it around)—and it wasn't just the clothes, the hair, the makeup, the lighting, and the distorted lens.

2. *I* didn't chicken out. *I* showed up, and virtue is my middle name.

3. All's well that ends well. The performance didn't go at all badly, considering that Flo and I weren't on speaking terms at the time. And afterward, we kissed and made up. In the non-lesbian sense.

4. That's the last time I ever attempt to make moussaka. Which is fine by me because I prefer being a slut in the bedroom anyway.

5. The love I receive from my "fan club" compensates for all the brutality and the loneliness in the world.

6. Well, maybe not *all*, but a lot of it.

7. Felicia does have a heart, after all, and I have discovered the way to it: empanadas. Easy!

8. It could be worse than dancing with a cod. I could be dancing with a halibut, say—or worse still, dancing with neither cod nor halibut. And then I'd have no reason for being in the *culo del mundo*. None at all.

9. When you think about it, it's a blessing that Santiago doesn't want a relationship. One can only go for so many rolls in the hay per day. Think of all the boring horsey talk you've spared yourself in between!

10. And finally, the people of Argentina have risen and taken charge of their destiny! They have said no to corruption! no to incompetence! and no to eating very expensive sandwiches outside banks everywhere. Happy, happy New Year!

January 3, 2002

Everything is exactly how I left it before I ran away like a headless chicken. My building has neither been bombed nor pillaged and the windows are all intact. Not an overturned table, not a vandalized chair nor even a ripped pillow! What an anticlimax! That's the story of my life, really. I do have one piece of interesting news, though. We have a new president, the fifth in two weeks, and his name I *do* remember: Eduardo Duhalde (no comment).

At work, things are also pretty much as I left them, which is a huge relief. The Statue of Liberty gets off his pedestal as soon as he sees us and immediately starts to unravel his yards and yards of green bandaging. Tower Records is still pumping out its really bad (and loud) music, which it is now my job to try to minimize through pleading with the store manager. I think he does it on purpose to force me into his store in my ridiculously short skirt, fishnet tights, and stiletto heels.

The automated doors of the C&A continue to slide open and closed as the shoppers stream in and out of the store, thus sending me the delicious gusts of air-conditioning that help me recover from my heatstroke between sets. The gypsy urchins are still up to their usual antics, running in and out of our circle during the show and driving Felicia as nuts as ever. Our regular cast of characters is back on its bench and in its usual place, the old man in the gray anorak—no matter how hot it gets—sitting next to the old woman with no teeth sitting next to the man I suspect has a mild case of Down syndrome sitting next to the founding (and only?) member of the official "La Griega" fan club, who as usual holds up his cardboard sign whenever he deems it appropriate to show support and generate cheers from the rest of the audience.

The only thing that is a bit abnormal are the sounds of banging pots and pans that you hear every so often, in the distance. But they are far off enough that it is possible to ignore them.

"Careful! Not like that! You're going to dirty my trousers!" That's Pablo telling me off when I accidentally lift his trouser leg, showing some sock—oops!—but more interestingly, some suspender holding up the sock. This faux pas occurs as I am doing a standard tango embellishment that consists of stroking the guy's shin with your shoe in a kind of mock-wiping action. But he can hiss at me all he likes today, I am so thrilled to be back on Florida that nothing will upset me.

Instead, I smile and go back to dancing with my eyes closed and to making believe that I am dancing with Santiago. Until I open my eyes and I see Ernesto standing in the crowd with his bike leaning against his hip and a pouch on his back. I blow him a kiss in the middle of a *giro* and as I do, I catch Felicia giving me one of her dirty looks. I know I'm going to hear it from her as soon as the set is finished. But I don't care. I'm back where I belong!

"*Ciao, Princesa!*" shouts Ernesto as he blows me a kiss and hops onto his bike, off on his merry way.

I close my eyes again and go back to dancing with Santiago. Until I tell myself that it's not healthy and that I really ought to stop. And so I focus on what I am doing and as I do, I think: "*This* is what I am still doing in the *culo del mundo*!"

January 9, 2002

Overnight, Argentina has turned into a Banana Republic. And I don't mean the store. It happened the day before yesterday: the dreaded devaluation that everybody has been predicting since I came here almost three years ago. It's the first thing that Duhalde has done since he took over. The peso, which had been pegged to the dollar— *"el uno por uno "*—has been unpegged, and as a result it has already dropped in value by 30 percent. Which means that I am no longer earning $15 bucks a day, but $5!

This has sent everyone into a frenzy of speculation—of the monetary kind. Most people are trying to get their hands on dollars before the peso falls even further down the tubes. Others are out to make a buck and have made a full-time occupation out of buying and selling dollars according to the fluctuating market prices. Suddenly, all the exchange bureaus that were as good as dead have come to life again. I used to wonder why they were still around, since they were always empty. Now I know. They were hanging around, waiting for times like these.

It has suddenly turned into a queue country. If they are not lining up outside the embassies, they are lining up inside the *casas de cambio*. But money changing isn't restricted to these sordid interiors. It is going on all over the place, in broad daylight. Currency hawkers everywhere—there are suddenly lots of them on Florida—approach you and whisper furtively: *"Cambio?"* I don't understand why they look so nervous. It's not as if anybody is going to stop them. The police certainly don't seem to care.

Another visible result of the devaluation is that shopkeepers have already put their prices up—preemptively in many cases. I ran out of moisturizer today, so I went to the pharmacy. I couldn't believe it: a bottle of Neutrogena Combination Skin Moisture (oil free) now costs eighteen pesos! That's more than a day's salary and what I call extortion! It's not even my usual brand, but I couldn't find my usual brand, so they had me cornered. That bottle had probably been sitting on the shelf for six months, judging by the dust on the wrapping. But it *was* an emergency, so I coughed up the eighteen pesos even though it made me angry.

I'm not really entitled to complain. I'm a spoiled brat compared to the Felicias of the world. I have a handy debit card linking me to a bank account in New York. Even though these days, that's no guarantee that I'm actually going to get my hands on any of *my* dollars. The serious shortage of green bills means that the banks don't have enough of them to pass on to me. As a result, it's hit or miss these days when I go to a cash machine—often miss.

Nevertheless, the fact is that life is going to be cheaper from now on for those of us with dollars—unless things spiral out of control and the country goes into hyperinflation, which is what happened in 1989 and why they pegged the peso to the dollar in the first place. People are terrified that it will happen again. They don't look forward to wheelbarrowing worthless bits of paper about to pay for a cup of coffee. But that is not my greatest concern right now.

My greatest concern is that the divide between Felicia and me has just widened by 30 percent. Overnight, she has become 30 percent poorer—or I, 30 percent richer, depending on how you look at it. Which is going to make it a lot more than 30 percent more difficult to work with her. It was hard enough omitting certain details about my background. Now it's going to be even harder to pretend that I am poor. And my guilt over it has already appreciated by far more than 30 percent.

January 24, 2002

Last night, I went out to dinner and I packed a toothbrush, just in case. It's always a bit iffy whether I'll make it back to the apartment. You never know when they are going to cordon off the square due to a spot of rioting. Between you and me, it's becoming a bit of a drag.

The tension has escalated since they went and stole everybody's money. It's called *"pesificación"*—i.e., they have converted all dollar savings into pesos. In other words, people who thought they had, say, ten thousand dollars in their savings account have woken up to find that their ten thousand dollars have turned into three thousand dollars, and tomorrow they could easily be worth twenty-five hundred dollars, and who knows what they will be worth the day after that. This has not done much to bolster people's confidence in the banking system. Especially when the banks won't let panicked depositors take their money out. Or get inside, for that matter. On my street, every branch of every bank is boarded up to protect itself from ransacking. But they can't protect themselves from the grannies turned graffiti artists, armed to the teeth with canisters of spray paint. They have sprayed the word *"ladrónes"* (thieves) all over the banks' facades. It makes me shed tears of frustration when I think that this is the only possible outlet for their rage.

It's not the Juan Carloses of the world that I'm worried about. They have never kept their money in this country and never will. And now I see why.

It's the middle class who is worst hit. Those who had savings but not enough to put in Swiss or Uruguayan banks. Those who had no alternative but to trust the banks here. Luckily, I don't know too many of those.

And then there are those who either didn't have any savings to lose, or who have had the sense to keep the little they have under the mattress. I asked Felicia whether she had been affected by this latest turn of events—I couldn't bring myself to say "theft."

"If you think I was going to trust those *boludos* with even a penny, you must be joking!" she said.

Thank God! I thought.

But when I asked Pablo whether things were okay on his end, he didn't answer. There was nothing unusual about that. But his eye twitched and that twitch said more than a thousand words. I felt awful. Don't cry for me, Argentina. I am crying for you.

February 2, 2002

This morning, before we started on our trek down Florida, Pablo announced to me that he was going to quit.

No! I cried silently. You can't do this to me! Not now! I'm not ready! He had threatened to leave on a number of occasions, it was true. But I had always brushed it aside, thinking that push would never come to shove.

"Why?" I asked. I thought he was going to say that he was fed up with Felicia bossing him around.

"I'm out of here! I'm not staying in this shithole! With that bunch of thieves!" I knew he meant the government and what they had done to his savings. But before I could find a diplomatic way of asking him if he needed me to lend him any money, he said: "I've got a gig in Oman. It's for six months. The pay's good. We leave next week." "We" is him and his "real" partner, Patricia, who is above dancing in the street.

It's not happening! What's to become of me? I thought as I mumbled all sorts of stuff about seeing and understanding and about quitting too, since if he goes I go, etc. He hadn't given me a choice, really. There was no way I could stay on all by myself with Felicia. Who knows who she'd make me dance with? She'd probably bring Ruben back. No, I couldn't risk that. If Pablo went, then I had to go. Fuck.

It was not a pretty scene when we broke it to her that she was losing not one but two dancers. Leaving the *Pacífico Tango Show* with one dancer: her. And just in case people haven't figured it out by now, it takes more than one to dance the tango. But it wasn't ugly in the way I expected it to be. I was afraid she would scream and shout and pull me through the streets by my hair. Instead, she looked at us both, dumbfounded, and then once she had recovered, she said: "Sure. Okay. Fine. I'll find a couple to replace you."

I couldn't believe it: she had pulled a *me*—making it much more difficult to feel indifferent. How could I not empathize with her when I could see through to her heart? When I knew all about the devastation she was hiding behind that bravura of hers—of mine? I wish she had told us to piss off in no uncertain terms. I would have felt much better.

The deed was done. After Pablo and I had jointly turned our backs on Felicia, we came to our own crossroads and the way we parted was typical of our relationship:

"Good luck in Oman, then!" I said, not knowing what else to say.

"Good luck to you too!" he said, giving me a chilly kiss for the sake of form before we turned our backs on each other for good.

Today, the name "Florida" is enough to make me feel queasy. I feel so sad—among a thousand other things. And as bad luck would have it, I'm going to have to do more than hear the name tomorrow. It's too soon to go back, but I must. I can't get out of it. Monica has asked me to go shopping with her for some bridal stuff, and of course, it had to be Galerías Pacífico. I made sure to suggest we go during the Statue of Liberty's shift so as not to run into Felicia. But still, just walking down that street is going to bring back feelings I can't handle right now.

Of course, I could have stayed on, had I really wanted to. But I knew that sooner or later I was going to have to move on. I couldn't make the gutter my home forever. No matter how familiar it had become—in the family sense of the word. It was certainly dysfunctional enough to qualify as a family!

Without realizing it, I had become attached to Felicia, and even to Pablo with his silly mustache. To Mauricio and to Ruben, even though I got to know them less. I had become accustomed to their faces, in the words of my favorite musical. And habits die hard, even when they're shit.

I will miss the street, the beggars, the gypsies, the living statue, and the "supporting cast" on the bench; the sounds of chaos and squabbling; the music blaring from the loudspeakers; and of course, the applause. I will miss the kind of love you get when you are "famous."

Life was good in the gutter. But at the end of the day, I couldn't settle in there. As much as I want to settle somewhere. As tired as I am of moving on. Of always searching. Of never finding. But with the Pacífico show over, I have lost my reason to stay. And once again, the time has come to pick up my belongings and say good-bye. Good-bye to the dream. Good-bye to Buenos Aires.

February 10, 2002

I called Mummy yesterday to tell her.

"I'm leaving Buenos Aires," I said.

"Don't tell me: you're moving to Australia," she said. She has come to expect the worst from me. I don't know why.

"I hadn't thought of Australia, but now that you mention it . . . ," I said. I am nothing but a tease. My partners were right.

I finally put her out of her misery and told her my plans.

"Thank God!" she exclaimed. I was happy that she was happy.

"And what about tango?" she asked me.

"What about it?"

"You're still going to keep dancing, aren't you?" she said.

"Well, no, actually, I'm not," I said.

"You can't give it up, after all the work you've put into it," she said.

"I know, you're right, but—"

"What will I tell my friends? That you've suddenly gone and stopped being a tango dancer?" she said. (Tango has become the sound track to her bridge parties.)

"Don't worry, Mummy, you'll find something to tell them. I know: you can say that I'm going to get married and have lots of babies and live happily ever after."

"I can't tell them that! They'll never believe it," she said.

Next, I called Daddy:

"Oh no, you've joined an ashram," he said morosely.

I remembered a conversation we'd had once when I was sixteen. I have grown up a little since then, haven't I?

Anyway, I reassured him that I have *not* joined an ashram but that I *am* leaving Buenos Aires. He didn't say "Thank God!" but I'm sure that's what he was thinking. He's been bombarding me with e-mails lately about the unrest in Argentina, in case I hadn't noticed the tear gas in my lungs.

"And what about the tango?" he asked me.

"I'm going into early retirement," I said.

"That's a shame," he said. And I'm sure he meant it.

I was expecting him to give me a lecture about pension plans, but he didn't.

"So what are you going to do now?" he asked.

"I don't know," I told him, "but I'm going to look for it," I said.

"I'm sure you'll find it," he said, topping the "I'm proud of you" moment.

"You know you can always stay with us if you need to," he added. No, *that* topped it. I thanked him and told him that would not be necessary. I told him my plans and he sounded happy, which made me happy.

February 26, 2002

I put on my purple ring before setting out to La Glorieta for what would be my last tango. I couldn't bring myself to tell most of my partners that I am leaving. Only a select few. The others, I have left with the impression that they will see me again next Sunday. I think it's because I'm afraid to hurt them with the news of yet another defection. I felt like a ghost haunting her favorite spot.

Until I spotted a triplet—it was Javier! I hadn't seen him in ages. God, I'd forgotten how sexy he was. Those dark, swarthy looks . . . yum! And then I thought about how ironic it was that in the end, I hadn't slept with the most promiscuous triplet of the three. How on earth had I managed to resist the temptation? This brought back the memory of cold showers. And of his girlfriend. I looked around for Romina, but she wasn't with him. The ghost instantly turned into flesh and blood.

"*Che,* I left a message on your answering machine. Did you get it?" he asked nonchalantly. I could tell, though, that his inquiry was anything but.

"No, I didn't. What does it say?" I asked.

"It doesn't matter. You're here now," he said as he took me by the waist and led me to the floor.

He must have heard through the grapevine that I am leaving. I blushed at having been caught attempting to flee the country without saying good-bye. But I knew it was too dangerous. I was afraid of awakening the desire once more and then once more being left dangling. (I have sworn off cold showers for good.) But what I didn't know was that Javier had no intention of letting me leave the country (a) without lighting the fire again, and (b) without extinguishing it himself.

I don't know if people realize how difficult it is to dance tango while on the brink of orgasm.

"Come on! Let's get out of here!" he groaned.

"No!" I moaned.

"Why not?" he whimpered.

"Do I need to remind you that you have a girlfriend?" I said, ruining the mood somewhat.

"What's that got to do with anything?" he said testily.

"If you can't behave, we'll have to stop dancing," I threatened.

He behaved (i.e., he stopped talking) and we went back to dancing the "hidden" tango in peace and quiet. Until remorse set in. Mine.

"What if . . . ?" I started.

"Yes?" he answered eagerly.

"What if . . . we did it . . . just once. Before I leave Buenos Aires."

"Are you leaving?" he asked, pretending to be shocked. I'm sure he knew. But still, it made me sad to hear somebody else say it.

We finished the tango, which had turned into a silent handshake on a deal.

"Thank you, *mi amor*," I said. "Patience is a virtue," I added. There were a number of partners I wanted to dance with one last time. I wanted to experience the different shades of sublime sadness, the many textures of blissful melancholy that each one of my partners afforded me. One last time.

No sooner had the *milonga* ended than Javier was by my side. I got the impression he didn't trust me.

As we walked over to his truck, I glanced over my shoulder at the bandstand amidst the jacaranda and let out a sigh.

"Where do you want to go?" he asked me (where did *I* want to go?). He was hoping I'd say "my place." I was going to disappoint him, though. You see, I had one last fantasy that I wanted to fulfill before I left.

"I've never been to a *telo* [a love motel]. Will you take me?" I asked him.

"I don't have any money," he said.

"I'll pay," I said.

"Okay then," he said as he started the engine.

Now, just in case you think it was ungentlemanly of him to refuse to pay, let me defend him by saying that he did pull out a voucher from the glove compartment of his truck, which gave us a $5 discount on a *telo* in Belgrano, not far from La Glorieta. I was touched by the gesture: "Perfect, let's go there then."

The flickering red and green lights above the entrance indicated that we had arrived. We pulled into the covered garage, ensuring the privacy of the clientele. This way there is no risk of the car of somebody who is not supposed to be there being spotted. Two other cars were parked inside. I hoped the rooms were soundproofed. I would feel self-conscious if they weren't. We made our way into the reception area through the garage. Behind a smoked glass window, a faceless receptionist checked us in. I had slipped the $10 to Javier before we entered the motel. I didn't want him to look bad. Or maybe it was me I didn't want to look bad. He handed the money and the voucher over to the thing on the other side of the glass.

"Do you want the room for a shift or for the night?" the thing asked us. Javier took my cue and replied: "A shift." That's two hours. More than ample time.

We entered the den of evil and . . . it was exactly the same room I have stayed in at every cheap hotel I have ever been to, from Bangladesh to Bratislava (I haven't been to Bangladesh, but I couldn't think of anything else that goes with Bratislava). It had the same used carpet; the same frayed wallpaper; the same chipped bedside furniture; the same porno on the TV that you can't see very well because it had the same poor reception (so you're left to guess what the flickering forms are on the screen, which is actually quite erotic); the same cracked pink tiles in the bathroom; the same missing shower curtain, which doesn't make a difference anyway because the water splashes all over the place given the shallowness of the tub, if you can call that a tub; the same abrasive towels that are never long enough to wrap around your waist fully, no matter how thin you are; the same little soap bars that make you smell worse than before you washed. It was all so disappointingly familiar and reassuring at the same time. The only novelty was the overhead disco lights. And perhaps a few more mirrors than need be. I asked Javier for his POV:

"So, is this a typical room, then?"

"Yeah, I s'pose so. There are some really posh *telos*. The rooms have themes like 'safari' or 'A Thousand and One Nights' and that kind of thing. And then there are the flea motels. This is somewhere in between."

I can't say that this room did much for me. I was worried I'd have trouble getting my juices flowing. I needn't have. We had run out of small talk. It was time to get down to business.

Rough and tumble is the way I would describe the kind of business that Javier and I got down to. In the good sense. I don't know who surprised me more: Javier or myself—and I'm not easily surprised. Because Javier's talent, as I discovered last night, is not the tango. I've never been with anybody whose sexuality was so pure, so raw, so exciting, and so unadulterated by feelings. I was at the mercy of a man-turned-monster. And what surprised me, as I said, was that I loved it! He took me to the threshold of pain and then beyond it to find pleasure on the other side, completely unraveling my body so that its secrets lay out on open display. It's scary how close I came to never knowing them. I wonder how many things I will never know about myself before I die. Too many, I suspect.

We took a break. Javier picked up the phone and ordered a Coke for himself. After he had hung up, he asked me: "Did you want anything?"

"No, no. That's okay," I croaked through parched lips. "I'll share with you." Minutes later, a hand holding a can of Coke popped through a hole in the wall.

"How clever!" I thought. Everything about this room had become a source of rapture and delight.

We took turns sipping from the can. Javier asked me if I wanted to spend the night. No, I didn't. I don't think he did either, but he asked out of politeness. We went back to business. Now, he flew me to a place I have never been flown before. And I mean "fly" in the acrobatic sense of the word. He seemed to be taken over by a spirit that accomplished feats impossible for a mere mortal. He was in the kind of trance that makes people pierce their cheeks with arrows, walk on burning coals, lift trucks and even 105-pound girls *with one arm*, under a shower, turning her into a helicopter. You had to be there.

Once we had finished spending the $10, we got dressed in silence. Apart from a loud "Ouch!" when I pulled my dress over my ribs. I hope I haven't cracked one. They do feel awfully sore. And today, they've gone a deep purple-green. I'll have to have them x-rayed if they don't feel better in a few days.

I popped my head through the door a last time before we closed it behind us. If you can call that a head. It was more like a crow's nest (from all the hair pulling. Actually, I'm lucky I have any left). Anyway, as I was saying, the room had grown on me. On the surface, it hadn't changed in two hours. But it now kept my XXX secrets inside its walls. I smiled at the thought that a part of me will remain between them forever. Or was I smiling at the thought that I will take them with me wherever I go? Or was it because I had a slight concussion? I don't know.

What I do know is that if I get hit by a cab tomorrow, I don't care. If I never have sex again, that's fine with me—well, maybe not exactly fine, but I could live with it. Because in two hours, Javier made up for all the bad or nonexistent sex I've had to endure the last three years. He has single-handedly put Buenos Aires back on the map as the World Capital of Latin Lovers. At the eleventh hour, Argentina's reputation has been saved! (SFX: sounds of crowd cheering at a soccer stadium.)

For some reason, this makes leaving Buenos Aires less difficult.

"*Vamos,*" I said with a huge grin.

"*Vamos,*" he said, looking like he'd spent worse evenings in his life.

February 27, 2002

I hate packing. I wish I could skip this bit altogether. I wish everything would find its way into the suitcases on its own. I wish I didn't have to face the tango gowns I will never wear again. The skimpy black dress I wore for my first-ever exhibition with Chino; the silver sequins I wore when Gustavo stood me up at the audition; the black velvet catsuit that by some miracle did not make my ass look too big despite clinging to it like cellophane wrapping to a lamb chop; the red-and-white polka-dot skirt I wore on the merry-go-round-gone-mad (Pablo); the indecently short one that had its very own fan club on Florida—and all the others. They all wink at me from their hangers.

"We had some good times together, didn't we?" they say.

I close the door as quickly as I can and make a mental note: sell tango outfits.

"It's silly to keep them. They'll only collect dust," I say to myself. But I know I won't get rid of them. I could never.

It's the same story with the shoes. I open the rack, and here too, I cannot avoid the sight of the eight pairs of black suede heels. They have been my most true and trusted companions. I have relied on them more than I have on my partners (that's not saying much, I know). Some are more worn out than others. The veterans are the heels that I wore to La Glorieta every Sunday: they are absolutely covered in dirt. They deserve a medal. On the top rack, my red glitter "Dorothy shoes" catch my eye. I hadn't been able to resist those. Next to them, the patent-leather ones that almost killed me before I discovered Vaseline. Beneath them, the two pairs of purple suede shoes and next to them, the black-and-white ones, and next to them, the black-

and-red ones that I battered daily on Florida's cobblestones. They are almost as badly wounded as my Glorieta heels. But they do not bear a grudge.

"Please will you take us out to play today? We're bored in here," they call out to me.

The sight of them is too upsetting, so I close the door and send them back to their new life out of the spotlight and in the shadows.

I'll pack later.

March 1, 2002

As I waited for takeoff, I put a tango disc in my portable CD player and wrapped the headset around my head. That way, nobody would talk to me and/or throw up on me. As I did, my hand brushed my cheek, triggering as it did a sharp pain. I remembered the bruise there and smiled. I may even have let out a chuckle. I can't be sure.

But as I closed my eyes and floated back into the collective arms of the partners I was leaving behind, my lip started to quiver and I felt my throat constricting. I tried hard to keep it in—like when you're watching a sad movie with other people in the room, so you don't want to break down. But I couldn't keep it in, and soon I was giving in to a lament that even a *bandoneón* could not rival.

I cried as the flight attendant reminded us to buckle our seat belts, stow away our trays, and bring our seat backs into their upright positions. I cried during the demonstration of how to inflate the life vests, what to do in the event of an emergency landing, how to adjust the oxygen masks to our faces, and where to locate the emergency exits should all else fail. I cried during the dinner service, and when asked if I wanted chicken or pasta, I sobbed, "Chicken." I cried as I tried unsuccessfully to cut off a piece of the chicken with the little plastic knife they had placed in the wrapping alongside the stainless-steel spoon and fork. (How did the airline know I was contemplating suicide?) I cried as I mixed one mini-bottle of vodka with one can of Bloody Mary mix after another. (What is it about airplanes that makes one order Bloody

Marys?) But they didn't drown my sorrow. There weren't enough mini-bottles in the world to do that. I was prepared to cry for the remaining nine hours of the flight, since I had forgotten to bring a book and I had a lot to cry about:

For all the men I will never dance with again.

For the mes that each of them has the key to, the mes that will remain locked inside forever now that I have lost the keys.

But most of all, for the tango, which has given me more joy than I knew the world contained.

I was so busy crying that I didn't notice it at first: the hand that was holding the hankie. Until it nudged me. I looked up (God only knows what my tear-stained face looked like, but I can guess) and there he was.

Since when does Hugh Grant travel in cattle? I wondered.

He really was the spitting image of Hugh Grant, but he couldn't have been. That's not the kind of thing that happens to me. I'm the type of person who sits next to people who are sick all over her. I'm not the type of person the airline computer puts next to Hugh Grant. I gave this person who looked like Hugh Grant but couldn't possibly be a thank-you nod and took the Kleenex. I blew my nose loudly, while keeping my headset firmly in place. But the clone did not take the hint. He tapped me on the shoulder:

"Is everything all right?" he asked me. I think that's what his lips were saying, though I'm not 100 percent sure because of the tango that was blasting in my ears. I agree, it wasn't the cleverest thing to say, but he did get points for bravery. By starting a conversation with someone in my state, he was putting himself at high mucus risk.

I took off my headset to reassure him that I had "never been better." I can't remember what he said, but it must have been funny because I caught myself giggling. He certainly had a good sense of humor—as good as the original, I thought. They had really outdone themselves to-day in the guardian-angel department. I don't know if it was his doing or the Bloody Marys that finally kicked in, but I dozed off and was soon dreaming of angels that bore an uncanny resemblance to Hugh Grant.

When I opened my eyes again, it was dawn and the captain was saying:

"If you look out of the right side of the plane, you can just about catch a glimpse of the Acropolis in the early morning light."

The weight of the passengers shifted to the right side of the plane, sending the right wing of the aircraft into a dip that felt more like a dive.

"There are worse places to die, I suppose," I sighed morosely.

"But I want to live!" cried out another voice, more adamantly.

My stomach did one backflip after another, while the captain reassured us that it was "nothing to worry about," it was just a "touch of turbulence." That's when I realized I would very much like to experience life after tango, if such an opportunity were to arise. I glanced over at Hugh Grant, who looked equally attached to life at the moment—leading me to suspect that he might not be an angel after all.

It was in preparation for death that I was able to appreciate the immensity of tango's legacy. Tango had connected me with ME. It had revealed the flame of passion burning within, which nothing could extinguish—other than a plane crash. It had revealed the ME that I was particularly attached to at this moment and that I hoped to take many places before the grave. The ME that had loved once and that would love again. Many times, perhaps.

We were making the approach for landing, and as I looked out at the salmon-pink Acropolis, I reflected on how it stood there, thousands of years later, having survived ransacking and fire, pillage and plunder. Though it was not intact, it was more beautiful today in its naked vulnerability than it had been in past days of pomp and glory.

We touched down, the wheels screeching to a halt on the runway. I was going to live! And when at last I set foot on the soil of Athens, I waved good-bye to Hugh Grant. And as I made my way inside the terminal building to the beat of *"Volver,"* the tango that was now playing on my portable CD player, I knew that everything was going to be all right. And I smiled.

Afterword

Almost two years had passed since I fled Buenos Aires—twenty months to be precise—but I could still feel tear gas in my lungs. I had fled in humiliation with no thought of ever coming back. Of course it was the tango I had run away from. It wasn't the city itself or the country's economic collapse—though the strain of living in the former during the latter had certainly helped in my decision to leave. And while I had taken comfort in the promise of *Volver*, the tango that I had listened to as I flew away, I hadn't really believed in its prophecy of return. I knew that it was merely a lie I had told myself to make the separation less painful. Leaving is easier when you tell yourself it's not forever.

But then I wrote the book. I don't know if you've seen the movie *Something's Gotta Give*, but picture Diane Keaton, crying and laughing, laughing and crying as she writes. That was me! In my case, writing had also been therapeutic, and while it had undoubtedly brought me closer to giving up the ghost of tango, I still wasn't one hundred percent there.

There was no avoiding it. If I wanted to exorcise the ghost once and for all, I was going to have to go back. I wasn't too keen on the idea at first. In fact, I think it was scarier this time around than it had been the first. Those nasty knots that turned my stomach into a gas chamber came back with a vengeance when I thought about it. But now I also had another reason to go back.

I needed to find a Happy Ending.

I wasn't thinking *only* of myself when I came to this realization. I was also worried about my friends and family. If I didn't bring them back a Happy Ending, I would be letting them down. Or worse still: they would pity me. This was the dreadful thought that finally got me over the hump of my resistance. Having said that, there was one thing I was NEVER EVER prepared to do again as long as I lived and that was dance the tango. It was simply too dangerous for a recovering addict like me.

"Take a pair of heels with you just in case. Not that you'll ever need them, but you never know," said the not-as-fully-recovered-as-one-would-have-hoped junkie as she packed her suitcase, bound for Buenos Aires.

No sooner had I popped my head out of the taxi to receive the city's balmy evening kiss as it raced me from the airport into town along *9 de Julio* than it hit me: I was home.

I was going to stay in a flat in *Recoleta* that friends were lending me while they were away. As I unpacked, I shook with fear and excitement. "What day is it today?" I wondered. "Tuesday," I replied. And then, *"La Catedral!"*

Twenty minutes later I was waving down another cab, after a quick shower, pasting on the old make-up, and fishing out the only non-crumpled item of clothing from my suitcase:

"Why didn't you bring any decent tango gear? It's a good thing you packed your fishnets," I said to console myself.

As I climbed up the steep and unlit flight of stairs to the *milonga*, I wondered who would be there, and would they remember me? It had been such a long time. And so many foreigners come and go from the scene. Was I just one more to them?

That's when I spotted *el Gato* and his trademark whiskey tumbler, which he carried with him when he came over to me. I thought how reassuring it is that some things never change. But hang on! What was that I saw in his glass? It couldn't possibly be. . . . But it *was*: seltzer water?!

"I haven't had a drop in five months and three days—and thirteen hours," he added with a gruff chuckle. "It's the early wake-up calls: they kill you," he sighed as he blew out the smoke from his cigarette. Ever since he had been cast as a crooked cop in a hit movie, he had become somewhat of a celebrity.

"So what are you doing back here then, *rubia?*" he asked me.

"I'm on holiday. Just for three weeks. I've written a book, actually," I said, even though I already knew that I wouldn't be leaving again so soon.

"Yeah? What's it about?" he asked suspiciously.

"Oh . . . nothing . . . about my life as a tango dancer," I said as casually as I could.

"What did you say about me?!" he asked. I wasn't sure how to interpret his tone. Was he being playful or threatening?

"Don't you worry, my *Gatito*! It's all good!" I said before changing the subject: "Dance with me!"

And once again I felt the delicious softness of his paws against my back as together we prowled across the floor like one feline on four legs. And once more I tasted that bliss—the bliss that I thought I would never taste again.

As it turns out, not only had I not forgotten how to dance but I couldn't forget how to dance the tango even if I tried. It was a part of me now and nothing could eradicate it from my body/my soul/whatever it is you want to call it. And when I rolled into bed at 6:30 A.M., my last sleepy thought before I finally passed out was: what happier ending than this? And for the life of me I couldn't think of one.

Buenos Aires, 30 September 2005

Tango FAQs

1. What should I wear?

Most tango dancers like to wear black, with red following closely behind as their second favorite color. A skirt or dress with a high slit and fishnet tights are also considered de rigueur in most dancers' wardrobes. When it comes to tops, the field opens up but the trend is low-cut, open-back, and sleeveless—with the idea being to show as much skin, skin, skin as possible! It's true that it does help to feel sexy when you're not wearing much. Especially when you're starting out and want to make sure the guys spot the newcomer. It's one of the best ways to ensure you get lots of practice from the get-go. But in reality, you don't need to get dolled up if you don't want. And you'll find that the longer you dance, the less effort you'll feel like making. Because tango is a spirit you exude no matter if you're wearing a pair of jeans and a simple T-shirt. It is about the way you move, not what you wear.

2. Are heels really necessary?

As you know by now, I'm not much of a *Rules* girl. But you will find that it's much easier to dance the tango in heels rather than in flats. I know this is hard to believe but it's true. Odder still, it's easier to dance in heels than it is to walk in them—I guess it's because one tends to walk forward in real life, while one mostly walks backward when dancing the tango. I find that the heels give me the support I need when I am on the balls of my feet—which is ninety-nine percent of the time. But girls, it's not a competition: don't go out and buy four-inch heels until you're ready. Slowly does it. Most importantly, make sure to wear heels that fit properly. I lost all feeling in my toes on both feet for over a year because my shoemaker insisted that they should fit me "like a glove." Although I had cried out in agony when trying them on, I had not had the courage to return the pair to their maker. Instead, I hobbled around until it became clear that my toes—they had turned blue—would have to be amputated if I continued wearing the heels that in retrospect must have been at least three sizes too small for me.

3. Will I turn into a vampire?

It's true that most milongas do take place in the later hours. But not all. In Buenos Aires there are plenty of matinees (afternoon dances) to choose from. Also, many lessons and practicas are held in the early evening. So it is perfectly possible to take a class and catch the earlier part of a milonga without feeling like death the following morning. The key is to dance in moderation—admittedly, this is hard to do. But if, unlike yours truly, you manage to keep your addiction somewhat under control, you will be able to dance and hold down a job at the same time.

4. Do I need to be very fit?

The nice thing about the tango is that you can dance it well into your eighties or hundreds —remember Carmencita Calderon, whom I watched dance in the exhibition she gave on her hundredth birthday? It's a great, low-impact form of exercise and I recommend it highly to people of all ages and fitness levels. If, however, you're looking to turn it into a serious hobby or to go professional, requiring a more athletic approach to the dance, I recommend stretching before and after each session to avoid injury. Many dancers practice yoga, swear by Pilates, do classical ballet to improve their line, or martial arts like Tai Chi to work on their body awareness. Whatever works for you is good.

5. How often do I need to practice?

Never, if all you want is to enjoy dancing at a milonga. Or everyday, if you are aiming to become the world's best tango dancer. Most of us learn most of what we know by dancing with lots of different partners at the milonga. The more you practice leading and following different people, the better it is for your tango, providing you in turn with the best excuse to dance with a dozen or so partners a night—this is practice enough for most people.

6. Do I really need a partner?

No you don't. Not at first. In ninety-nine percent of tango classes, the teacher will ask you to rotate to insure that everyone gets a chance to dance with everyone else. Think of the tango as a language: the more people you speak to, the better you'll become at communicating. On the other hand, if you reach the point where you are considering a career in tango, or want to take your dancing to another level, it does help to have a steady partner. Similar to life, there comes a point where you think, "If I have to go through all that first date rigmarole one more time, I'll shoot myself." When you're having thoughts like these, the time has come to find a steady partner.

7. What music do you recommend?

Francisco Canaro, Osvaldo Fresedo, Pedro Laurenz, Carlos Di Sarli, Alfredo De Angelis, Juan Darienzo, Rodolfo Biagi, Angel D'Agostino with Angel Vargas, Ricardo Tanturi with Alberto Castillo, Miguel Caló with Raúl Berón, Aníbal Troilo, and Osvaldo Pugliese are just a few of my favorite tango orchestras.

8. Where can I go for lessons?

If you live in a major city in the United States, there is more than likely a thriving tango scene going on right beneath your nose. Big tango hubs include New York, San Francisco, Seattle, Portland, Chicago, Boston, Miami, Atlanta, Houston, and Santa Fe, among others, where you can dance the tango every day of the week if you want, and on most nights you'll need to choose between at least two if not more studios, classes, and/or *milongas* competing for your patronage. Check out information online regarding schedules and programs in your city. In smaller towns, where the tango is not as well established, chances are you will also find a budding tango community. Tango organizers often invite visiting teachers from Argentina or from other countries or cities in the United States to give workshops. I've met a number of brave tango pioneers who have built their own tango communities from scratch. Hats off to them!

9. Don't you have to be Argentine to do the tango?

I'm Argentine, you're Argentine, we're all Argentine . . . if to be Argentine means feeling the need to "reach out and touch someone" from time to time. You're also Argentine if there are days when you feel sad, lonely, and depressed. Or if you are searching for a soulmate. Or looking for a spark to ignite your fire. You're also Argentine if you like to flirt. And to dance. Or to flirt while dancing. And to hold someone in your arms. And be held by that person in return. If any of these apply, you've qualified as being Argentine-enough-to-dance-the-tango. Congratulations!

10. I don't speak Spanish.

So what? Neither did I. And anyway, you don't need to speak it in order to perform an "ocho." Tango is a universal language. It transcends all language barriers. I have no doubt that you will understand it, whether or not you and your teacher speak the same language. Trust me.

11. How long does it take to learn?

It doesn't take long to learn the basics—in fact, the basics are child's play since by definition: Tango = Walk + Embrace, and we all know how to do those two things, don't we? The real difficulty is not feeling self-conscious while we do these things with another person there to watch. As a rough guideline, I'd say a leader needs about three months before he feels at ease on the dance-floor. For a follower, it's relatively easy in the beginning: as long as she's dancing with a good leader, she can enjoy herself right from the start. The problem for followers is that they are usually forced to dance with fellow beginners, which can result in arms being torn out of sockets (see lesson 1) While it gets easier for leaders once they have understood the basics, it gets tougher for followers as their focus shifts to improving their technique, which requires a lifetime. But as I said, this is only a guideline since it all depends on the individual's ability and on how much time he or she dedicates to the dance.

12. When's the best time of year to go down to Buenos Aires?

Just because it's in the Southern Hemisphere does not make Buenos Aires a tropical city. There are definite seasons here, with January-February being the hottest summer months. If you don't like sweating or being sweated on, avoid coming at that time. Also, the city has emptied out since anybody who can get away is away at the beach— on the Argentine coast in Mar del Plata, say, or at Punta del Este in Uruguay to name two of the most popular resorts. Conversely, July–August are the wettest and coldest winter months. Though it never reaches the ridiculous sub-zero temperatures of Chicago or New York, it still gets far too cold for my old bones. Having said that, you'll find it does heat up on the dance floor in July and August since many tourists from the States and Europe flock here for their summer vacation. The most pleasant months weather-wise are the Spring and Fall months, i.e. March–May and October–December. If you ask me, it's always a good time to come down to Buenos Aires!

13. Shouldn't I wait to be more advanced before making the trip down there?

I don't think so. But do make sure to pack a thick skin. Men especially. Be prepared for women to pretend they didn't see your *cabezeo* or to straight out reject you, which would never happen to you at home, where you are everybody's favorite partner, I'm sure. I'm afraid it's one of those Catch-22s since a girl generally won't dance with you unless she has seen you dance with someone else before. But with a lot of patience, a bit of luck, and a good dose of humor, you'll find an exception to the rule who will be more than happy to help get your foot through the door. As for women coming down here for the first time, you'll remember that I was just as terrified as you. But remember this: you have a huge advantage over all the other women at the *milonga*: you are NEW FLESH, and there is nothing more enticing to a *Porteño*—I should know. They will be lining up to taste the new dish on the menu: YOU!

Glossary

A is for *Alfajores*—It is impossible to eat only one of these delicious cookies at a time, hence the plural.

Asado—A barbecue, and the meaning of life in Argentina. Vegetarians had better get with the program—or starve!

B is for *Bandoneon*—The high-pitched instrument similar to an accordion that gives the tango its soulful lament.

Boludo/a—Depending on the tone of voice, can either signify a term of endearment, roughly equivalent to "dude!" or alternatively might mean "fucker!"

Bonbon—A sweet pick-up line that may be applied to both sexes, though more often than not, it is old men in Panama hats who apply it to barely post-pubescent girls.

Bronca —A potent mix of anger, frustration, and impotence that Argentine taxi drivers, among others, feel on a daily basis.

C is for *Cabezeo*—The nod that a man gives a woman across the dance floor when he wants to dance with her.

Chanta—In the broadest sense, someone who is not of his word, so that's more or less everyone.

Che!—Hey! This is how all Argentines address each other. Now you know how Ernesto Guevara got his nickname.

Compadrito—A "wiseguy" of the early twentieth century, and legendary originator of the tango dance. In fact, male tango dancers today continue to imitate the swagger and style of this prototype.

Compromiso—1) Commitment. 2) Something that Argentine men are particularly loathe to do.

Cortado—A cup of espresso coffee "cut" with milk that the average Argentine drinks four to five times a day, providing him with the perfect excuse to spend hours at the café instead of the office.

D is for *Desencuentro*—A failed encounter. You'd be surprised how difficult it is to meet up with people in Argentina.

Despues!—Meaning "Later!" and the correct form for refusing a man who has had the audacity to ask a woman to dance directly instead of resorting to the *cabezeo* (see above). Not only will he get the hint, but he is ninety-nine percent sure never to ask her to dance again.

Dulce de Leche—A caramelized milk topping they put on everything from bananas to pancakes to yogurt to ice cream to *medialunas* to. . . . And one of the things that makes life in Argentina so very sweet.

F is for *Flaco/a*—Thin. Given the entire Argentine population fits this description—a puzzling phenomenon considering the amounts of *dulce de leche* consumed (see above)—the term is also used as a form of address, as in *"Che, flaca!"* Not to be taken literally but without a doubt, far better than being called *"gorda," "negra,"* or *"loca."*

Funyi—The wide-brimmed hat once worn by the *compadrito*, and a traditional part of the male tango costume. Also very handy for collecting money on *calle Florida*.

G is for *Giro*—A tango figure whereby the man makes the woman draw a "circle" around him, and Pablo de las Pampa's Alpha and Omega.

Gomina—Hair gel and a vital part of both male and female tango dancers' kits.

Griega—Greek. My stage name, as well as the most frequent response to the question "What is your nationality?" Better than the alternative: *Gringa*. See below.

Gringa—A foreigner, especially of the North American persuasion. It's not great to be called this, but better than being called *"Yanki."*

H is for *Hinchar las Pelotas*—When you nag an Argentine man, his balls don't bust—they swell.

Histérico/a—Applies equally to men and women in Argentina, all pros at flirting in order NOT to have sex.

L is for *Ladrones*—Thieves: beware of grannies armed with spray paint canisters!

Lentejuelas—Sequins, and there's nothing more humiliating than being stood up when wearing these. Trust me.

Lunfardo (or *Lumfardo*)—Most tangos are impossible to understand if you don't speak this rich, colorful, and oh-so-poetic argot of Buenos Aires.

M is for *Mas o Menos*—Literally, it means "more or less" or "sort of," but in most instances it really means "no, not at all." For example, in response to the question "Do you speak English?" if the person answers "mas o menos," translate this as "Not a bloody word."

Mate—A bitter leaf tea that is drunk out of a gourd, using a metallic straw, and usually passed around a group like a joint. Warning: it's an acquired taste.

Medialuna—A croissant-style pastry. Also the name of a tango figure, in which the man leads the woman into a half-turn reminiscent of a half-moon.

Medias de Red—Fishnet stockings. A must. (Try on a pair and you'll see why.)

Milonga—Is it a tango party? Is it a rhythm? Have you been paying attention?

Mina—Literally goldmine, and slang for "girl." Personally, I don't mind being called this at all.

Mugre—This is the tango version of "dirt"—as in "Dirty Dancing."

N is for *Novia*—There isn't a *Porteño* who doesn't have one of these hiding somewhere, so don't believe him when he says he doesn't.

O is for *Ombu*—An enormous bush that frankly looks like a tree and is very nice to kiss under.

P is for *Piel*—It means "skin" literally and "chemistry" figuratively. It's heaven if you and your partner have it—and hell if you don't.

Piropo—One of an endless repertory of flirtatious pick-up lines in verse that Argentine men learn to say before they can talk, and which they throw out at unsuspecting women on the street, at a café, at the movies, at the *milonga*, at the . . .

Planchar—To iron; also means "to be a wallflower"—neither of which are my favorite pastime.

Plantado/a—To get stood up. Something I've had plenty of practice in.

Porteño/a—What the inhabitants of Buenos Aires call themselves.

Pucho—Slang for cigarette. As a matter of fact, I think I might have permanent lung damage from secondhand smoke at the *milonga*.

R is for *Rubia*—Blonde. Whether natural or fake makes no difference.

S is for *Salida*—Exit. Also the term for the initial step a couple takes at the outset of their tango journey. Until one of them trips and falls due to lack of Vaseline on her shoes.

Sanguichito—A tango figure inspired by the snack of the same name, where the leader traps his partner's feet between his so that she remains stuck there. Not my favorite figure.

Sentimiento—That special feeling whereby (Nostalgia + Regret) x (Desire + Frustration) = Tango Passion.

T is for *Taco*—The heel of your tango shoe. Not to be confused with "*Tajo*" which means the slit in your tango skirt.

Tango—The most frustrating partner dance of all time. But as they say, you don't choose it. The tango chooses you. . . .

Index of Partners

Name	AKA	Occupation	Age	Strength	Weakness
1. Dragon	Herr Two Left Feet	Torturer	40+	Giving directions: "Cross now!"	Hygiene
2. Oscar	Mr. Perspiration	Overeater	Too young to die	At least he didn't smell bad	Is killed by a pizza shortly after dancing with me
3. Armando	Mr. Latin Lover	Psychiatrist/Gigolo	Too old	Nice year-round tan	Doesn't understand meaning of the word "no"
4. Frank	Mr. Verbally Challenged	Assistant Tango Instructor	30	Fluent in body language	Prefers stick insects to me
5. Hector	The Collector	International Poet	Geriatric	Teaches me the benefits of Vaseline	He has had 3,996 partners before me
6. Marcelo	The Big Tease	Translator of Tango Lyrics	21	His whiskers: they tickle!	Cold showers and a psycho girlfriend
7. Guillermo	Mr. James Dean	Fashion Student	Too young to take Viagra	He is rock hard....	...except for where it counts
8. Claudio	Mr. Piropo	Molester	Old enough to be MARRIED	Looks like Ben Affleck	My right tit still hurts
9. José Vargas	God's Gift To Female Dancers	La Rosarina's Partner	Has yet to grow out of his acne	His religiousness is cute ...	...until he jumps out of bed and into a confessinal
10. ???	El Chino	Thief	Middle-aged	Never stole anything from me (except my heart)	It's hard to practice tango in jail
11. Pancho	Triplet 1	Flan	24	First triplet out of the gate....	...but he has the worst timing!
12. Jorge	Triplet 2	Taoist	24	Didn't lie to me (about wanting a relationship)	He should have lied to me (about wanting a relationship)

Name	Nickname	Role	Age		
13. El Gato	The Multicolored Hulk	Dealer	Between 35–65	Only man ever to propose to me	Perpetually stoned/drunk
14. Diego	Cupid's Arrow Is Bent	Doctor	Early thirties	Practicing with him is HOT, HOT, HOT!	Likes to play tug-of-war while dancing
15. Ezequiel	My Half Orange	Construction	25	Love is blind	He doesn't like me very much
16. Julio	Mr. Blind as Two Bats	My Leading Man	26	Only kicks my shin very occasionally and by accident (because he can't see where it is)	Tells ME off about it afterwards
17. Gustavo	Mr. Never Forever	Runs a dance studio	32	Is not afraid to use the C-word	Has no idea what it means
18. Florencia	Ms. Lesbo Tango	Ally/Foe	29	Is not a man	Is not a man
19. Pablo de las Pampas	The Moustache	Rudolph Valentino Impersonator	28 (looks 38)	Beggars can't be choosers	If you thought a trout was cold . . . .
20. Ruben	The Veteran	Street Dancer	Younger than he looks	Dancing with him is better than passing the hat around	Tries to corrupt youth (me)
21. Cecilia	Fagin	Mother of S-I-X!	Too scared to ask her	Unbelievably flexible (thanks to very short skirt)	Has a serious cocaine habit
22. Ernesto	Subway Boy	Bike Messenger	21	Sweeter than a *dulce de leche* pancake	His broom is too short
23. Javier	Triplet 3	World's Best Lover	24	XXX (Censored)	Makes me pay for the telo